Verney L. Cameron

Across Africa

in Two Volumes - Vol. 2

Verney L. Cameron

Across Africa
in Two Volumes - Vol. 2

ISBN/EAN: 9783348054171

Hergestellt in Europa, USA, Kanada, Australien, Japan

Cover: Foto ©Andreas Hilbeck / pixelio.de

Weitere Bücher finden Sie auf **www.hansebooks.com**

ACROSS AFRICA

BY

VERNEY LOVETT CAMERON, C.B., D.C.L.

COMMANDER ROYAL NAVY

GOLD MEDALLIST ROYAL GEOGRAPHICAL SOCIETY, ETC.

IN TWO VOLUMES

VOL. II.

WITH NUMEROUS ILLUSTRATIONS

LONDON

DALDY, ISBISTER & CO.

56, LUDGATE HILL

1877

CONTENTS OF VOL. II.

CHAPTER I.

Nyangwé.—The Headman's Harem.—Syde Mezrui is a Fraud.—A
Slow Set.—The Markets.—The Weaker Sex.—Their Lordly Masters.
—Difficulty in obtaining Canoes.—Native Opinion of the White Man.
—As others see us.—An Anti-Slavery Lecture.—A clear-headed Man
of Business.—An old Impostor.—No Guides.—Fighting on the Road.
—Ulegga.—The Lualaba and the Nile.—Lake Sankorra.—Tipo-tipo.
—Crossing the Lualaba.—A Fever Den.—Bad Quarters.—Fishing-
weir Bridges.—Russûna.—A Brush with the Natives.—Blood-Money.
—A Check upon Looting.—Russûna's Wives.—Not Bashful but
Inquisitive.—A State Visit.—Russûna's private Village.—The Cares
of a Mother-in-law 1

CHAPTER II.

Tipo-tipo's Camp.—Kasongo visits us in State.—The Ceremony.—
Kasongo's ready Assistance.—I become a Gunsmith, Bone-setter, and
Soap-boiler.—Kasongo at Home.—Sankorra Traders.—Am forbidden
to proceed.—Reasons for not using Force.—I take another Route.—
Warua Guides.—Export of Slaves from Manyuéma.—Their Disposal.
—Cause of Increase of Slave-holding.—Ants as a Delicacy.—Mode of
trapping them.—A lazy Leader.—Kifuma Hospitality.—A desirable
Residence.—Carved-Door-posts.—A Rifle is stolen.—Fear of Consequences.—Thankfulness and Gratitude.—Leaving my "Guide" to
his own Devices I strike out a new Course.—My Men will not
follow.—I will not return.—Their Scruples are overcome.—Attack on
the Caravan.—Fists versus Archery.—Peace.—Kasengé.—Hundreds
flock to see me feed.—Kwarumba 20

CHAPTER III.

PAGE

My Goat is stolen.—The Natives become hostile.—We are fired upon.—Preparing for the worst.—An Exchange of Shots.—Wounding an important Personage. — A Parley. — Negotiations broken off.—Renewal of the Fighting.—Allowed to depart in Peace.—More Treachery.—At it again.—Storming a Village.—The Inhabitants bolt.—My brave Army.—Fort Dinah.—Barricades.—Prisoners of War.—We capture an Angel of Peace.—She makes it.—Leaving Fort Dinah.—An Explanation of my Intentions.—The Cause of the Attack.—Convivial Mourning.—Painted Faces.—My Guide's Craftiness.—Dried up.—Green Water as Refreshment.—My Guide meets his Mother and forsakes me.—Reception of a Headman.—Another queer Guide.—He also bolts.—Salt-making.—A March in a Marsh 39

CHAPTER IV.

Jumah Merikani.—Coal.—A Portuguese Trader.—His Followers.—Kasongo's Chief Wife.—José Antonio Alvez.—His History.—Warned against Mata Yafa.—Lake Mohryá.—An Inquisitive Lady.—Peculiarity respecting Names.—Alvez' Habitation.—Consuming your own Smoke.—Taking Bilâl down a peg.—Well-fortified Villages.—View of Lake Mohrya.—Huts on Piles.—An amphibious Race.—No Visitors allowed.—A Spiritualistic Medium.—Skulls of old Enemies.—Urua.—Kasongo's Dominion.—Its Government.—The Social Scale amongst Warua.—Mutilation for small Offences.—Kasongo professes to be a God.—His Morals.—His Family Harem.—Unfaithful Wives.—Kasongo's Bedroom Furniture.—Rule as to Fires and Cooking.—Devil-huts and Idols.—The great Idol Priests.—The Idol's Wife.—Dress and Tattoo Marks 55

CHAPTER V.

A Fair Deceiver.—Marriage Ceremony.—The youthful but unblushing Bride.—A Mountain Gap.—Grand Thunderstorm.—Lake Kassali.—Not allowed to visit it.—Return of a Chief.—Medicine Men.—Their Dress.—Ventriloquism.—They impose upon the public.—Am suspected of possessing Power to dry up the Lake.—Narrow Escape of my Messengers. — Manufacture of Floating Islands. — Jumah Merikani's Kindness.—Strange Tales.—Lion Tamers.—Deadly Shade.—Sculpture.—Cave Dwellings.—Poisonous Water.—A Tribe of Lepers.—My Occupations.—Kasongo's Wives.—Their shocking Behaviour. — A Performer of Tricks. — Kasongo returns. — An Afternoon Call.—His Appearance.—His Band plays me home.—Their excruciating Performance.—They will not "Move on."—My Anxiety to do so 74

CHAPTER VI.

PAGE

A Horde of Ruffians.—A thorough Blackguard.—A King amongst Beggars.—Wives and Families visit me.—Mutilated Men.—Kasongo's Vanity.—His Message to Her Majesty.—He takes me for a Ghost.—No Guides or Escort obtainable.—Abandonment of my fondest Hope.—Honest Alvez.—He lies like Truth.—Plotting. —The Levée.—Warned and armed.—The Ceremony.—Salaams of the Chiefs.—Biting the Dust.—Speeches.—Deceit.—Sleeping with Deceased Wives.—Obliged to build Kasongo's House.—Cruelty of Portuguese Slave-traders.—Delays.—Desertion.—Jumah Merikani sends Deserters a Warning.—Funeral Rites of a Chief.—Wives buried alive with him.—Blood shed over his Grave.—Kasongo's harsh Rule.—His demoniacal Frenzies.—Fire in Camp.—My Servant's good conduct.—Delicate Attention of Mrs. Kasongo   95

CHAPTER VII.

Making "Medicine" against Fire.—An elaborate Operation.— Kasongo's importunate begging.—Disgraceful Conduct of Alvez' people.—No Mercy for the Weak.—Cringing to the Strong.— Jumah Merikani's Generosity.—The "Fiend Stream."—Strange Trees.—My Men mistake Pombé for Water.—Swamps and Bogs.— Many Slips.—"Sloughs of Despond."—Enormous Ant-hills.—A Monarch dreaded by his People.—Surpassing his Predecessors in Cruelty.—The Biter bit.—A welcome Present.—Playing with Firearms.—I frighten a Chief out of his Village.—Alvez' Tactics. —A new Arrival.—Endeavours to obtain Allies.—Driven to Desperation I determine to march alone.—Result of Firmness   117

CHAPTER VIII.

Another Fire.—"Medicine" a Delusion.—Havoc and Desolation. —Coimbra's Captures.—Unmerciful treatment of Women.—He calls himself a Christian.—Misery and Loss of life.—Abuse of the Portuguese Flag.—Alvez shares the Flesh and Blood.—The Lovoi. —Limit of Oil-palms.—Composition of the Caravan.—Fire again.— Fortification of Msoa.—Mshiri.—"A very bad Man."—His power. —His Followers.—Trade in Slaves increasing.—Its Result.—Fate of the Women Slaves.—Probable Export.—Gods of War.—Excessive Heat.—Our coldest Night.—Alvez loses Slaves.—His Lamentations. —Am taken for a Devil.—Mournful Procession of Slaves.—A weird Grove.—Mata Yafa.—Vivisection practised on a Woman.—Rebellion of his Sister-wife.—Marshes.—A sumptuous Meal.—Burning a Roadway.—Lagoons.—Bee-keeping   134

CHAPTER IX.

PAGE

Ulûnda.—Born in Slavery.—Elephant Ragout.—Alvez dodges me.
—Compelled to follow him.—The Walunda.—A dirty Race.—Curious
Fare.—Returning Thanks.—Remarkably small Huts.—I drop into a
Pitfall.—My Rifle gives Satisfaction.—Zebra.—A cold Dip.—Ice in
August.—Lovalé People pushing eastward.—Cowardly Demeanour
of Bihé men. — Kafundango. — Escape of a Slave Gang.—Their
cruel Treatment.—Maternal Affection.—Savage Manners of Lovalé
Men. — Extortion. — Rudeness of Dress. — Clever Iron Workers.—
Arrow-heads and Hatchets.—Beef once again : but not for me.—
Numerous Fetishes.—The Zambési and Kassabé.—Interlocking of
their Systems.—Available for Traffic.—Mode of fishing.—Katendé
in State.—Recollection of Livingstone.—The Legend of Lake Dilolo 153

CHAPTER X.

João the White Trader.—Putrid Fish.—Dishonesty of the Noble
Savage.—Festive Natives.—Scanty Apparel.—Elaborate Hair-dress-
ing.—Cataracts.—Sha Kélombé.—Alvez proves fickle.—Exchanging
a Wife for a Cow.—An attempted Burglary.—Baffled.—The Thief's
Complaint.—Unparalleled Audacity.—Revengeful Threats.—Smelting Furnace.—High-flavoured Provisions.—Sambo chaffs a Chief.—
Forest.—A well-dressed Caravan.—Wanted, a Dairy-maid.—Friendliness of Mona Pého.—A well-ventilated Suit of Clothes.—"Sham
Devils." — Blacksmiths. — Am believed to be a Lunatic. — Alvez'
Reputation amongst Traders.—I sell my Shirts for Food.—A Village
eaten up by a Serpent.—An Eclipse.—Kanyumba's Civility.—Alvez
tries to rob the Starving.—Natural Hats.—False Rumours of Fighting
on the Road   174

CHAPTER XI.

The Kwanza.—Its Navigation.—Neat Villages.—Convivial Gather-
ing.—A Head of Hair.—Cattle Plague.—The Kokémas.—Filthy
Villages.—A lively Chase.—Reception of Alvez.—Payment of his
Porters.—Soap and Onions.—My Ragged Crew.—Alvez cheats me
at parting.—A Man in Tears.—An Archery Meeting.—A Tornado.—
The Town of Kagnombé. — Its Size. — Kagnombé's Officials. — A
Secretary unable to write.—Mshiri's Men.—Their Journeys from
Coast to Coast.—Kagnombé's Levée.—My Seat of Honour.—Kag-
nombé's best Clothes.—His full Style and Title.—Strong Drink.
— Fetish place.—Skulls.—Graves.—His Guards.—His Hat.—Senhor
Gonçalves.—His House.—Breakfast.—He tells me his History.—
His Kindness and Hospitality.—The Influence of Men of his Type . 196

CHAPTER XII.

PAGE

João's Settlement. — His official Position. — Openly trading in
Slaves. — Bad Specimen of the White Man. — A Fetish Man. — Fortune
telling. — Charms. — Infallible Cures. — Arms for Kasongo. — Probable
Result. — Belmont. — Miserable Work. — Buffalo Herd. — Opposition by
Bibé People. — Civility of the Chiefs. — The Kutato. — An extraor-
dinary River. — Dangerous Crossing. — Subterranean Streams. —
Lungi. — Suspected of the Evil Eye. — A Fetish Man declares me
free. — Untrustworthy Postmen. — Making and mending Clothes. — A
Portuguese in Pawn. — A Festival. — Drink and Debauchery. — A
superior Chief. — Rheumatism. — A Glimpse of Paradise. — Visit to
King Kongo. — Housed and fed by the Prime Minister's Wife. — The
King's own Hut. — His Dress. — Strongly guarded. — A drunken Con-
ference. — Pounding Corn. — My Beard excites Curiosity. — Hungry
Times. — Caterpillars a Delicacy. 216

CHAPTER XIII.

My dispirited Crew. — Native Bridges. — Bad Weather. — Secure
Dwellings. — Breakdown of my Men. — A Man missing. — Fallen out
by the Roadside. — A fearful Night. — Searching for the Straggler. —
Delay dangerous. — The Straggler arrives. — Past Recovery. — His
Death and Burial. — Locusts. — The Slave-trade on the Coast. — Mode
of Embarkation. — Failing Strength of my Carriers. — I throw away
Tent, Boat, Bed, &c. — A Rush for the Coast. — Our highest Camp. —
Gay Umbrellas. — A Mulatto Settlement. — Cascades. — Numerous up
Caravans. — Their Trade. — No Food left. — Search for a Camp. — Dead
beat. — A tedious March. — Skeletons of Slavers' Victims. — Starvation
and Exhaustion. — The Sea. — Leaving the worn-out Men behind. —
The final Effort. — Scurvy attacks me. — Help. — A Good Samaritan.
— A Haven of Rest 239

CHAPTER XIV.

Peace and plenty. — Katombéla. — My Illness increases. — Carried
to Benguella. — Medical Advice and good Nursing. — My Recovery. —
Arrival of my Stragglers. — Death of another Man. — Bombay's Objectionable Behaviour. — An original Character. — Benguella. — Its tumbledown Fort. — Convict Soldiers. — Their Loyalty. — My Men indulge
too freely. — Arrival at Loanda. — Reception by the Consul. — Courtesy
of the Governor. — An amusing Incident. — My Men object to their
Quarters. — Preparing to send them Home. — Liberal Offers. — Purchase of a Schooner. — Fitting her out. — Visit to Kisembo. — No
Charts obtainable. — A Windfall. — Departure of my Crew in the
Frances Cameron. — Leaving my Loanda Friends. — Homeward-bound.
— Meeting old Faces. — Safe at Home 265

CHAPTER XV.

PAGE

Formation of the Continent.—River Basins.—Deserts.—The Watersheds.—Zambési.—Kongo.—Physical Geography.—Useghara Mountains.—Fertile Soil.—The Lugerengeri Valley.—The Kungwa Hills. —Gum-copal.—Timber Trees.—Fauna.—Snakes.—The Mukondokwa Valley.—Lake Ugombo.—Mpwapwa.—Barren Soil.—The Marenga Mkali.—Ugogo.—A dried-up Country.—Ziwas.—Kanyenyé.—Usekhé.—Granite.—Khoko.—Vale of Mdaburu.—The "Fiery Field."—The Mabunguru.—Jiwé la Singa.—Urguru.—Unyanyembé. —A cultivated Country.—Ugunda.—Ugara.—The Kawendi Mountains.—Uvinza 281

CHAPTER XVI.

The Lake-system of Central Africa.—A Flaw in some ancient Upheaval.—Correct Position of the Tanganyika.—Kawélé.—Ras Kungwé.—Kabogo Island.—Ruguvu.—Coal.—Rapid Encroachment of the Lake upon its Shores.—Formation of Cliffs.—Remains of an Inland Sea.—Mukukomo Islands.—Gradual disappearance.— Constant Additions from Mainland.—Ras Musungi.—Loose Masses of Granite.—Weather-worn Cliffs.—Fantastic Forms.—Numerous Landslips.—Black Beaches.—The West of Tanganyika.—A new Geographical Region.—The Rugumba.—Black Speculum Ore.—The Kilimachio Hills.—Affluents of the Lualaba.—Underground Dwellings.—The Lualaba and Kongo.—Changes in River Channels.—Bee Culture.—A Barren Waste.—A Fertile Flat 302

CHAPTER XVII.

Africa's Future.—Slaves and other Articles of commerce.—Trade Routes.—Export of Indiarubber increasing.—Internal Slave-trade. —Ivory Supply.—Products.—Sugar-canes.—Cotton.—Oil-palm.— Coffee.—Tobacco.—Sesamum.—Castor-oil.—The Mpafu-tree.— Nutmegs.—Pepper.—Timber.—Rice.—Wheat.—Kaffir Corn.— Indian Corn.—Indiarubber.—Copal.—Hemp.—Ivory.—Hides.— Beeswax.—Iron.—Coal.—Copper.—Gold.—Silver.—Cinnabar.—Mission Work.—Commercial Enterprise.—Establishment of Depôts.— Scheme for advancing into the Interior.—Light Railways.—Steamers on Rivers.—Probable Results.—Shall Slavery continue?—How to stamp it out and make Africa free 320

APPENDIX I. 340
        „   II. 347
INDEX 357

ILLUSTRATIONS TO VOL. II.

FULL-PAGE PLATES AND FACSIMILES.

SCENE IN ALVEZ' BOMA . . . . *Frontispiece*
CROSSING THE RUVUMU RIVER . . . . . *To face p.* 14
CROSSING THE LUKAZI RIVER 34
FORT DINAH 44
LAKE MOHRYA, OR REALMAH 63
WARUA WAGANGA 82
JUMAH MERIKANI'S TEMBÉ 86
KASONGO'S MUSSUMBA 93
SCENE IN CAMP 106
CAMP AT LUPANDA 145
PAGE OF JOURNAL WHEN PAPER WAS RUNNING SHORT (*facsimile*) . 152
CROSSING THE LUKOJI 159
VILLAGE OF SONA BAZH 161
THE HOSPITABLE SETTLEMENT OF SENHOR GONÇALVES, BIHÉ . 212
MOUNTAINS BETWEEN BAILUNDA AND COAST 230
HILL AND VILLAGE OF HUMBI 241
MAISON CAUCHOIX 266
PART OF A BILL OF LADING FOR SLAVES FROM LOANDA (*facsimile*) 323

SMALLER WOODCUTS.

	PAGE		PAGE
Pottery	4	African Adjutants at Kasengé	36
Russûna and a Wife	17	Village Forge	38
Russûna's Shield and Drum	18	A Native of Mpanga Sanga	46
Sub-Chief	19	Salt-making	53
King Kasongo	22	Birds	54
Warua Guides	27	Hut in Mohrya	65
Hut at Kifuma	31	Warua Slave-driver and Slave	73

	PAGE		PAGE
Wedding Dance	76	Game Traps	172
Chief of Kowédi	80	Hair-dressing	173
Kasongo's Band	94	Arms and Ornaments	177
Coimbra	96	Crossing a Stream	183
Bird	109	Sham Devil at Mona Pého's	188
Jumah	114	Sham Devil	189
Kasongo's House	115	Head-dress of Kimbandi	193
Hair-dressing	116	Sham Devils	195
Njivi Marsh	125	Head of Hair at Kapéka	199
Heads	128	Alvez' Settlement	203
Lunga Mándi's Son	131	Village in Bihé	205
Pottery	133	Knives	209
Scene on the Road	136	Trap for Game	215
Village of Kawala	143	Porters from Bihé	223
Slave Gang	147	People of Kisanji	258
Hut in Ulúnda	152	Scene on Road	264
Village in Ulúnda	156	Custom-house at Benguella	279
Bow, Spears, Hatchets, and		Sierra Leone	280
Arrow-heads	163	Victor Emmanuel Mountains,	
Head-dress at Lovalé	165	Lake Tanganyika	301
Head-dress and Hatchet	166	A Group of Pagazi	319
Village in Lovalé	167	Colour Party	339
Fetish Hut	170		

CHAPTER

NYANGWÉ. — THE HEADMAN'S HAREM. — SYDE MEZRUI IS A FRAUD. — A
SLOW SET. — THE MARKETS. — THE WEAKER SEX. — THEIR LORDLY MASTERS.
— DIFFICULTY IN OBTAINING CANOES — NATIVE OPINION OF THE WHITE MAN.
— AS OTHERS SEE US. — AN ANTI-SLAVERY LECTURE. — A CLEAR-HEADED MAN
OF BUSINESS. — AN OLD IMPOSTOR. — NO GUIDES. — FIGHTING ON THE ROAD. —
ULEGGA. — THE LUALABA AND THE NILE. — LAKE SANKORRA. — TIPO-TIPO. —
CROSSING THE LUALABA. — A FEVER DEN. — BAD QUARTERS. — FISHING-WEIR
BRIDGES. — RUSSÚNA. — A BRUSH WITH THE 'NATIVES. — BLOOD-MONEY. — A
CHECK UPON LOOTING. — RUSSÚNA'S WIVES. — NOT BASHFUL BUT INQUISITIVE.
— A STATE VISIT. — RUSSÚNA'S PRIVATE VILLAGE. — THE CARES OF A MOTHER-
IN-LAW.

NYANGWÉ has been well chosen by the Zanzi- August, 1874. bar traders as a permanent settlement on the _____ Lualaba. It takes the form of two villages, each set on an eminence above the river, divided by a small valley watered by a little marshy stream and affording admirable rice grounds.

The right bank of the river, on which Nyangwé is situated, being well raised is free from malaria and fever; whilst the left bank is low and over-flowed by the annual floods which leave festering, stagnant backwaters. It is about as pestilential a place as it is possible to imagine, notwithstanding which the Wagenya live and flourish there, apparently feeling no ill effects from the miasma.

Of the two settlements, the western one is occu-

August, 1874. pied entirely by Wamerima from Bagamoyo and its neighbouring district.

The headman among them is Muinyi Dugumbi, who, finding himself a far greater personage here than he could ever hope to be in his native place, gave up all idea of returning to the coast and devoted his attention and energies to establishing a harem. He had collected round him over three hundred slave women, and the ill effects of this arrangement and his indulgence in bhang and pombé were plainly noticeable in his rapid decline into idiotcy.

The eastern part, where I stayed, is the abode of the Wasuahili and Arabs, but Tanganyika was the only one then there; the factories of Syde ibn Habib and others being under the charge of confidential slaves.

Tanganyika showed me the house he lent to Livingstone. It belonged to, and was occupied at that time by, one of his wives whom he turned out of her home for the convenience of the doctor.

That part of my caravan which journeyed by land arrived two days after me, and I instantly made endeavours to collect canoes for the attempt at floating down the river to the sea.

Syde Mezrui, notwithstanding his boasted acquaintance with the chiefs, proved to be of very small consequence, and contented himself with constantly asking for beads. When refused by me, Bombay and Bilâl, in spite of my positive orders to the contrary, gave him what he wanted, until I detected the little game and locked my beads up in Tanganyika's ivory store.

Tanganyika offered to assist me in everything in his power, but said that Muinyi Dugumbi was regarded as headman by the natives and therefore must be consulted. That individual altogether failed to understand the object of being in a hurry, and as I had only arrived a few days thought that surely a month or so hence would be time enough to think about canoes.

I would not leave him till he promised that he would try to persuade the natives to sell me some canoes on the first market-day.

Others made some show of affording aid, but they always said, " Slowly, slowly; don't be in a hurry; to-morrow will do as well as to-day." And so the matter dragged along.

Every fourth day large markets were held in each part of the settlement; and as the neighbouring chiefs and canoe-owners came to them, I had great hopes of getting what I required.

At the first that occurred after my arrival I found cowries, goats, and slaves were the only currency available in large purchases, and being without these I could do no *trade*. Tanganyika induced some men to promise they would think about selling their canoes if I obtained cowries, and also arranged to take Bombay across the river and through the strip inhabited by the Wagenya to the woods where canoes were made.

August,
1874.
Early in the morning of market-day canoes appeared on the river in every direction, bringing people with pottery, palm oil, fish, fowls, flour, salt, grass cloth, slaves, and everything produced in the country.

They were crowded and laden to such an extent as to render the presence of a black Mr. Plimsoll highly advantageous to passengers and cargo ; but as the crew were oftentimes the owners, perhaps they would have objected to his watchful eye.

POTTERY.

At the landing-places the canoes were hauled ashore, when the men shouldered the paddles and sauntered slowly to the market-place, leaving the women to bring up the merchandise. This they carried in large baskets slung on their backs by a strap across the forehead, like the creels of the Scottish fish-wives.

The men moved about the market-place doing nothing, unless something important—such as the sale of a slave—occurred to attract their attention.

The women, on the contrary, addressed all their energies to the momentous work of bargaining and chaffering, and as soon as they had selected the spot where they intended to locate themselves, down went the basket, and the articles for sale were arranged on the ground. The saleswoman then, sitting in the basket, squatted on the ground and looked like some extraordinary specimen of shell fish ; the basket doing duty as shell and preserving their delicate persons from contact with the damp earth.

The whole of the purchasers and vendors jammed themselves in a compact mass, none standing a yard from the main body although there was plenty of room for them to have moved about in comfort. But they seemed determined to squeeze together for three or four hours in a screaming, sweating, and I may add stinking, crowd, the savour of which ascended on high. Suddenly a move would be made by some person, and in another twenty minutes the two thousand that had been assembled were dispersed.

Every day these markets take place on some neutral ground, and the feuds in which the people are constantly engaged cease for the time the market is being held as also during the passage of buyers and sellers to and from their villages.

Except at Nyangwé the market-places are in uninhabited spots; and here there were only the houses of traders and the huts of their slaves and porters who had settled there principally on account of the market.

The neighbouring chiefs are always to be seen on these occasions, and at Nyangwé they lounged about the Arabs' verandahs talking of the price of ivory, goats, and slaves.

I tried every means to persuade the people to sell me canoes, but without avail. One hoary-headed old fellow said that no good to the Wagenya had ever resulted from the advent of strangers, and he should advise each and all of his countrymen to refuse to sell or hire a single canoe to the white man. For if he acted like the strangers who had gone before him, he would only prove a fresh oppressor to the natives, or open a new road for robbers and slave-dealers.

Others said they would bring canoes if I paid for them in slaves; but I replied that as an Englishman I could not deal in slaves. Englishmen did not recognise the status of slavery, and in our opinion all men should be free. I added that of course I was powerless to make alterations in the customs or laws of a country where slavery was allowed; but that if my sovereign heard of my being engaged in the slightest degree in any transaction that might savour of trading in slaves I should get into great trouble on my return to my own country, as the whole idea of our government was opposed to any form of slavery whatever.

Some of the chiefs then agreed to accept an

equivalent for slaves, taking their current price in
cowries, but only one ever came again about his
bargain.

When I counted out before him the correct
number of cowries—which I had purchased at about
threepence or fourpence a piece—he quietly looked
them over and then returned them, remarking that
if he took home such a quantity of cowries they
would only be appropriated by his wives as ornaments, and he would be poorer by a canoe; and
his wives wearing numbers of cowries would not
provide him with better food or clothing.

So anxious was I to close this bargain that I
offered double the value of his canoe in cowries,
saying that surely his wives could not possibly
wear such an amount.

But he had a wonderfully keen idea of trading,
and replied that the cowries would be lying idle
and bringing him in nothing till he managed to
buy slaves with them, whereas if he received slaves
in payment he could set them at work at once
to paddle canoes between the markets, to catch fish,
to make pottery, or to cultivate his fields; in fact,
he did not want his capital to lie idle.

Muinyi Dugumbi used to "sell" me when I
went to ask his assistance on a market-day.
His reply was always, "Stop in the verandah. I
will go and see if there are any people who have
canoes to sell;" and he would leave me apparently on this errand. But I afterwards found

that he used to slip into one of the houses of his harem by a back way, and remain there until the market people had gone.

Tanganyika tried his utmost to find men willing to part with canoes; but builders even would not dispose of their craft. Two or three promised to do so and received part payment in advance, but they afterwards returned the cowries.

What further to do, Tanganyika did not know, but he assured me I was welcome to the only one he possessed; and he held out as some encouragement the possibility of my obtaining canoes on the return of a large party then making war on the natives on the other bank. They had canoes, and it was likely that when the natives saw I had some, they would not object to my getting more.

Waiting was weary work, but I lived in hope and spent many tedious hours in talking with Tanganyika about his different journeys. From him I heard that the river flowed W.S.W. from Nyangwé, and fell into a great lake to which men, bringing cowries and cloth for sale, came in large vessels capable of containing two hundred people.

Some distance west of Nyangwé was Meginna, and to that place people owning boats traded, according to statements made to me by Arabs who had been there. I tried to engage guides and men to escort me to Meginna by land, our party being far too small in the eyes of my people to make the journey by itself, as the high-handed manner in which large armed parties of traders travelled had set all the natives against them. But the settlers at Nyangwé declared themselves to be too short of powder and guns to spare a sufficient force to accompany me and return safely by themselves, so no volunteers were forthcoming.

In addition to this they were very much afraid to travel by the roads north of the Lualaba; for several strong and well-armed parties had been severely handled by the natives in that direction, and had returned to Nyangwé with the loss of more than half their numbers.

One party, which had been a long way to N.N.E., and reached Ulegga, had especially suffered, having lost over two hundred out of their total strength of three hundred. They described the natives as being very fierce and warlike and using poisoned arrows, a mere scratch from which proved fatal in four or five minutes unless an antidote, known only to the natives, was immediately applied.

Ulegga was, they said, a country of large mountains wooded to the summits, and valleys filled with such dense forest that they travelled four and five days in succession without seeing the sun.

From the natives they had heard that people wearing long white clothes and using beasts of burden came to trade far to the north of the furthest point they had reached. These, no doubt, were the Egyptian traders in the Soudan.

All the streams seen by them on these journeys flowed towards the Lualaba, which, west of Nyangwé, received three large rivers from the northward, the Lilwa, Lindi, and Lowa. This last, which I believe to be the Uelle of Dr. Schweinfurth, was reported to be as large as the Lualaba (the Ugarrowa of the Arabs) at Nyangwé, and to be fed by two important affluents, both called Lulu, one from the east, the other from the west.

The levels I obtained at Nyangwé conclusively proved that the Lualaba could have no connection whatever with the Nile system, the river at Nyangwé being lower than the Nile at Gondokoro, below the point at which it has received all its affluents.

The volume of water also passing Nyangwé is 123,000 cubic feet per second in the dry season, or more than five times greater than that of the Nile at Gondokoro, which is 21,500 feet per second. This great stream must be one of the head-waters of the Kongo, for where else could that giant amongst rivers, second only to the Amazon in its volume, obtain the two million cubic feet of water which it unceasingly pours each second into the Atlantic? The large affluents from the north would explain the comparatively small rise of the Kongo at the coast; for since its enormous basin extends to both sides of the equator some portion of it is always under the zone of rains, and therefore the supply to the main stream is nearly the same at all times instead of varying, as is the case with tropical rivers whose basins lie completely on one side of the equator.

After I had remained at Nyangwé rather more than a fortnight one of the expeditions that had been looting slaves, goats, and everything they could lay their hands on to the south of the river returned, and with it the men who owned canoes. I offered anything in reason for a few canoes, but they would not part with one even, and my hopes were rapidly falling to zero. But on the 17th of August I heard the sound of firearms drawing near and was told that another party of marauders was returning.

This proved, however, to be the advanced guard of Tipo-tipo (Haméd ibn Haméd). He was coming to Nyangwé from his permanent camp about ten marches off, in order to settle a difference between the plunderers and a friend of his, a chief called Russûna who had begged him to interfere when the Nyangwé people attacked him.

In conversation with the leader of this guard I ascertained that Tipo-tipo's camp was close to the banks of the Lomâmi, an important southern affluent of the Lualaba, and that the lake into which that river flowed was within fourteen or fifteen marches of the camp; and he said that there were people with Tipo-tipo who had been to this lake, the Sankorra, and had met traders there with large boats.

Two days afterwards Tipo-tipo arrived and came
to see me. He was a good-looking man and the
greatest dandy I had seen amongst the traders.
And, notwithstanding his being perfectly black, he
was a thorough Arab, for curiously enough the
admixture of negro blood had not rendered him
less of an Arab in his ideas and manners.

He marched to his present camp from Katanga,
and, although he had been settled there for nearly
two years, had no idea of the proximity of the
settlement at Nyangwé.

He advised me that to reach Lake Sankorra the
best method would be to return with him to his
camp, and then, procuring guides and crossing the
Lomâmi, to march straight for the lake. Natives
were constantly passing backwards and forwards
in small parties and he did not think the journey
would prove difficult.

With him were two natives of the country west
of the Lomâmi, who confirmed his views and also
gave me some particulars of a lake named Iki,
situated on the Luwembi, an affluent of the Lomâmi,
and which is probably the Lake Lincoln of Livingstone.

Tipo-tipo was accompanied by some of Russûna's headmen, and the palaver concerning the
attempted raid on that chief was quickly settled
by the declaration of Tipo-tipo that he would side
with Russûna if he were again attacked. As his
caravan, and those of five or six traders who recog-

nised him as their head, could have brought more guns into the field than the Nyangwé people, and as the traders at Kwakasongo were also likely to have sided with Tipo-tipo—he and his father being two of the richest and most influential of the travelling Zanzibar merchants—it was thought wise to promise to leave Russûna alone in future.

On the 26th of August, having bade farewell to Muinyi Dugumbi, I set about getting my men across the river in readiness for starting with Tipo-tipo early the following day. Tanganyika provided canoes and assisted me much; but in the afternoon a bad attack of fever laid him up and I was thrown upon my own resources. I saw nearly every man away from the Nyangwé side, and then, being very tired, left Bombay with a canoe containing a portion of my kit, to bring the remaining men across after me.

On landing on the other side I found the village where we had to camp situated on the bank of a stagnant, muddy backwater, reeking under the sun's rays. The place was inhabited only in the dry season by the fever-proof Wagenya, owing to its being flooded for four or five months of the year.

In vain that night did I look for Bombay and the remainder of the stores and men; and when he joined me at noon the next day, Asmani, his chum Mabruki, and another pagazi had deserted, taking with them guns and ammunition. I heard that the moment I was out of sight Bombay un-

loaded the canoe and coolly returned to the settlement to indulge in a big drink. My bed, cooking-
gear, provisions, and medicine chest were all in
that canoe, and to the want of them may in a great
measure be attributed the heavy attack of fever
I had after sleeping on the low left bank of the
river.

Fever or no fever I determined to go on ; and
at one o'clock started to meet Tipo-tipo, who had
crossed the river rather lower down.

Our road led through many villages, the inhabitants of which were employed either in catching
fish in the backwaters, or making large egg-shaped
pots used for storing palm oil.

Nearly every hut had a pig tied to the door-
post, and their odour combined with that of mud,
rotten fish, &c., made a *bouquet d'Afrique* not to be
imagined.

Soon after joining Tipo-tipo we left the river
and began to ascend a gentle slope ; and, passing
a market in full swing, arrived after four hours'
marching at the river Rovubu, a large stream
which we crossed on a gigantic fishing-weir bridge.

The weir was composed of poles, in many
instances over forty feet in length, and from the
number used it was evident that a great amount
of patient and well-directed labour must have been
required in its construction. Here we halted and
most of the people took the opportunity to have
a bathe ; but I was obliged to lie down and rest,

CROSSING THE ROVUBU RIVER.

[Page 14, Vol. II.]

being completely exhausted by fever. After a time we moved on, passing many deserted villages with their crops destroyed by the late marauders from Nyangwé, and camped about nine in the evening.

During the last part of the march the fever so increased that I reeled like a drunken man and was scarcely able to drag one foot after the other. To my fevered vision and ideas the large, white, pyramidal ant-hills which were plentiful often seemed to be my tent; and when I found myself mistaken, the hope that each in succession might really prove to be it kept me moving, although I was thoroughly beaten. I was somewhat better the next day and managed to get along; but it was weary work and my feet were so blistered that I was obliged to slit open my boots.

Russûna's was reached on the 29th of August, the country passed through being very fertile with many fine trees, mpafu, gum-copal, African oak, teak, and others. In one place there was a large grove of nutmeg-trees, and for forty or fifty yards the ground was literally covered with nutmegs.

During this march a very unpleasant fracas occurred, owing to some Nyangwé people who were accompanying us to Tipo-tipo's to buy copper being recognised as old enemies by the natives, who let fly a volley of arrows in the midst of them.

In an instant all was confusion, and two or three

September, natives were shot down before a parley could be
1874. begun ; but Tipo-tipo appearing on the spot, they
recognised him and were reassured. Some, however, did not recover from their fright until I
induced them to sit round me and guaranteed their
safety until matters were settled.

Tipo-tipo compelled the Nyangwé people to pay
blood-money for those natives who were killed, as
he argued that it was owing to their folly in going
in front of his men—who were well known to the
natives as friends—that the trouble arose. I was
delighted to see his leading men serve out sound
and well-deserved thrashings to some Wanyamwési porters from Nyangwé who had taken advantage of the row to commence looting a village.

We camped about two miles from Russûna's
village, yet he, together with his brother and half-
a-dozen wives, came to stay with us during our
two days' halt. He visited me very often, bringing a different wife each time. They were the
handsomest women I had seen in Africa, and in
addition to their kilts of grass cloth wore scarves
of the same material across their breasts.

On the second day all fear of me and bash-
fulness had vanished, and they came in a body
to see me. I soon had them all sitting around me
looking at pictures and other curiosities ; and after
a time they began to wax so much more familiar
that they turned up the legs and sleeves of my
sleeping suit, which I always wore in camp, to

iscover whether it was my face alone that was Septembe
1874.
vhite. Indeed, they ultimately became so inquisi-
tve that I began to fear they would undress me

HUSSENA AND A WIFE.

ltogether; to avoid which I sent for some beads
ind cowries and gave them a scramble, and thus
vithdrew their attention from my personal pecu-
iarities.

VOL. II.   C

When Russûna came to see me he brought a large and handsomely carved stool, upon which he sat, while he used the lap of one of his wives who was seated on the ground as his footstool.

Whilst he remained here a sub-chief visited him in state, accompanied by people carrying shields ornamented with cowries and beads and fringed

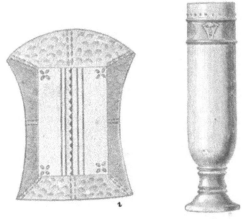

RUSSÛNA'S SHIELD AND DRUM.

with black monkey-skins, and a woman bearing on a spear the skin of a tippet monkey as a standard. Russûna, in equal state, went a short distance from the camp to meet and welcome him.

This chief and Russûna then had a palaver with Tipo-tipo and the Nyangwé Arabs, and after swearing eternal friendship the caravan was free to reached without any further adventure on the 3rd of September.

Russûna's private village, inhabited only by himself and his wives, was passed on the road. It consisted of about forty comfortable square huts in two rows, with a large one in the centre for himself. Each hut contained about four wives, and Russûna's mother had the pleasant task of keeping them all in order.

CHAPTER II.

TIPO-TIPO'S CAMP—KASONGO VISITS US IN STATE.—THE CEREMONY.—
KASONGO'S READY ASSISTANCE.—I BECOME A GUNSMITH, BONE-SETTER AND
SOAP-BOILER.—KASONGO AT HOME.—SANKORRA TRADERS.—AM FORBIDDEN
TO PROCEED.—REASONS FOR NOT USING FORCE.—I TAKE ANOTHER ROUTE.
—WARUA GUIDES.—EXPORT OF SLAVES FROM MANYUÉMA.—THEIR DISPOSAL.
—CAUSE OF INCREASE OF SLAVE-HOLDING.—ANTS AS A DELICACY.—MODE
OF TRAPPING THEM.—A LAZY LEADER.—KIFUMA HOSPITALITY.—A DESIRABLE
RESIDENCE.—CARVED DOOR-POSTS.—A RIFLE IS STOLEN.—FEAR OF CONSE-
QUENCES.—THANKFULNESS AND GRATITUDE.—LEAVING MY "GUIDE" TO
HIS OWN DEVICES.—I STRIKE OUT A NEW COURSE.—MY MEN WILL NOT
FOLLOW.—I WILL NOT RETURN.—THEIR SCRUPLES ARE OVERCOME.—
ATTACK ON THE CARAVAN.—FISTS *versus* ARCHERY.—PEACE.—KASENGÉ.—
HUNDREDS FLOCK TO SEE ME FEED.—KWARUMBA.

September, 1874.

TIPO-TIPO'S camp was well arranged and situated on a slight eminence; but not being a really permanent settlement no large houses had been built although Tipo-tipo and the other traders had good huts. They provided me with a very comfortable one having two small apartments and a bathroom, besides sheds for my servants and cooking arrangements.

Before making preparations for crossing the Lomâmi we had to receive a visit from Kasongo, the chief of the district, which took place two days after our arrival. At eight o'clock on that morning Tipo-tipo, myself, and every leading man of his and the Nyangwé parties, arrayed ourselves in our best—although I confess mine was not much of a turn-out—and assembled in an open shed, which was the general meeting-place of the settlement during the day and often far into the night.

An individual authorised by the chief to do duty as master of the ceremonies then arrived carrying a long carved walking-stick as a badge of office, his advent being the signal for all porters and slaves in camp and people from surrounding villages to crowd round to witness the spectacle. The M.C. drove the anxious sightseers back and formed a space near the reception-room—as the hut may be termed—and then different sub-chiefs arrived, each followed by spearmen and shield-bearers varying in number according to rank, a few of the more important being followed also by drummers.

Each new comer was brought to the entrance, where the Arabs and myself had taken our seats, and his name and rank proclaimed by the master of the ceremonies, who further informed him the position he was to occupy in order to be ready to welcome Kasongo.

After some time spent in this manner, much drumming and shouting heralded the approach of the great man himself. First in the procession were half-a-dozen drummers, then thirty or forty spearmen followed by six women carrying shields, and next Kasongo, accompanied by his brothers, eldest son, two of his daughters and a few officials,

 the rear being brought up by spearmen, drummer
and marimba-players. On his reaching the entranc
to the hut a ring was formed, and Kasongo—dresse
in a jacket and kilt of red and yellow woollen clot
trimmed with long-haired monkey skins, and wit

KING KASONGO.

a greasy handkerchief tied round his head—pe
formed a jigging dance with his two daughters.

The Terpsichorean performance being conclude
in about a quarter of an hour, he then entered th
hut and we had a long conversation.

I acquainted him with my wish to cross the
Lomâmi and proceed to Lake Sankorra, and found
that the country and road presented no great diffi-
culties and that we should be almost certain of
meeting people who owned large boats on the lake;
but it would be necessary to obtain permission
from the chief on the opposite bank of the Lomâmi,
before passing through his territory.

Kasongo kindly offered in the first instance to
confer personally with this chief on the matter; but
afterwards coming to the conclusion that he was too
old for the journey, decided to despatch some of his
people with a party belonging to Tipo-tipo and
myself to obtain the necessary permission.

He made many enquiries as to my nationality
and business, and I informed him that it was
from my country that cloth and other articles used
in trading in Africa were sent; and my object was
to visit the people who purchased these things and
to see their countries, so that I might be enabled
to tell my Sultân what they wanted, and increase
the trade for the benefit of both sides.

When Kasongo had taken his departure, which
was conducted with much the same ceremony as
that observed on arrival, I asked Tipo-tipo to lend
me a few-men and detailed an equal number of
my own to accompany Kasongo's people to the
Lomâmi.

Next morning the party started, and I settled
down for two or three days' rest.

I was, however, occupied with doing many things for the benefit of the camp. All broken locks of muskets were brought to me for repairs; I was asked to doctor people for fever and dysentery; and in one instance to perform a surgical operation upon a man who had been shooting with copper slugs and had lodged the charge in his hand. I cut the slugs out, put splints on the broken fingers and dressed the whole with carbolised oil, and before I left had the satisfaction of seeing the unfortunate fellow on the high road to recovery. I could not make him hold his hand steady whilst extracting the slugs, so had to adopt rather a rough and ready course and lashed his wrist firmly to an upright post during the operation.

Not content with making me gunsmith and surgeon, they begged me to try my hand at the manufacture of soap from palm oil, having heard that the English used it for that purpose. Not being sanguine as to the result I did not care to make the attempt, but they pressed it so upon me that I consented; and after much trouble succeeded in manufacturing a sort of soft soap—which would wash clothes—of palm oil and lye made from ashes of the stalks of Indian corn.

Two days after Kasongo's visit I returned his call and found him sitting on an open grassy space in the middle of his village, which was composed of good-sized comfortable huts. He was dressed only in native grass cloth, but looked far cleaner and more respectable than when tricked out in his tawdry finery.

Some people then with him had just returned from Lake Sankorra and said that traders had been there very recently ; and, to prove the truth of their statements, showed me new cloth and beads they had bought there, quite different in kind and quality from any coming from Zanzibar. Another proof, and an unwelcome one, was that the cowries I purchased at Nyangwé had fallen from the abnormal price they obtained there to considerably below par, when compared with beads. This was owing to the large quantities brought into the country by traders to the lake, who were described to me as wearing hats and trousers and having boats with two trees (masts) in them.

All my hopes of an easy journey to this mysterious lake were dashed to the ground on receiving the answer from the chief whose territory I desired to cross.

"No strangers with guns had," he said, "ever passed through his country, and none should without fighting their way."

Although I could have obtained sufficient men from Nyàngwé and Tipo-tipo to have easily fought my way through, I recognised it as my duty not to risk a single life unnecessarily ; for I felt that the merit of any geographical discovery would be irretrievably marred by shedding a drop of native blood except in self-defence.

My direct road to the lake being thus closed, I enquired if it were possible to get there by some circuitous route.

Tipo-tipo had heard of Portuguese having been close to the chief of Urua's capital, which lay about a month's journey S.S.W. from us, and showed me a Portuguese soldier's coat bought from a native who stated that he received it from a white man who was with the chief of Urua. After consultation with Tipo-tipo and carefully weighing the *pros* and *cons* I decided on proceeding to the chief of Urua in search of the white traders—who had I thought most probably come from the lake —and thence to work back to Sankorra by a road to the westward of the country through which I was forbidden to pass.

When I decided on taking this course Tipo-tipo offered me the services of three Warua guides who had come from the south with him. They were Mona Kasanga, headman and son of a chief on Lake Kowamba; M'Nchkulla, one of the headmen of a village called Mukalombo; and Kongwé, of no particular rank or status.

Wages and rations for the three were arranged and, according to custom, paid in advance to Mona Kasanga.

From them I gathered information about Lake Iki; another called Mohrya, reported to have huts on it built on piles, and yet another, named Kassali, on which there were floating islands.

Septemi
1874.

At first I was unable to make much use of this
nformation owing to their imperfect knowledge of
Kisuahili; but afterwards, when I obtained the
key, it proved most valuable.

Besides these, Tipo-tipo also sent one of his
eading men to journey ten days with me on the
road.

The only drawback I experienced to the comfort
of Tipo-tipo's camp was the number of slaves in

WARUA GUIDES.

chains who met my eyes at every turn; but,
except being deprived of their freedom and con-
ined in order to prevent their running away, they
had a tolerably easy life and were well fed.

Tipo-tipo and many Arab traders asserted that
they would be glad to find other means of transport for their goods instead of trusting to slaves;
but not regarding slave-dealing as a sin in the
abstract, they availed themselves of the means at
their disposal.

Very few slaves are exported from Manyuéma by the Arabs for profit, but are obtained to fill their harems, to cultivate the farms which always surround the permanent camps, and to act as porters.

By the time a caravan arrives at Tanganyika from the westward nearly fifty per cent. have made their escape, and the majority of those remaining are disposed of at Ujiji and Unyanyembé, frequently as hire for free porters, so that comparatively few reach the coast. Slavery nevertheless is increasing, owing to the number of coast people settling in the interior who fancy that it adds to their dignity to possess large numbers of slaves.

We left the camp on the 12th of September, with the usual amount of trouble caused by men skulking and pretending to be unable to carry anything, and on halting after a very short march, I had to send for men and loads remaining behind. In the night two men deserted, but I went on without them, not finding out until afterwards that they had stolen a quantity of snider cartridges. To this they had been incited by Syde Mezrui, who also left at Nyangwé, by "accident," a rifle I had lent him during the journey from Ujiji.

For some days we journeyed through a fairly populated country, with large villages of well-built and clean huts disposed in long streets with bark-cloth trees planted on each side. All the streets ran east and west, but the reason for this custom I was unable to discover.

The people seemed friendly, and the chiefs usually brought small presents of corn or dried white ants—which are eaten here with porridge as a relish on account of the scarcity of animal food—and they were perfectly satisfied with very small presents in return.

The ants are caught in rather an ingenious manner. A light framework of cane or twigs is built over a large ant-hill and covered with leaves cleverly fastened together by sticking the mid-rib of each into the one above it. A very small entrance is left open at the bottom, and under this is dug a round hole a foot in diameter and two feet deep. When the winged ants come out of the hill ready to migrate they all make for this entrance and hustle each other into the hole, where they lose their wings and are unable to get out. In the morning they are collected by the natives who smoke them over slow fires to preserve them.

The country was wonderfully full of oil-palms, which in some places grew in extraordinary abundance.

After two or three hours' marching each day, Tipo-tipo's man declared that the next camping-place was too far away to be reached until late, and therefore we had better stay where we were. His orders were merely to accompany me for ten days, and not to any specified place, and it was of

September, 1874. course to his advantage to make a day's march as short as possible.

Each of the affluents of the Lomâmi with which the country was intersected had hollowed out for itself a small deep valley in the nearly level plateau we were traversing, and, shaded by fine timber, their dark depths were rich in the most beautiful mosses and ferns it is possible to imagine. Sometimes one side of a valley was steep and cliff-like, exposing the various strata; at the top, a shallow layer of vegetable mould, then about fourteen feet of sand and from fifty to seventy feet of water-worn pebbles of granite and quartz resting on the solid granite. The pebbles were occasionally divided into two parts by a stratum of soft yellowish sandstone of ten or twelve feet; but all lay level except the granite, which was very irregular.

Two days after Tipo-tipo's man left us we arrived at a village named Kifuma, from which the people bolted on our approach; but on the peacefulness of our intentions becoming apparent the chief came to me, and even offered his hut—a delightfully clean place—for. my use. It was ten feet square, and a large portion of the space was occupied by a bed-place made of split mid-ribs of the raphia palm.

The two doors—but especially the front one—were wonderfully good specimens of carpentering, each having two leaves working on pivots fitting into holes in the lintel and threshold. Where the leaves met they overlapped and were halved into each other. The front door was also carved on the outside, with the pattern traced in red, white and black, and on each side were three carved pillars.

The floor was of clay, raised eighteen inches from the ground and polished until quite slippery. The

HUT AT KIFUMA.

walls were seven feet in height and built of poles about a foot apart, with stout slabs adzed out of logs between them, and kept in place by battens. The roof ran up in the form of a dome twenty feet high on the inside, and was made of slender

September,
1874.
rods fitting at the apex into a round piece of wood
carved in concentric circles and painted black and
white, while two or three horizontal rows of rods
gave strength and rigidity to the structure. This
framework was covered with fine long grass laid
quite smoothly in horizontal lengths, and over this
was a heavy thatch about two feet thick, coming
down to the ground and evenly trimmed, the thatch
over the doors being so cut and arranged as to form
porches.

During the night a rifle and cartridge-pouch
being stolen I spoke to the chief respecting the
theft. He declared he knew nothing about it, and
begged and prayed me not to destroy his village on
account of it.

Of course I had no intention of doing this, and
so I told him ; but he could hardly believe such
forbearance on my part possible. And when he
saw us depart without having done any harm his
delight knew no bounds, and to show his gratitude
for what he evidently considered my unwonted
lenity, he brought some goats to our next camp as a
gift. I only accepted one and gave him a present in
return, on which he knelt down and fairly covered
himself with mud in token of thankfulness.

I told him Englishmen did not punish indiscriminately for theft, and that even if I had caught
the thief I should only have compelled him to
return the stolen rifle and have given him a sound
flogging.

He had never before heard of such merciful treatment, and said the inhabitants of villages fled on the approach of the caravan because the only strangers they had any previous knowledge of were those who came slave-hunting and seized the slightest pretext to make war and destroy villages for the sake of obtaining slaves and plunder.

For another few days we marched along by the Lomâmi, and then my guides became doubtful about the road and endeavoured to work east.

One day, after the road had been declared lost and found again three times in an hour, my patience was so tried that I decided to walk on in the direction I wanted to go, whether the guides were satisfied or not. For some time not a man followed me ; still I went forward by myself and then sat-down and smoked a pipe quietly waiting to see the turn events would take.

Soon four men came running after me without their loads, saying I was going the wrong way. I replied that the only right way was the road I wanted to travel, and that was in the direction I was then walking.

On hearing this and seeing my determination they left me, and I continued on my way. Bombay then followed and endeavoured to frighten me by declaring that every man would run away if I persisted in going by this road; but I only answered, " Where will they run, you old fool ? "

September, 1874.

He tried by every means in his power to induce me to return, but I obstinately refused; and after a time the whole party followed me, and in the evening we arrived safely at a village on the banks of the Lukazi, a branch of the Lomâmi.

The guides now insisted that we were in a *cul-de-sac* formed by the winding of the river and should have to retrace our steps, and on my sending them forward to discover whether the path did not lead to a bridge they reported that it was only the way to a watering-place.

This statement was so apparently false that I declined to put any faith in my "guides," and after walking twenty minutes along the path came upon a fishing-weir bridge. The day following we crossed and had not proceeded far before I perceived natives moving about amongst the long grass, but all attempts at inducing them to come near failed.

Very soon afterwards, when I was in front accompanied by two or three men looking for the road, I was unpleasantly surprised by some arrows being shot at us through a narrow strip of jungle. One of them glanced off my shoulder, and catching sight of the fellow who had shot at me lurking behind a tree I dropped my rifle and started in chase.

Fortune favoured me, for my enemy tripped and fell and before he could regain his feet I was down on him, and after giving him as sound a thrashing

s ever he had in his life smashed his bow and
arrows. This finished I pointed to some of his
riends who were now in view and considerably
assisted him to join them by means of stern pro-
ulsion, the kick being a hearty one.

A large party of natives occupying the path
n front seemed inclined to attack us; but I made
igns and overtures of peace and offered them a

AFRICAN ADJUTANTS AT KASENGÉ.

ew strings of beads, and after some hesitation they
:ame forward in a most friendly spirit and escorted
is to Kasengé, the village of their chief, before
vhom they performed a kind of war-dance on
ıringing me into his presence.

On enquiry I learnt that we were on an
sland formed by a bifurcation of the Lomâmi,
ıaving crossed the Lukazi—one of the two branches

—which rejoined the Lomâmi a little further down.

The village of Kwarumba, a sub-chief of the great King of Urua, which had been named as one of our stations was very near here, so had I taken Mona Kasanga's advice respecting the route I should certainly have been misled.

That intelligent being, not satisfied with having given trouble on the road, now commenced to assume airs of authority and declined to march the following day on account of himself and wife being fatigued and requiring rest. I objected to this, upon which he asserted that being the son of a chief he was accustomed to act as he pleased, and that when travelling with Arabs they always halted if he wished it.

Being mainly dependent upon him for communication with the natives I was obliged to submit to his demands, and when the next day came I was not sorry to be quiet as I had a touch of fever.

On the 27th of September we again moved, and crossing the Lukazi by another fishing-weir bridge made a long march to a large and populous village.

The people had never before seen a white man and gathered round me in crowds, staring and indulging freely in remarks on my appearance, manner of eating, &c. Whilst I was having my evening meal there must have been upwards of five hundred standing round in a dense ring and

September, 1874.

some of their observations were no doubt the reverse of complimentary, but being unable to understand them I was not embarrassed by this free criticism.

We passed through Kwarumba's own village the next day, and as no strangers were allowed to sleep near the chief camped in a wooded dell just beyond.

In the afternoon he called on me, and seemed to be a dirty, drunken old man without much sense. He could give me little or no information, but from some of his followers I heard that people who carried guns and umbrellas, and though not white were known as Wasungu, had been fighting near here two months previously and had now returned to the town of the great chief of Urua, into which country we had now fairly entered.

On leaving Kwarumba's I found Mona Kasanga still unaccountably trying to work away to the eastward. So I took my own line again, and, camping in the jungle one night, arrived at a large village called Kamwawi. Here the people were dressed, tattooed, and wore their hair exactly like the Waguhha.

Although we were obliged to camp a short distance from the village, women and children selling food were in and out all day long. The men, too, came and talked to us and one volunteered to show the road to the capital of Urua, which he said was only three or four days distant.

Everything seemed *couleur de rose*, and I tur
in happily and sincerely hoping to make a g
march on the morrow on the direct road. But
these hopes were destined to be frustrated.

VILLAGE FORGE.

CHAPTER III.

MY GOAT IS STOLEN.—THE NATIVES BECOME HOSTILE.—WE ARE FIRED
UPON.—PREPARING FOR THE WORST.—AN EXCHANGE OF SHOTS.—WOUND-
ING AN IMPORTANT PERSONAGE.—A PARLEY.—NEGOTIATIONS BROKEN OFF.
—RENEWAL OF THE FIGHTING.—ALLOWED TO DEPART IN PEACE.—MORE
TREACHERY.—AT IT AGAIN.—STORMING A VILLAGE.—THE INHABITANTS
BOLT.—MY BRAVE ARMY.—FORT DINAH.—BARRICADES.—PRISONERS OF
WAR.—WE CAPTURE AN ANGEL OF PEACE.—SHE MAKES IT.—LEAVING FORT
DINAH.—AN EXPLANATION OF MY INTENTIONS.—THE CAUSE OF THE
ATTACK.—CONVIVIAL MOURNING.—PAINTED FACES.—MY GUIDE'S CRAFTI-
NESS.—DRIED UP.—GREEN WATER AS REFRESHMENT.—MY GUIDE MEETS HIS
MOTHER AND FORSAKES ME.—RECEPTION OF A HEADMAN.—ANOTHER QUEER
GUIDE.—HE ALSO BOLTS.—SALT-MAKING.—A MARCH IN A MARSH.

A S we were preparing to start I missed my goat
which usually slept at my feet or was the
first to pay her respects in the morning; and on
enquiring where she was, found that she had been
seen between the village and the camp late in the
evening.

I thereupon went to the village with two men
and a guide to look for her; and so confident did I
feel of the friendliness of the natives towards us
that we were unarmed. Some men whom we saw
I told of my loss and stated my willingness to pay
a reward if she were brought back, but I could
get no answer whatever from them.

It soon became evident that we were in for a row,
for all the women had disappeared and there were

October,
1874.

far more armed men about than the size of the
village would account for.

Those with whom I had been trying to have some
conversation bolted from us suddenly, and immediately others at a short distance commenced shooting their arrows at us. At that moment some of my
men with rifles fortunately arrived, and Jumah
coming behind me put my trusty twelve-bore rifle
into my hand.

None of my people were hit in this preliminary
skirmish, but I sent orders for the remainder to
join me at once with the stores so as to form one
body ; and no sooner had they quitted the camp
than the natives set fire to it.

The greater number of my people I placed under
shelter of huts and posted others as pickets to
prevent our being taken in rear or flank, and then,
with the guides, went into the centre space of the
village to declare our peaceable intentions and to
enquire the cause of our being attacked ; but the
only reply vouchsafed was a dropping fire of arrows.
I was much astonished that none of us were hit,
for at least half-a-dozen arrows fell within a yard
of me in a couple of minutes.

Being unable to obtain any satisfactory answer
I returned to the caravan, and at that moment a
body of about five hundred men, who had been
posted in ambush on the road we were to have
taken, joined the natives.

Encouraged by this reinforcement and our pacific

October,
1874.

attitude, the natives closed in and commenced hurling spears at us. And as matters were now becoming rather serious I reluctantly allowed a few shots to be fired.

One of these fortunately took effect in the leg of a native who happened to be a person of consideration and was standing in what he imagined was a position of safety. This circumstance made such an impression that a parley was proposed by the chief of the village, and I gladly acceded.

After some talk the following agreement was entered into, namely, the goat should be found and returned ; I should make a present to the chief of a piece of scarlet cloth ; Bombay or Bilâl should make brothers with him ; and we were to be furnished with guides and permitted to depart in peace.

I at once proceeded to carry out my part of the agreement, and having fetched the cloth was returning with it to the chief of Kamwawi, when another arrived with more armed men and said to him, "Don't be such a fool as to make peace with these people for the sake of one piece of cloth. We are strong enough to eat them, and can easily get every bit of cloth and every bead belonging to them, and themselves we can kill or make slaves of. How many tens are they ? You can count their tens on one hand ; whilst our tens would take more hands to count than we could number afterwards."

The councils of the newly arrived chief unhappily prevailed; negotiations were broken off, and arrows again began to fly about.

I now determined to make some show of retaliation, so burnt down one hut, threatening at the same moment that if not allowed to leave peaceably I would set fire to the entire place and let them know what bullets really were.

This decided action resulted in permission being given for our departure, but only by a road leading in an opposite direction to that we proposed going.

My guides said that a village under a separate chieftainship, where we should be hospitably received, was situated on the road we were ordered to follow, so I decided to go there to avoid any further argument or trouble with these treacherous people and gave orders to march.

The road was through tangled grass, scrub, belts of thick jungle and open plains, and as we marched along we were surrounded by crowds of yelling savages who kept out of range of our guns in the open, but closed in and shot at us whenever there was cover.

The whit! whit! of the long arrows going through the trees created a very unpleasant sensation; but notwithstanding the number flying about none of us were wounded. I therefore would not allow a gun to be fired, being determined not to shed any blood unless driven to do so in self-defence.

About five o'clock the natives drew off; and at

sunset we arrived at a strip of jungle with a
stream running though it, and on the opposite bank
was the village that we hoped would prove a haven
of peace and rest.

With the guides I went to hail the village and
enquire whether we could be received. And here
again our only answer was a volley of arrows.   ·

I then called upon my men to follow me, a
summons to which Jumah, Sambo and one or two
others responded, and firing our guns, we dashed
through the jungle, across the river, and entered the
village at one side while the natives disappeared at
the other.

The rest of my brave army, excepting four or
five who remained with Bombay in charge of the
stores, bolted ; and for thus turning their backs on
the enemy retributive justice furnished two of
them with artificial tails looking remarkably like
arrows. ·   ·

I knew that not a moment was to be lost in
preparing for the return of the hostile natives, so
ordered the loads to be brought into the village
immediately.   ·

My runaways speedily followed and now, Falstaff-
like, began to boast of their great deeds and of the
still greater performances they intended in future.
But it was no time for talking, and I set cowards as
well as heroes at work in fortifying our position.

Four huts in the centre of the village forming
an imperfect square I had loopholed as block-

October,
1874.

houses, and between them built a barricade of
doors and poles from the remaining huts, which
were either torn down or burnt to prevent their
affording cover for our enemies. The barricade
being formed, a trench was dug inside and roofed
over, and, notwithstanding our being disturbed by
several volleys of arrows, the morning saw us
fairly protected.

It was plain that matters were serious, and that
to get away from our present situation we should
be obliged to return the fire of the natives.

During the next two days we were constantly
shot at and some half-dozen of my men were
wounded whilst fetching water from the stream;
but the natives grew afraid of our guns as two or
three had been killed and a few wounded, and did
not come near the fort, which I had named Fort
Dinah in memory of my poor goat.

I next sent out reconnoitring parties, and they
soon returned after having destroyed some barricades erected by the natives across the paths,
but which were not manned when my people
found them.

On the third day a party going further afield
captured two men and a woman and brought them
into camp. The woman proved to be a relation of
Mona Kasanga, and we gladly despatched her with
one of the men to tell the natives that we wanted
peace, not war, while we detained the other man
as a hostage.

FORT DINAH.

She returned the following morning with a neighbouring chief, who was also a relation of Mona Kasanga, and peace was soon concluded.

Fort Dinah was left on the 6th of October, and in villages which we passed many temporary huts built to accommodate the fighting men who had assembled in order to share in plundering us were still remaining. These men had now returned to their homes, and the villages had resumed their normal state, and women and children ran alongside the caravan, chattering and laughing.

When we camped the chief of the district brought me a large bundle of grass cloth and some goats as payment for having attacked us without provocation. .

I accepted one goat and gave him some beads as a token of friendship, remarking that, unlike some other travellers, we were not looking for slaves and endeavouring to pick quarrels, but only desired to see the country and be friendly with the people. But I took the opportunity of informing him that we should always defend ourselves if attacked, and, as they had already learnt, we were quite strong enough to take care of ourselves.

I afterwards found that Mona Kasanga, although acting as interpreter during this palaver and hearing my remarks, tried to extract something from the chief on his own account. Fortunately I discovered his little game, or the chief would have come to the conclusion that the white man was

given to talking about friendship and pretending
to be generous, and yet allowed his men to take
the offering in a roundabout manner.

The actual reason of our being attacked was
that a party from a Portuguese caravan had been
within five miles of Kamwawi, destroying villages,

murdering men, and carry-
ing off women and children
as slaves. The natives na-
turally connected me with
the slave-hunters, more especially as I had made particular enquiries respecting
them and whence they came;
and no doubt they were
supposed to be friends whom
we wished to join in carrying
on these barbarities.

We now marched through
the districts of Munkullah
and Mpanga Sanga, over a
plain country with occa-
sional valleys, through the
Kilimachio range—a semi-

A NATIVE OF MPANGA SANGA.

circular sweep of granite hills of every shape and
form—and crossed several considerable streams,
which flowed eastward to the Lualaba—not to
that branch of the river seen by Dr. Livingstone
quitting Lake Moero, but the one of which the
sources were passed by the Pombeiros on their

journey to Tété from Kassanci in the beginning of October, this century. 1874.

At the principal village of Mpanga Sanga I met a very intelligent fellow who offered to conduct me in two or three days' journey to the principal place of Kasongo, the chief of all Urua. For some private reasons Mona Kasanga dissuaded him from fulfilling his promise and assured me he was not speaking the truth, for in the direction pointed out by him the people were very troublesome, and taking that road would lead to more fighting.

We therefore continued our journey under Mona Kasanga's guidance, and arrived the next day at a village the headman of which—M'Nchkulla—was a friend of Mona Kasanga. Here we halted, and remained whilst these worthies and their friends got drunk in honour of some mutual acquaintance who had departed this life about three months previously.

The headman visited me in a very maudlin state and insisted on shaking hands with me times without number. From him I ascertained that the camp we were occupying had been built by the plundering party we heard of near Kamwawi, and that Kasongo's capital was only three or four days distant.

When their convivial manner of mourning for their dead friend was completed and Mona Kasanga was ready to march, he again refused to take the direct road but led us in an E.S.E. direction,

and we camped by a village situated on the
banks of the Luvijo, a large stream running to the
Lualaba.

Near the source of this river is found a large
quantity of cinnabar, used by the natives for
painting themselves.

Their faces they colour in the most ludicrous
manner. A red dot on the tip of the nose is a
favourite embellishment, and some who also use
a kind of pipe-clay as white paint give their
faces a very close resemblance to that of a circus
clown.

Their ornaments are principally beads, worn in
great numbers round the arms and legs and in two
ropes of several strands disposed across the breast
and back like cross-belts, and also a few copper·
and iron bracelets and anklets.

The fashion of dressing the hair was rather different to that outside Urua, but it was still worked
elaborately and decorated with iron ornaments.

Another march in the wrong direction, along the
northern base of the Nyoka hills, had to be under-
gone the day following; and all the water-holes
being dry we were compelled to continue our
walk until late in the afternoon, suffering from the
pangs of thirst. We had become so accustomed
to constant streams of running water since leaving
the Tanganyika that we failed to take the precaution of carrying a supply with us.

At last we reached Hanyoka, a village where

the only obtainable water was of a dark green
colour and as thick as peasoup; but, notwithstanding its objectionable appearance and still more
nauseous taste, we were glad to drink it, for—

> The way was long, the day was hot,
> The pilgrims were a thirsty lot.

The mystery of Mona Kasanga's behaviour in
dragging us eastward was now revealed. He had
doubtless heard of his father having neglected to pay
tribute to Kasongo, and that he, according to his
custom on such occasions, had looted the village
and killed most of the inhabitants. Mona Kasanga's
father and brothers were amongst those killed, but
his mother, who had escaped, met her son at this
village soon after we arrived.

Mona Kasanga refused to go any further, and
M'Nchkulla being a headman of Mukalombo said
he must first visit that village, which was three
or four miles from Hanyoka.

On our arriving on its outskirts the whole of the
inhabitants turned out, and some hoisted M'Nchkulla on their shoulders and chaired him round the
place, yelling and shouting, while he looked very
foolish and uncomfortable. This performance being
ended we were conducted to a camping-place
destitute of all shade near a pool of muddy water,
and we gladly shifted to a more suitable spot the
following day.

Mona Kasanga hurried off with his mother and

October.
1874. wife, being anxious to put as great a distance as possible between himself and Kasongo.

The duty of guiding us to Kasongo's now devolved on M'Nchkulla, who, in company with the chief of the village, made demands for increased payment. They stated that Mona Kasanga, as headman, received the lion's share of that given by me at Tipo-tipo's, and as M'Nchkulla had now succeeded to the position of principal guide he should properly receive the same amount as his predecessor.

It was further maintained that as this new engagement was entered into at the village of his chief that personage was entitled to a fee; besides which M'Nchkulla refused to proceed without half-a-dozen of his fellow-villagers who also expected payment for their services.

Kongwé would willingly have taken upon himself to show the road but feared his countrymen, for being of lower rank than M'Nchkulla he would have been punished had he dared to supersede him.

No sooner were arrangements made to M'Nchkulla's satisfaction than he returned to the village and made merry on pombé. The next day he also devoted to the worship of the African Bacchus, and he proved a very poor specimen of a guide when brought into camp on the third day, being so drunk at starting that two friends were obliged to help him along.

We reached the village of Munza on the 21st of October, passing on our way over the rocky Kilwala hills, and through plains, partly forest, with other portions more park-like with open meadows and many streams.

There were also small hills of gneiss and granite, much weather-worn, the effects of sun and rain having split large blocks into fragments which lay more as though they had been piled together instead of being 'originally part of one shattered mass.

Charcoal-burners' fires were frequently seen and some villages had foundries, the hæmatite ore being obtained by digging pits sometimes twenty and thirty feet deep.

At Munza we found a party belonging to Jumah Merikani, who had a large permanent camp at Kasongo's head-quarters, and they said that a Portuguese trader from the West Coast was also there. They had heard nothing of our approach and were much astonished at seeing us.

This meeting was fortunate since M'Nchkulla and his friends had taken the opportunity of bolting; but Jumah's people promised me a guide to his camp, for which I started after remaining a day to obtain provisions, as Kasongo's place, Kwinhata, was reported to be hungry.

The guide was a Mrua named Ngoöni, who had been lent to Jumah by Kasongo during his stay, and who had learnt to talk Kisuahili very fairly.

We made two marches through fertile and open
country, with many villages lately destroyed by
parties reported to belong to Kasongo and the
Portuguese. The people had been carried off as
slaves, the country laid waste, and banana-trees
and oil-palms cut down.

Situated in the middle of an extensive plain
we saw a few huts occupied by people employed
in the manufacture of salt.

This plain I was informed was Kasongo's own
especial property, and worked by his own slaves
and retainers. There were many others in the
surrounding country which were the property of a
chief who paid heavy tribute to Kasongo for the
right of manufacturing salt.

There is scarcely any vegetation in these plains,
the soil, springs, oozes, and pools being all salt.
In one instance a small running stream is also
salt, but it soon falls into a fresh-water river.

The manner in which salt is manufactured here
differs somewhat from that already described.

A frame shaped like an inverted cone made of
sticks joined together by hoops at short intervals,
is fastened to four or five stout stakes planted in
the ground. The inside of this cone being carefully
lined with large leaves, and grass being put into
the apex to act as a filter, it is filled with the soil.
Boiling water is then poured into it, and the salt
being dissolved oozes through the grass and drips
out at the apex of the cone into a gourd or earthen

t. The water is then evaporated, and the salt, ııch is impure and dirty and usually contains ıch saltpetre, is formed into small cones averaging ree pounds in weight. ·

This salt is carried long distances for purposes

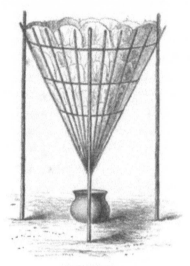

SALT-MAKING.

trade and is greedily sought after by tribes who ve none in their country.

After a hot afternoon march through an extensive ırsh, with water and mud waist-deep in the only acticable passage through the dense vegetation which it was overgrown, we arrived on the nks of a small stream shaded by fine trees, and on the other side was Kilemba, Jumah Merikani settlement.

We halted until a messenger had been sent t apprise Jumah Merikani of our arrival, accordin to Arab etiquette, and when he returned w crossed the stream.

As I reached the other bank my hand wa warmly grasped and shaken by a fine, portly Ara with a slight dash of the tar-brush, who gave m the benefit of the only two English words he knew " Good morning."

This was Jumah Merikani, who proved to be th kindest and most hospitable of the many friends found amongst the Arab traders in Africa.

He conducted me to his large and substantiall built house, situated in the midst of a villag surrounded by large plantations of rice and cor and did everything in his power to make me fee thoroughly at home and comfortable.

CHAPTER IV.

JUMAH MERIKANI.—COAL.—A PORTUGUESE TRADER.—HIS FOLLOWERS.—
KASONGO'S CHIEF WIFE.—JOSÉ ANTONIO ALVEZ.—HIS HISTORY.—WARNED
AGAINST MATA YAFA.—LAKE MOHRYA.—AN INQUISITIVE LADY.—PECU-
LIARITY RESPECTING NAMES.—ALVEZ' HABITATION.—CONSUMING YOUR OWN
SMOKE.—TAKING BILÂL DOWN A PEG.—WELL-FORTIFIED VILLAGES.—VIEW
OF LAKE MOHRYA.—HUTS ON PILES.—AN AMPHIBIOUS RACE.—NO VISITORS
ALLOWED.—A SPIRITUALISTIC MEDIUM.—SKULLS OF OLD ENEMIES.—URUA.
—KASONGO'S DOMINION.—ITS GOVERNMENT.—THE SOCIAL SCALE AMONGST
WARUA.—MUTILATION FOR SMALL OFFENCES.—KASONGO PROFESSES TO BE
A GOD. — HIS MORALS. — HIS FAMILY HAREM. — UNFAITHFUL WIVES.—
KASONGO'S BEDROOM FURNITURE.—RULE AS TO FIRES AND COOKING.—
DEVIL-HUTS AND IDOLS.—THE GREAT IDOL PRIESTS.—THE IDOL'S WIFE.—
DRESS AND TATTOO MARKS.

JUMAH MERIKANI had been here nearly two October, years, trading chiefly in ivory, which was fairly 1874. plentiful and cheap.

Being an intelligent man and having travelled much since leaving Tanganyika, he and some of his men were able to give me a vast amount of geographical information, and the key to what Mona Kasanga and others had told me while travelling from Tipo-tipo's camp.

He had been to the gold and copper mines at Katanga; to Msama's country, where he found coal of which he gave me a small specimen; had taken the road between Lakes Moero and Tanganyika, crossing the Lukuga, and had formed a per-

October, manent camp at Kirua on Lake Lanji—the Lake
1874.
Ulengé or Kamorondo of Livingstone—whence he
had come to this place.

. The Portuguese,, who had been up here rather
less than a year and were principally engaged
in the slave - trade, were acquainted with my
arrival and sent a messenger to say that the
leader of the caravan would call upon me the
following day.

A number of his people came over and were a
wild rough-looking set of nearly naked savages,
carrying old Portuguese flint-lock guns with
inordinately long barrels ornamented with an
immense number of brass rings.

They were very inquisitive and wanted ·to see
everything I possessed, and expressed much delight
on recognising any object similar to what they
had seen near the West Coast, such as cups, books,
or anything European. These they pointed out
to the Warua, who had joined them in staring at
me and my belongings, as being quite common
in their country, and claimed superiority on that
account.

Kasongo, accompanied by many people both
from Jumah Merikani's and the Portuguese caravan, was absent, being engaged in travelling about
his kingdom collecting tribute and punishing such
villages as did not pay.

During his absence he was represented by his
chief wife, who lived in a quadrangle of con-

siderable size containing a large hut for Kasongo, another for herself, and many smaller ones for members of the harem.

Jumah Merikani, when he heard of an Englishman being near, thought that he must be Livingstone, whom he had once met, having heard nothing of his death or of Stanley's journey to relieve him. He also met Speke and Burton at Ujiji, and they gave him some percussion caps (Eley and Joyce's), which were still perfectly good, though the French caps he had received from Zanzibar within the last five years were entirely useless from the effects of climate.

Kendélé, as the Portuguese trader was called by the natives though his true name was José Antonio Alvez, visited me the next day. He came in state, being carried in a hammock with an awning by two bearers with belts covered with brass bells round their waists, and followed by men with flintlock muskets, and a boy carrying his gun—a worthless Birmingham double-barrel—and his stool.

I had almost taken it for granted from the manner in which he came, and as I had hitherto only heard him spoken of as a Msungu, that he was a white man who might possibly give me some information. Great was my disappointment, however, when an old and ugly negro turned out of the hammock.

Certainly he was dressed in European fashion and spoke Portuguese, but no further civilisation

could he boast of, notwithstanding his repeated
asseverations that he was thoroughly civilised and
the same as an Englishman or any other white
man.

One point upon which he specially insisted was
that he never lied, his word being as good as his
bond ; and, indeed, that he was altogether the most
honest man on the face of the earth.

When we had exchanged greetings and I had
informed him of my name, nationality, and the
object of my journey, I enquired into his history
and learnt that Dondo on the river Kwanza, in
the province of Angola, was his native place. He
left there more than twenty years ago and had
spent the greater portion of that period in travelling and trading in the interior, formerly as agent
for white merchants but latterly on his own account.
He gave me to understand that his head-quarters
were at Kassanci, and he intended to start on his
homeward journey on the return of his men, who
were away with Kasongo, as his stores were nearly
expended.

I asked whether he knew anything of Lake
Sankorra, but he had only heard of it, and informed me that people trading there followed a
very dangerous route through Mata Yafa's country.

Mata Yafa is the native pronunciation of the
title of the chief generally called Muata Yanvo
by writers on Central Africa.

I felt much inclined to attempt a visit to Mata

Yafa's capital, respecting which some strange accounts have been written, but was told that the rains having set in the roads would be well-nigh impassable.

Even if I reached the capital I was warned that I should never return, as the last white man known to have visited his sable majesty was forcibly detained to instruct the people in the art of European warfare, and after four years of dreary captivity died there, having had no opportunity of escaping.

On enquiring whether a more direct route to the lake existed, I heard that men belonging to Jumah Merikani and Alvez had been within a few days of its shores, but finding no ivory they had turned back. The road they traversed was only practicable in the dry season as it led across vast treeless plains intersected by many rivers, and in the rainy season they were converted into swamps.

Alvez offered to conduct me to Loanda or Benguella, for, in his opinion, my party was far too small to travel alone through the intervening countries in safety, and it was agreed that on arrival at the coast I could make him a present proportionate to the value of his services.

As it was improbable, according to his statement, that he would move for at least a month, I decided to explore such portion of the neighbourhood as might be possible in that time, going in the first place to Lake Mohrya to see its lake dwellings.

Before starting on this cruise it behoved me to call on Fumé a Kenna, and to return the visit of Alvez, and on this errand I went the next day with Jumah Merikani and some of our men.

We first proceeded to Kasongo's settlement, or Mussumba, which was six hundred yards long by two hundred wide and surrounded by a neat fence of sticks five feet high, lined with grass and having only one door.

On entry we found a large clear space, in the centre of which, about a hundred yards from the doorway, stood Kasongo's dwelling, and a little further along were three small compounds enclosing huts in which Fumé a Kenna and some other principal wives lived. On each side of the quadrangle ran a triple row of smaller huts, the residences of αἱ πολλαί of the harem.

When we were ushered into Fumé a Kenna's compound, her ladies-in-waiting entered her hut to announce our arrival, and spread a fine lion's skin on the ground for her to sit upon. She soon appeared dressed in a smart tartan shawl, and seating herself on the skin at once began the conversation.

She enquired whence I had come, where I was going, and put a variety of questions to me, and then became curious as to whether I was white all over.

With much laughter she insisted on my boots and stockings being taken off in order that she might examine my feet, and when satisfied with this inspection looked at my gun and pistols and had them explained to her.

After some time I asked her name, being unaware that I was thereby transgressing the rules of etiquette. She replied Mké Kasongo, which may be translated Mrs. Kasongo, as no Warua dare tell their own names.

They are also extremely shy about giving those of any person who may be present, though they have not the slightest objection with respect to people who are absent. But, unlike some tribes in South America, they do not object to be accosted by name.

I requested her to provide me with guides to different places in the neighbourhood which I wished to visit, but she said I ought to remain until Kasongo returned, for although she was vested with supreme power during his absence, yet he might be displeased if I went away before seeing him. Finally I overcame her scruples and she promised to give me a guide to Mohrya.

I afterwards called on Alvez, and found his camp a wretchedly dirty place. His own was the only hut more substantially built than those temporarily erected day by day when travelling. It had puddled walls and a high-thatched roof, being thus made more secure against fire than the ordinary grass hut. Inside it was dirty and close, the only light and air being admitted through the door; and, with a fire burning in the centre whilst the thermometer ranged from 90° to 100° in the shade, the temperature of this dwelling may be imagined.

Alvez was profuse in his offers of assistance and assured me he desired to get as quickly as possible to Kassanci, which would be a march of about two months, and thence Loanda might be reached in thirty days, or less if a passage in a Kwanza steamer was obtained.

On the 30th of October I started with a small party for Lake Mohrya. The guide given me by Fumé a Kenna had one arm amputated at the elbow, and he was ·very careful to inform me that this operation had been performed on account of a wound from a poisoned arrow and not as a punishment.

Although I required only eight or ten men altogether, I had much trouble in getting them. Bombay certainly assisted somewhat, but Bilâl, was strutting about on a pair of high clog-like sandals, doing nothing, and when spoken to even laughed at me. So I had to take him down a peg by knocking him off his clogs and throwing them at his head.

Bombay asserted that the men wanted to break up the caravan and go no further, and the trouble on this occasion was a tentative attempt at forcing me to abandon going to Mohrya. Had they succeeded they would then have endeavoured to prevent my making any other excursions whilst waiting for Alvez, and also to compel me to al-

LAKE MOHRYA, OR REALMAH.

together give up the idea of travelling to the West November, 1874. Coast.

We marched over hilly and well-wooded country, with several large villages situated in patches of dense jungle, and only approachable by narrow and tortuous paths closed by gateways constructed of a series of logs planted like inverted V's. These formed a tunnel so low that it was almost necessary to creep along on hands and knees to enter them, and in case of attack they could be barred by falling logs arranged at the inner end like a portcullis, and no enemy could well hope to get inside.

Yet these villages are frequently surprised by some neighbouring people during the absence of the men; for, although the whole of Urua and its dependencies are under the nominal rule of Kasongo, there are often internal dissensions and fights between villages and districts.

Lake Mohrya, situated in a small basin surrounded by low and woody hills, was sighted on the 1st of November, and in the lake were three villages built on piles, and also a few detached huts scattered over its surface.

My guide gave trouble here, having a notion that his belonging to the court entitled him to take whatever he pleased from the country people. I gave him beads to purchase food so as to prevent his thieving whilst with me; but upon the appearance of a small party of men carrying large baskets 'of provisions he at once commenced plundering

them and would not restore what he stole until I
paid him for it.

He declared it was the custom of the country
for Kasongo and his immediate retainers to take
whatever they required from the villagers, and he
would not forego his rights when with me.

After arranging this matter I proceeded to a
large village near the western end of the lake
and camped.

I asked the chief to supply me with canoes for
the purpose of visiting the lake villages, and he
promised to try to obtain some from the inhabitants, as neither he nor any of his people who
lived on shore possessed canoes. He said there
would probably *be great difficulty, as the lake
villagers were very chary of allowing strangers to
visit their houses.

He was right in his conjecture, for no canoes
were forthcoming the following day, and I had
to content myself with taking a good survey
through my field-glasses and making a sketch.

The lake was small, the open surface of the
water being an oval of two miles long by one wide,
the longer axis lying E.N.E. and W.S.W., and
around the margin was a belt of floating vegetation.

I could easily distinguish the huts and noticed
that they were built on platforms, raised about
six feet above the surface of the water, supported
on stout piles driven into the bed of the lake.
Some were oblong and others round, the former'

usually having a projecting roof over the door.
Their roofs and walls appeared to be constructed in
a manner precisely similar to that of the huts on
shore. Underneath the platforms canoes were
moored, and nets hung to dry.

Men were swimming from hut to hut, notwith-

HUT IN MOHRYA.

standing reports I had heard of enormous snakes,
whose bite was fatal, inhabiting the lake. The
people live entirely in these huts with their fowls
and goats, and only come ashore to cultivate provision grounds and bring goats to graze.

Their canoes were simple " dug-outs," twenty or
twenty-five feet in length, and their paddles were

like large circular shallow spoons with long straight handles.

No chance of obtaining canoes offering, we started the next morning on the return march to Kilemba, and seeing some lake villagers working in a field I attempted to talk with them, but they scampered off to their canoes near at hand and paddled away.

We followed them across a rotten piece of tingi-tingi to the very edge of the lake where their canoes had been moored, slipping through holes in the treacherous vegetation more than once owing to our not knowing the right path. But hailing the people and holding up cloth and beads to entice them to come to us was of no avail, and I had reluctantly to abandon all idea of making myself more intimately acquainted with their manners and habits.

Kilemba was again reached after two marches, the second being through pouring rain which commenced ten minutes after we started and did not cease for a moment until after we arrived.

The previous night we camped at what had formerly been the head-quarters of Bambarré, Kasongo's father. In the old enclosure devoted to his harem his chief wife still lived, and was not permitted to receive any visitors except one of Kasongo's magicians who consulted her on all important occasions. She was supposed to be a spiritualistic medium, holding communication with her deceased husband, and, consequently, inspired with prophetic powers.

Fowls and goats roamed unmolested near her habitation, for he would indeed have been a bold man among the Warua who dared to touch anything supposed to belong to her. The few people living near were slaves of her late husband, who nightly placed provisions for her use and then retired.

On the road we passed a peculiar little hut, very well built and finished, and having sheets of grass cloth hanging over the roof to hide its contents from prying eyes.

I was determined to discover what this hut contained as it was said to be a great "medicine;" so lifted the cloth and looked in, when a quantity of skulls decorated with beads and ranged in circles met my view. Afterwards I heard that these skulls were those of brothers and chiefs of Bambarré, who, having rebelled against him, were conquered and killed.

Kasongo was still away when I returned, and no one knew his exact whereabouts; so I asked Fumé a Kenna for guides to Kassali, a large lake on the Lualaba, and also to Kowamba, the first of a chain of small lakes on the Kamorondo or true Lualaba—that seen by Dr. Livingstone to the north of Moero being really called the Luvwa, although the Arabs and others from the East Coast commonly call both branches Lualaba.

November,
1874.
Before proceeding further, it will be well to give a description of the extent of Urua and some of the customs of its inhabitants.

Urua proper commences just south of Tipo-tipo's camp and extends to nine degrees south latitude. It is bounded on the west by the Lomâmi, and on the east by the tribes fringing the shores of the Tanganyika. In the centre of this country lies the territory of Ma Kazembé, who is tributary to Mata Yafa, the chief of Ulûnda.

Kasongo also claims dominion over some tribes on the Tanganyika, including the Waguhha, the northernmost of his subjects settled on that lake. Miriro and Msama, chiefs of Itawa, are tributary to him, as also are the Kasongo at Tipo-tipo's camp and Russûna. Ussambi, lying to the west of the Lomâmi, is likewise part of the dominions of Kasongo; but many of the Wassambi pay tribute to Mata Yafa as well, for being close to his dominions they are subject to the raids of his people if they refuse to comply with his demands.

The vast territory claimed by Kasongo is divided into many districts, each (mis-) governed by a Kilolo or captain.

Some of these are hereditary governors, and others are appointed by Kasongo for a term of four years. At the expiration of that time they may either be reappointed or transferred to another district if they have given satisfaction, or be relegated to private life; but if Kasongo is displeased with them he orders them to be deprived of noses, ears, or hands.

The ranks of the Warua are well defined, and great deference is exacted by superiors from those below them in the social scale.

An instance of this which came to my notice specially impressed itself on my memory. A person, of some rank himself, ventured to sit down when in conversation with me, forgetful that one of his superiors was standing by. Instantly he was called aside and lectured on the enormity of his offence, and I afterwards heard that had it not been for my presence this would probably have cost him his ears.

The punishments inflicted by Kasongo, and those high in authority amongst his chiefs, are death and mutilation.

A nose, finger, lip, half or the whole of an ear, are cut off for mere peccadilloes; whilst for serious offences hands, toes, ears, nose, and all are taken.

Kasongo, or the chief for the time being, arrogates to himself divine honours and power and pretends to abstain from food for days without feeling its necessity; and, indeed, declares that as a god he is altogether above requiring food and only eats, drinks, and smokes for the pleasure it affords him.

In addition to his chief wife and the harem maintained in his private enclosure, he boasts that

he exercises a right to any woman who may please
his fancy when on his journeys about the country;
and if any become *enceinte* he gives them a
monkey-skin for the child to wear, if a male, as
this confers a right to live by taking provisions,
cloth, &c. from any one not of royal blood.

Into the enclosure of his harem no male but
himself is allowed between sunset and sunrise on
pain of death or mutilation; and even if one of the
harem should give birth to a male child during the
night, the mother and infant are bundled out
immediately.

His principal wife and the four or five ranking
next to her are all of royal blood, being either his
sisters or first-cousins; and amongst his harem
are to be found his step-mothers, aunts, sisters,
nieces, cousins, and, still more horrible, his own
children.

As might be expected from such an example,
morals are very lax throughout the country, and
wives are not thought badly of for being unfaithful;
the worst they may expect being severe chastise-
ment from the injured husband. But he never
uses excessive violence for fear of injuring a
valuable piece of household furniture.

When Kasongo sleeps at home, his bedroom
furniture consists of members of his harem. Some
on hands and knees form a couch with their
backs, and others lying flat on the ground provide
a soft carpet.

November, 1874.

It is the rule for all Warua to light their fires themselves and cook their own food, Kasongo being the only one exempt from its observance; but should either of the men appointed to do this service for him by any chance be absent he then performs these duties for himself.

No Warua allow others to witness their eating or drinking, being doubly particular with regard to members of the opposite sex; and on pombé being offered I have frequently seen them request that a cloth might be held up to hide them whilst drinking.

Their religion is principally a mixture of fetish and idolatry. All villages have devil-huts and idols before which offerings of pombé, grain and meat are placed, and nearly every man wears a small figure round his neck or arm. Many magicians also move about with idols which they pretend to consult for the benefit of their clients; and some, being clever ventriloquists, manage to drive a flourishing business.

But the great centre of their religion is an idol named Kungwé a Banza, which is supposed to represent the founder of Kasongo's family and to be all-powerful for good and evil. This idol is kept in a hut situated in a clearing amidst dense jungle, and always has a sister of the reigning chief as a wife, who is known by the title of Mwali a Panga.

Round the jungle live a number of priests who

guard the sacred grove from profane intruders and receive offerings for the idol, and also a large portion of the tribute paid to Kasongo. But although they hold this official position, and are thus intimately connected with all the rites and ceremonies pertaining to the deity, they are not permitted to set eyes upon the idol itself, that privilege being reserved for its wife and the reigning sovereign, who consults it on momentous occasions and makes offerings to it upon his accession and after gaining any great victory over his adversaries.

Notwithstanding my efforts I could not discover the exact position of this idol's habitation, but am perfectly convinced of its existence, as all the accounts I received were precisely similar on all material points.

As a means of testing its truthfulness more than once I tried the experiment of saying "Kungwé a Banza" close behind a man, when he would jump as if he were shot and look round with every outward sign of terror, as though afraid that the dreaded deity were close at his heels ready to carry him off. From the nature of the natives it was an impossibility for them to turn pale or for their wool to stand on end with fright, but they made the attempt; and there can be no doubt that they hold this great idol in such awe that they dared not breathe the name of Kungwé a Banza without fear and trembling.

The people dress like the Waguhha and tattoo
themselves in the same fashion, but wear their
hair differently, the majority drawing it back from
the face and tying and binding it together behind,
so that it projects in a most curious fashion re-
minding one much of a saucepan handle.

The men wear plumes, frequently made from
the red tail-feathers of the grey parrot, varying in
size and shape according to rank. They also have
aprons made of a single skin, and it is worthy of
remark that each clan or family has a distinguish-
ing skin which it is customary to wear in the
presence of the chief.

WARUA SLAVE-DRIVER AND SLAVE.

CHAPTER V.

A FAIR DECEIVER.—MARRIAGE CEREMONY.—THE YOUTHFUL BUT UNBLUSH-
ING BRIDE.—A MOUNTAIN GAP.—GRAND THUNDERSTORM.—LAKE KASSALI.
—NOT ALLOWED TO VISIT IT.—RETURN OF A CHIEF.—MEDICINE MEN.—
THEIR DRESS.—VENTRILOQUISM.—THEY IMPOSE UPON THE PUBLIC.—AM
SUSPECTED OF POSSESSING POWER TO DRY UP THE LAKE.—NARROW ESCAPE
OF MY MESSENGERS. — MANUFACTURE OF FLOATING ISLANDS. — JUMAH
MERIKANI'S KINDNESS.—STRANGE TALES.—LION-TAMERS.—DEADLY SHADE.
—SCULPTURE.—CAVE DWELLINGS.—POISONOUS WATER.—A TRIBE OF LEPERS.
—MY OCCUPATIONS.—KASONGO'S WIVES.—THEIR SHOCKING BEHAVIOUR.—
A PERFORMER OF TRICKS.—KASONGO RETURNS.—AN AFTERNOON CALL.—
HIS APPEARANCE.—HIS BAND PLAYS ME HOME.—THEIR EXCRUCIATING
PERFORMANCE.—THEY WILL NOT "MOVE ON."—MY ANXIETY TO DO SO.

November
1874.

AS there appeared no prospect of Kasongo's return and no intelligence of his whereabouts could be procured, I anxiously asked his wife from day to day for guides to the lake of which I had heard.

She continually made fair promises, but never kept her word; and at last, tired of the delay and disappointment, I induced Jumah Merikani to provide me with men who knew the road, and started on the 14th of November for Lake Kassali.

Marching across the salt plain a little south of the route by which we had previously traversed it, we arrived the next day at Kibaiyéli, a village of fair proportions having in it numerous oil-palms and intersected by a stream of clear water.

Unfortunately for my repose and comfort the November, ceremonies attendant on a native wedding were _____ at their height when I arrived. As the bride was a niece of the chief and the bridegroom a headman, it was an unusually grand affair, and the shouts and yells with which it was celebrated continued both day and night and rendered sleep impossible.

A dozen men were constantly engaged in wheeling around and about two others playing drums. The dancers were provided with rude pan-pipes producing most discordant sounds, and an admiring crowd assisted with yells and clapping of hands. And this was continued without cessation, for no sooner was one man tired than another took his place.

On the afternoon of the second day the bridegroom made his appearance and executed a *pas seul* which lasted about half an hour, and on its termination the bride—a girl nine or ten years of age and dressed in all the finery the village could produce— was brought on the shoulders of one woman and supported by another to the place where the dancers were assembled.

A circle was now formed, and the women carrying the bride took up their position in the centre and jumped her up and down most vigorously, whilst she allowed her body and arms to sway about uncontrolled.

The bridegroom gave her fragments of tobacco-leaves and small quantities of beads, which she, keeping her eyes shut, scattered indiscriminately amongst the dancers, who scrambled eagerly for them, as they were supposed to bring good luck to those who obtained them.

After this ceremonial was concluded the bride was set down and danced with the bridegroom,

WEDDING DANCE.

going through most obscene gestures for about ten minutes, when he picked her up, and tucking her under his arm walked her off to his hut.

The dancing, yelling, and drumming was still continued, and, indeed, had not ceased when we left on the following day.

worked very hard, for I noticed that the skin was
actually rubbed off her back and shoulders.

Leaving here we crossed a plain with a fair amount of cultivation, and the river Chankoji, a considerable stream flowing south to the Lovoi, and came upon some rocky hills covered with trees and creepers.

Through this range we passed by a gap about four hundred yards wide, its precipitous sides composed of enormous masses of gneiss looking like giant walls. In the numerous cracks and crevices creepers and shrubs had taken root and clothed the massive rocks with a network of verdure. On the other side was some broken country, and then a steep range which joins the Kilwala hills.

We camped at Mwéhu, where the few surviving inhabitants of some destroyed villages were beginning to clear the ground and build temporary huts.

Soon after our arrival a thunderstorm, accompanied by violent squalls and torrents of rain, presented a ' grand sight. Although mid-day, there was little light except that afforded by the vivid and almost continuous streams of electric fire, blue and red, and often forked into three or four branches. Some flashes lasted an appreciable time, being wide and having an appearance of rippling like a running stream. The thunder crashed and roared without intermission, and the trees bent to the blast which threatened every moment to uproot them, whilst the rain was driven before the wind in sheets of water.

When this war of the elements had lasted two hours it suddenly ceased, the clouds cleared, and the western sun shone brightly on the dripping trees and grass, making them glisten as though studded with brilliants.

Our next halt was at Kisima, a partially deserted village, and here a violent paroxysm of fever attacked me without warning, but happily departed almost as suddenly as it came, thanks to liberal doses of Epsom salts and quinine. It so reduced my strength, however, that it was with much difficulty I dragged on for a short march the following day, —the thermometer at 100° in the shade—and reached a new settlement formed by the chief and the larger portion of the inhabitants of Kisima.

Turning sharp to the southward on leaving this, and camping one day in the jungle and another in Yasuki, we arrived on the 22nd of November at Kowédi, on the banks of the Lovoi, having crossed several affluents of that river. and passed over some hills of granite with particles of mica sparkling in the sun like diamonds.

From some rising ground close to this village I could discern Lake Kassali—often spoken of as Kikonja from the name of its chief—lying E.S.E. about twenty miles distant. Another portion of the lake was within eight miles, but was separated from Kowédi by the Lovoi and a range of hills.

I very much desired to visit the lake the following day ; but these sanguine anticipations were frustrated, and I was fated not to stand upon its shores or see the floating islands inhabited by its people.

The chief of Kowédi was with Kasongo, who was reported to be encamped on a large hill some sixteen miles W.S.W., having gone there to endeavour to capture his brother Daiyi, who had taken refuge with Kikonja after an unsuccessful attempt on the throne.

Of several of Kasongo's brothers who laid claim to the kingdom on the death of their father, Daiyi alone continued in open opposition. Some had been conquered and put to death and two had been received into favour on tendering their submission to Kasongo.

In the absence of her husband the chief's wife at Kowédi declared she had no power to permit me to pass, and therefore I could proceed no further. I instantly sent both to Kasongo and Fumé a Kenna, requesting them to give permission for me to cross the Lovoi and proceed to the lake, assuring them that I would give no assistance to Daiyi.

Nothing now remained but to wait patiently for the return of my messengers, and in a few days they brought me the unsatisfactory intelligence that Kasongo had broken up his camp and was moving to Kwinhata, his own settlement. I then despatched other messengers urging Jumah Merikani to press Kasongo to provide me with men for the journey to Kassali.

Kwinhata, in Urua, signifies the residence of the chief, and is the term always applied to his principal dwelling; but any place at which he or his head

CHIEF OF KOWÉDI.

wife may chance to stay, though but for a single night, becomes *de facto* Kwinhata during that time.

On observing much excitement amongst the people, many smearing themselves with mud and ashes and rushing along the road leading in the direction of Kasongo's camp, I enquired the cause and found that the chief of the village was coming, and shortly afterwards he appeared, heralded by shouts and yells from all the villagers.

I used my utmost endeavours to persuade him to grant permission for me to cross the Lovoi and proceed to the lake; but he replied that Kasongo had given him strict orders not to allow any person to go there on account of Daiyi's presence. If he disobeyed his village would be destroyed and all the people killed. It was therefore evident that there was no chance of assistance in this quarter.

My attention was attracted one morning by a tinkling, similar to that of a number of cracked sheep bells, and looking out I saw a Mganga, or medicine man, ambling round the village followed by his train.

He was dressed in a large kilt of grass cloth, and suspended round his neck was a huge necklace composed of pieces of gourd, skulls of birds, and imitations of them roughly carved in wood. His head-dress was a broad band of parti-coloured beads surmounted by a large plume of feathers; and his face, arms, and legs were whitened with pipe-clay.

On his back he carried a large bunch of rough conical iron bells, which jingled as he paraded the village with jigging and prancing steps.

He was followed by a woman carrying his idol in a large gourd, another with a mat for him to sit upon, and two small boys who bore his miscellaneous properties. ,

November,
1874.
When he appeared all the women turned out of their dwellings, and many collected around the village devil-hut and appeared to go through some devotions, bending down, clapping their hands, and making curious inarticulate moanings.

. Other Waganga soon followed until five, similarly dressed and attended, were assembled together. They then performed a general walk-round, and selecting an open space in the village seated themselves in a row, spread their mats and brought out their idols and other instruments of imposture.

The principal Mganga observing me sitting on my chair as a spectator evidently thought that his dignity was compromised and resolved that he also would have a high seat of honour, so sending for a mortar used for pounding corn he placed it on the ground upside down and seated himself thereon. But it proved very ricketty, and after two or three tumbles he preferred safety to dignity and again squatted on the ground.

The consultation was opened by the chief's wife, who gave them half-a-dozen fowls as an offering. She soon went away quite happy, the chief Mganga having honoured her by spitting in her face and giving her a ball of beastliness as a charm. This she hastened to place in safety in her hut.

The Waganga were now open to hear and answer questions put by the public, some of which were quickly disposed of while others evidently

WABIA WAGANGA.

raised knotty points resulting in much gesticula- tion and oratory.

When the Waganga pretended they could not find an answer the idols were consulted, and one of the fetish men who was a clever ventriloquist made the necessary reply, the poor dupes believing it to be spoken by the idol.

I noticed that large fees usually insured favourable replies, and the result of their day's divining must have been highly satisfactory to the Waganga. Two of them were so pleased that they came again the next day; but business was slack, for the people evidently could not afford to indulge any further in the luxury of having their fortunes told.

Day after day I remained here waiting for messengers from Kasongo or Fumé a Kenna, but as none returned I sent a few men to the lake, the chief consenting to this though not allowing me to go.

Directly after they started a message arrived from Kikonja, to the effect that he was very anxious to see me; but almost immediately other messengers arrived with the intelligence that Kikonja could not receive me, his diviners having warned him that if I looked upon the lake, its waters would dry up.

On this I pointed to the lake, telling them I had already seen it without producing any evil effect on its waters.

But I was assured that if I approached close to

its shores, either the lake would become dry or the
fish would die, thereby depriving Kikonja and his
people of a large portion of their food and much of
their wealth, as the fish, which are very plentiful,
are dried and sold to people living at a distance
from the lake.

Rumours reached me that the men whom I sent to
Kikonja had been detained by him and Daiyi, but
my fears for their safety were shortly relieved by
their arrival.

They told me, however, that they had been
warned by a woman that Daiyi intended to kill
them, and they had escaped this fate by taking a
canoe at night when the people were asleep, and
making their way from the floating island on
which Daiyi and Kikonja were then living to
the mainland, and thence by unfrequented paths
back to Kowédi.

They had seen Kikonja only for a few moments
on their arrival, for during their stay he remained
in his hut in a drunken condition.

Daiyi, with whom they had more intercourse,
was a tall, fine-looking man, elaborately dressed in
beads and coloured cloths, and seemed to have
complete control over Kikonja's people.

The floating islands on which the people live
are formed of large pieces of tingi-tingi cut from
the masses with which the shores are lined. On
these logs and brushwood are laid and covered
with earth. Huts are then built, and bananas

planted, and goats and poultry are reared upon the islands.

They were usually moored to stakes planted in the bed of the lake, but when their inhabitants desire to shift their position these are pulled up and the islands warped along by lines laid out to other stakes.

The tingi-tingi between the shore and the islands which lie along its edge is invariably intersected by small channels so as to be perfectly impassable on foot and only accessible by canoes.

The main plantations were necessarily on shore, and whilst the women were engaged in cultivating them the greater portion of the men were stationed as pickets to give notice of the approach of any enemies.

During my stay at Kowédi I suffered severely from dysentery, but doctored myself successfully, notwithstanding one or two relapses caused by Sambo's predilection for cooking with castor-oil; and when my men returned I was thoroughly tired of the place.

There was still no prospect whatever of guides coming either from Kasongo or Fumé a Kenna, so I determined to start for Jumah Merikani's on the 11th of December.

At Kibaiyéli, on the return march, there were a number of Warua who stated that they belonged to Kasongo, who was then at Munza, having again left Kwinhata. And when within ten minutes'

walk of Jumah Merikani's house I was met by
the messengers I had sent to Fumé a Kenna.

They were accompanied by a guide whom she
had that morning ordered to go with them; but
this was only an apparent civility on her part,
for when I wanted to avail myself of his services
on the following morning he was not forthcoming.

I then heard that Kasongo had given directions
that if I returned during his absence I was not
to be allowed to leave, and he was to be informed
immediately of my arrival.

Jumah Merikani, with the greatest consideration, was sending me rice and tobacco by these
men, knowing that the former was not obtainable
except from his plantations, and the latter grown
from Ujiji seed, which has the well-deserved reputation of being the best in Africa.

Immediately on arrival I visited Alvez to
ascertain our chances of making a move. He
informed me all was ready, ivory packed and
slaves collected, and that he was most anxious
to start, his stores being exhausted. Therefore
directly Kasongo returned and our adieux were
made, which might require two or three days, we
should take the road.

He assured me further that sixty days after
starting we should reach Bihé—to which place,
instead of Kassanci, I now found he was going—
and a fortnight or three weeks from that place
would take me either to Benguella or Loanda.

JUMAH MERIKANI'S TEMBE.

But I was again destined to experience grievous disappointment. Kasongo did not return until the end of January, 1875, and even then delays innumerable occurred, chiefly owing to the unparalleled falsehoods and cowardliness of Alvez.

During the many tedious hours which elapsed before Kasongo arrived I frequently questioned Jumah Merikani and his men about their various travels, and amongst his six hundred pagazi, besides slaves, there were very many representatives of different tribes, some being from the shores of Lake Sankorra.

I was therefore able to gather a fair idea of the positions of the various lakes and rivers of Central Africa and their relations to each other.

From them I also heard many curious stories which, although they may seem to be "traveller's tales," were vouched for by independent witnesses, and, I am convinced, thoroughly believed in by those who recounted them.

Amongst these narratives the palm may perhaps be given to one related by a native of Ukaranga. He asserted that in the village next to that in which he lived the people were on most friendly terms with the lions, which used to walk in and about the village without attempting to injure any one. On great occasions they were treated to honey, goats, sheep and ugali, and sometimes at these afternoon drums as many as two hundred lions assembled. Each lion was known to the

people by name, and to these they responded when
called. And when one died the inhabitants of the
village mourned for him as for one of themselves.

This village was reported to be situated on the
shores of Lake Tanganyika, not very distant from
Jumah Merikani's house; and he also told me that
this friendship between the natives and lions was
commonly spoken of, but he had never been
present at one of the gatherings. The Mkaranga,
however, asserted that he had often witnessed this
friendly intercourse between man and beast, and
brought several of his tribesmen to testify to the
truth of his statement.

Certainly, if this be true, our most famous lion-
tamers have yet something to learn from the natives
of Africa.

Another story had a curious resemblance to that
of the upas-tree. At a certain place in Urguru,
a division of Unyamwési, are three large trees with
dark green foliage, the leaves being broad and
smooth. A travelling party of Warori on seeing
them thought how excellent a shelter they would
afford and camped under them; but the next
morning all were dead, and to this day their skeletons and the ivory they were carrying are said to
remain there to attest their sad fate.

Jumah assured me he had seen these trees, and
that no birds ever roosted on their branches,
neither does any grass grow under their deadly
shade; and some men who were with him when

he passed them corroborated his statement in every particular.

He also told me that in the vicinity of Mfuto, a town near Taborah, figures of a man seated on a stool, with his drum, dog, and goat, were carved in the solid rock; and Arabs had informed him that in the Uvinza to the east of Tanganyika there was a large well with carved and perfect arches.

This work was ascribed by the natives to a former race of Wasungu, but the Arabs supposed it to have been executed by Suliman ibn Daood and the genii.

For the absolute truth of these stories I, of course, do not vouch, but simply relate them as I received them.

The following account of underground dwellings at Mkanna by the banks of the Lufira I obtained from Jumah. He had not actually entered them himself, being afraid of the devil reported to haunt the caves; but an Arab who accompanied him was more bold.

He reported them to be lofty and dry, with small rivulets flowing through them, and some were actually under the bed of a river in a place where there was a cataract. The inhabitants built huts and kept their goats and other stock inside these caves.

Numerous openings afforded outlet for the smoke from their fires, and there were several passages communicating with the interior; and upon being

December, attacked the inhabitants frequently sent out parties
1874. by different points of egress, to surprise and
assail their enemies in rear and place them between
two fires.

There are also underground dwellings at Mkwamba, a short distance further up the Lufira, but the
principal caves are at Mkanna.

During one of his cruises on the Tanganyika
Jumah passed a high rocky island named Ngomanza,
situated north of the islands of Kasengé and
separated from the mainland by a very narrow
channel, into which falls the river Ngomanza, and
to drink its waters for a week or ten days is supposed to be sufficient to produce leprosy.

The inhabitants are certainly leprous, the greater
number having lost a hand or foot, while nearly
all are deprived of the sight of one eye and many
of both, it being quite a rarity to meet a person not
suffering from blindness in some degree.

None of the neighbouring tribes intermarry with
these people, and when obliged by business to
travel through their dreaded country they hurry
along as fast as possible. The unfortunate lepers
are actually forbidden to emigrate.

It may possibly be a contagious leprosy with
which they are afflicted, and that the contagion
requires some little time to affect a healthy person.

Besides listening to these accounts of travel, I
employed myself in completing my maps and
journals, making a pair of slippers, and re-binding

my map portfolio. I also constructed a new double- fly tent of grass cloth rendered waterproof by being soaked in palm oil, my old one being completely worn out; and manufactured a new pair of colours for the march 'to the coast, those used hitherto being so tattered and stained as to be well-nigh indistinguishable.

Another important piece of work was darning my stockings, and as all my darning needles had been stolen on account of their having such conveniently large eyes, I was obliged to use a sail-needle which rendered the process even more tedious than usual.

Occasionally we enlivened the evenings by shooting at the innumerable fly-catchers and goat-suckers· which came swooping round after a hot day, and the uncertainty and swiftness of their flight afforded very good practice.

I also paid constant visits to Fumé a Kenna, urging her to despatch messengers to Kasongo to hasten his return ; and to Alvez begging him to be perfectly ready to start immediately Kasongo came.

Parties of Kasongo's wives frequently came to see us, and as they had usually been imbibing freely their manners and conversation were the reverse of moral and instructive. Sometimes they would dance, and their looseness of gesture and extraordinary throwing about of their limbs certainly exceeded anything I had ever seen.

One of Jumah's slaves amused us sometimes by

January, 1875. exhibiting extraordinary tricks. His particular performance was with a piece of heavy, hard wood shaped like an hour-glass, and two sticks each a foot in length.

Taking a stick in each hand, he would make the wood rotate rapidly and run backwards and forwards in the most extraordinary manner between the sticks, on a piece of string attached to their ends, then by a peculiar jerk he would send the wood flying up into the air, higher than a cricket ball could be thrown, and catching it on the string would again set it rolling.

Notwithstanding my occupations, the Christmas of 1874 and New Year's Day of 1875 passed drearily indeed, and right glad was I when I heard in the middle of January that Kasongo was really returning in answer to my numerous messages, and on the 21st of January he actually arrived, heralded by much drumming and shouting.

In the afternoon I went with Jumah Merikani to call on him, and on entering the enclosure appropriated to his harem looked in vain for any one having the appearance of so great a chief as Kasongo was reported to be. But when the assembled crowd opened to allow me to pass, I saw in front of the principal hut a young man, taller by nearly a head than any standing near.

This was the famous Kasongo, and behind him were some women carrying his shields, whilst he held a spear in one hand.

KASONGO'S MUSSUMBA.

Every care was taken that no uninvited person or objectionable intruder should find it possible to _____ be present unobserved. The entrance to the Mussumba, or enclosure, was now carefully guarded by sentries; and a porter clad in a huge leopard-skin apron, with an enormous crooked stick in his hand, examined every comer with the closest scrutiny before admitting him to the royal presence.

We were conducted by Kasongo into his hut, accompanied by his fetish men and a few of his wives, when we made him a small present and took our departure, this being merely a formal meeting, but Kasongo ordered his band to play me home as a mark of honour.

The band consisted of wooden drums, marimba, and globular gourds played as wind instruments and producing a sound resembling that of a bugle.

Kasongo's attention in directing so great a mark of respect as being marched home to the strains of his own band was of course most flattering, but the *tapage infernal* was well-nigh unbearable. I sent them a few beads in the hope that, like the organ-grinder of the civilised world, they would take the hint and move on. But the unsophisticated natives accepted this action as a mark of my appreciation, or else imagined that I had hired them for the rest of the day, for they continued until after sunset to play in front of Jumah's verandah, the only place I had in which to spend my days.

I now believed the time of starting to be near and sent to Alvez suggesting that he should bi farewell to Kasongo and make a move as soon a possible, since every day's delay was diminishing the stock of beads with which I had to make m journey to the coast.

CHAPTER VI.

A HORDE OF RUFFIANS.—A THOROUGH BLACKGUARD.—A KING AMONGST
BEGGARS.—WIVES AND FAMILIES VISIT ME.—MUTILATED MEN.—KASONGO'S
VANITY.—HIS MESSAGE TO HER MAJESTY.—HE TAKES ME FOR A GHOST.—
NO GUIDES OR ESCORT OBTAINABLE.—ABANDONMENT OF MY FONDEST HOPE.
—HONEST ALVEZ.—HE' LIES LIKE TRUTH.—PLOTTING.—THE LEVÉE.—
WARNED AND ARMED.—THE CEREMONY.—SALAAMS OF THE CHIEFS.—BITING
THE DUST.—SPEECHES.—DECEIT.—SLEEPING WITH DECEASED WIVES.—
OBLIGED TO BUILD KASONGO'S HOUSE.—CRUELTY OF PORTUGUESE SLAVE-
TRADERS.—DELAYS.—DESERTION.—JUMAH MERIKANI SENDS DESERTERS A
WARNING.—FUNERAL RITES OF A CHIEF.—WIVES BURIED ALIVE WITH
HIM.—BLOOD SHED OVER HIS GRAVE.—KASONGO'S HARSH RULE.—HIS
DEMONIACAL FRENZIES.—FIRE IN CAMP.—MY SERVANT'S GOOD CONDUCT.—
DELICATE ATTENTION OF MRS. KASONGO.

WITH Kasongo returned the horde of ruffians January, 1875. who had accompanied him on his plundering raids, and to Lourenço da Souza Coimbra, a son of Major Coimbra of Bihé, must be awarded the palm for having reached the highest grade in ruffianism amongst them all.

He lost no time in coming to see me in the endeavour to swindle me out of something, and commenced by advancing a claim to be paid as a guide, on the plea that he had shown Alvez the road by which we intended to reach the coast. And hearing that I had promised Alvez a gun when we had fairly started, he declared he was equally entitled to one.

To this request I most decidedly refused to accede ; and then Coimbra—who was known by the natives as Kwarumba—continually worried me with his importunate demands for cartridge-paper,

COIMBRA.

powder, beads, and in fact anything he imagined he might extract from me.

His attire and general appearance were worthy of his character. A dirty, greasy and tattered wide-awake hat, battered shapeless and so far gone that a *chiffonnier* would have passed it by as worthless, crowned this distinguished person. His

shirt was equally dirty, and a piece of grass cloth
bound round his waist trailed its end upon the
ground. His hair was short and kinky, and his
almost beardless face, where not covered with filth,
was of a dirty yellow colour. Even had he not
been always in a half-drunken state, his blood-
shot eye would have told the tale of debauchery.
In short, he was, true to his appearance, an un-
mitigated ruffian.

Alvez, his employer, was not behind in begging
for small things, besides the promised rifle, which
he said he particularly wanted to get possession
of at once in order to prove the existence of the
agreement between us. After constant appeals
made on this ground I allowed him to have it,
hoping that he might be induced to settle quickly
with Kasongo and start away without further
delay when he saw I was inclined to treat him
generously.

Kasongo's arrival was not the signal for our
speedy departure as I had hoped. After seeing
me and my wonders he began begging for all
I possessed—my own guns, hat, boots, pistols,
books—in fact everything new to him he fancied
and asked for, and was so very persistent and
difficult a beggar to get rid of that he would even
have bothered the agent of a mendicity society.

On returning my call he brought a crowd of
wives and followers, and sat for nearly three hours
under Jumah Merikani's verandah. Many of the

women had babies of tender age with them, and nursery kits being very limited in Urua some portion of the scene had perhaps better remain undescribed.

I was astonished to see Kasongo accompanied by a large number of mutilated men, and was still more so on finding that many had been thus mutilated simply for caprice or as an instance of his power.

His *fidus Achates* had lost hands, nose, ears, and lips in consequence of fits of temper on Kasongo's part; but notwithstanding having experienced such cruel treatment at his master's hands he seemed to worship the ground he stood upon. Several others equally badly maimed were scarcely less remarkable for their devotion.

Kasongo was inflated with pride and asserted that he was the greatest chief in the whole world.

The only one, in his opinion, who could in any way compare with him was Mata Yafa, the chief of Ulûnda, who was also a Mrua and belonged to the same family as Kasongo. He graciously informed me that, but for the obstacle offered by the great Lake Tanganyika lying in the way, he would visit England to see what the country was like.

I thought it possible his vanity might suffer a shock when I told him that the Tanganyika was nothing in comparison with the seas that lay between Africa and my home. But he merely remarked that he would defer his visit for the present, and directed me to tell my chief to pay him tribute, and to send me back with rifles, cannon (of which he had heard from the Portuguese), boats to navigate his rivers, and people to teach him and his subjects the manner of using them.

I then informed this self-important chief that those who understood how to make the things he required were not likely people to pay him tribute, and that my chief was far greater than he, and, indeed, that he could have no idea of the magnitude of her power.

I asked him how many fighting men he could muster, and the number that could be put into the largest of his canoes.

He said he was unable to count his fighting men, but that five or six was a very good number for one canoe.

I replied, laughing, that I had formed a good idea of the strength of his army, and that a very small chief in my country often commanded more men armed with rifles; whilst, instead of six men being as many as could go in one canoe, we had ships the size of islands, and although carrying more than a thousand men each they could remain away from land for many months.

Even after this conversation, although he admitted that what I had said might be true, yet he adhered to the opinion that he was a very great man, and I was still to convey his messages to my chief.

H 2

After this talk, however, the marvellous reports spread by my people concerning the power of the English reached his ears, and I heard that he came to the conclusion I was a ghost that had come from spirit-land to visit him.

I pressed him to permit Alvez to leave, telling him I had long been away from my home and wished to return, and that as I had a great distance to travel I was anxious to start as quickly as possible. He promised that directly he had held a levée of his chiefs, at which he desired me to be present in order that I might be impressed with his greatness, we should not only be free to depart, but he would also furnish guides to the boundary of his dominions.

My endeavours to induce him to provide me with guides to Sankorra were unsuccessful, for he always excused himself by saying that my people were too few to travel alone, and that my only chance was either to go with Alvez or to remain with Jumah Merikani until he returned to the Tanganyika.

Both from Alvez and Jumah Merikani I tried to obtain escort to the lake; but they said they were not sufficiently strong to spare any of their followers. Thus most reluctantly was I compelled to surrender my long-cherished idea of tracing the Kongo to its mouth.

The levée which I believed would at length bring my long period of inaction to a termination was postponed from day to day, and did not take place till the 10th of February.   .

Before this Alvez had demanded an agreement in writing as to the amount to be paid him for showing me the road to the coast.

The negotiations were carried on through the medium of one of my men, who, having been employed on board a Portuguese merchant ship, spoke the language well, but unfortunately understood nothing as to the money. Alvez unhesitatingly took advantage of this ignorance, and fleeced me outrageously.

When once the agreement was signed he changed his tone of almost cringing civility for one of impertinence, and it required considerable self-control on my part to avoid numerous rows with him. He had promised not to wait for the levée, but to start two days after signing our agreement. Yet as soon as he considered I was in his power he declared, notwithstanding my remonstrances, that he would not start until after the levée.

At last the momentous day arrived, and a messenger from Kasongo came to Jumah and myself at seven o'clock in the morning, saying that he hoped we would attend without delay as Alvez was already at his Muṣsumba.

Jumah warned me to be prepared for treachery, having heard that Kasongo had proposed to Alvez that he should join in attacking and looting us, and that although Alvez·had refused a large number of his people, headed by Coimbra, had agreed to assist in this plot. ʼ

"Once warned, twice armed;" so we posted fifty of Jumah's men with guns in different parts of his settlement, and taking sixty more and my own askari proceeded to the Mussumba.

There we found Kasongo and Fumé a Kenna almost alone in their glory, although large numbers of chiefs and their followers were collected outside. At first the entry of our armed party was objected to, but I overcame this by the assertion that they were brought merely in honour of Kasongo, as it would be disrespectful to visit so powerful a chief on a state occasion without a suitable escort.

I did not carry my rifle, contenting myself with keeping my revolver ready for action if necessary; but Jumah Merikani, contrary to his usual habit, dispensed with the services of a gunbearer and took the precaution of carrying his gun himself.

Soon after our arrival the jingling of bells announced the approach of Alvez in his hammock, and we then proceeded to business.

Alvez and his men, all of whom carried guns, were formed in line along one side of the open space near the entrance to the Mussumba, and Jumah Merikani and myself with our followers sat opposite. Midway between these two lines and towards one end stood Kasongo.

Facing him was a man supporting a curiously shaped axe, and immediately behind him were four women, one of whom also carried an axe similar in form to that of the man in front. Then followed two Waganga and women bearing Kasongo's shields, and behind them a party of men with all Kasongo's guns, standing in line and flanked on either side by executioners and other officials. In rear of all were his wives and children.

Opposite to Kasongo and close to the entrance of the Mussumba were the chiefs who had been summoned to attend with their followers all arrayed in their best.

The next stage of the proceedings consisted of a monotonous droning through a list of Kasongo's titles and a description of his greatness by the women immediately behind him, assisted occasionally by the people joining in chorus.

This long preamble being finished, the chiefs, commencing with the lowest in rank, came forward in turns and made their salaams.

Each one was accompanied by a boy carrying a bag of powdered pipe-clay or cinnabar, and when fairly in front of Kasongo, at about twenty yards' distance, the bag was taken from the boy by the chief, who rubbed its contents upon his arms and chest. Meanwhile he swayed about from one foot to the other, shouting at the top of his voice Kasongo's titles—Kalunga Kasongo, Kalunga, Moéné Munza, Moéné Banza, Moéné Tanda, and many others.

When sufficiently bedaubed the chief returned the bag to his boy, and drawing his sword rushed at Kasongo seemingly intent upon cutting him down; but just before reaching him he suddenly fell on his knees, driving the sword into the ground and rubbing his forehead in the dust.

Kasongo having acknowledged this salute with a few words, the chief arose, and passing to the rear was rejoined by his retainers.

After all the chiefs had saluted Kasongo delivered a long speech about himself, his divine rights, greatness and powers, declaring that the only person who could be compared to him was his relative Mata Yafa.

This was followed by an address from Coimbra and another from a man on our side who spoke Kirua. In these speeches there was much recrimination and self-laudation, and once or twice matters became threatening, but it passed away without any disturbance.

At the conclusion Kasongo formally confided me to the care of Alvez, telling him that should anything happen to me on the journey to the coast he would be certain to receive intelligence of it, and consequently Alvez had better look well after my interest or never again show his face in Urua.

Notwithstanding these parting instructions Alvez determined not to start until the mourning for one of Kasongo's wives who had just died was concluded. That occupied a week, at the end of which time I saw Kasongo looking very seedy and dirty, as well he might, for according to custom he had been sleeping nightly with his deceased wife. .

I expressed a hope that we might now leave, but he replied that Alvez had promised to build him a house and that I must follow his example and do likewise; but I excused myself on the impossibility of obtaining building materials suitable for a European house.

Alvez denied point-blank having made any such promise, but in a few days I ascertained that he had volunteered to do this service; and when I remonstrated with him on this breach of faith he declared that the house would be erected in four or five days and that Coimbra had already set about it with a party of men.

Coimbra returned soon after and I discovered that he knew nothing concerning the house, but had been engaged on some plundering or murdering expedition in company with a party of Kasongo's people.

Now I was told the whole caravan must move to Totéla, where the building operations were to be carried on, and which was two or three marches on our route to the coast. We were then obliged to wait until Kasongo was ready to select and clear the ground and prepare the necessary trees for building.

Day after day was wasted, puerile excuses of every kind were made, the fetish men, wives of Kungwé a Banza and the deceased Bambarré were consulted, and gave answers as ambiguous as those of the Delphic oracle. Kasongo could or would not decide upon starting until, at last, I promised him the rifle—which he had been begging for almost daily—as soon as a move was made, and thus persuaded he left for Totéla on the 21st of February.

It was equally difficult to get Alvez under way, but on the 25th we actually moved off, and after six dawdling marches and three days' halt, arrived at Totéla, where we found Kasongo with a number of Warua, but nothing done towards commencing the building operations.

On this march with Alvez I was disgusted beyond measure with what I saw of the manner in which the unfortunate slaves were treated, and have no hesitation in asserting that the worst of the Arabs are in this respect angels of light in comparison with the Portuguese and those who travel with them.

Had it not come under my personal notice I should scarcely have believed that any men could be so wantonly and brutally cruel.

The whole organization of Alvez' caravan was bad from beginning to end. The nucleus consisted of a small number of his own slaves and porters hired by him in Bihé; but the greater portion

SCENE IN CAMP.

was composed of independent parties from Bihé, and there were also a few people from Lovalé and Kibokwĕ who had joined *en route* in order to come to Urua to steal slaves.

These outsiders, who were all provided with guns, had been encouraged to join us to add to the apparent strength of the party. There was no discipline or authority over'them and they constantly hindered the caravan, as many as a hundred sometimes being present at a palaver about marching or halting.

At starting the whole caravan may have numbered seven hundred, and before leaving Urua they had collected over fifteen hundred slaves, principally by force and robbery.

Just before marching from Kilemba I heard, quite by chance, that a party had left for Kanyoka on the borders of Ulûnda, and that we should be delayed until they returned. I strongly urged the despatch of messengers to recall them at once, but this was not done until after our arrival at Totéla.

When leaving Jumah Merikani's house, where I had experienced the greatest hospitality during my long stay, he gave me a present of beads, two goatskin bags of good flour and one of rice, thus adding to the many benefits he had bestowed on me. And whilst at Totéla he constantly sent rice to me; so much, indeed, that it lasted me to Bihé.

It soon became evident that if the building
operations were left to Alvez and his motley crowd
years would elapse before the house would be
finished; so I set my men to work and completed
it in three weeks; excepting plastering and deco-
rating the walls, which was done by Kasongo's
women under the direction of Fumé a Kenna.

In the beginning of April the house was
finished but nothing was known of the Kanyoka
party. I therefore sent a few of my people with
some of Alvez' men to endeavour to ascertain
what had become of them.

Kasongo soon grew tired of remaining in one
place and on several occasions went away on
plundering expeditions, accompanied by Coimbra
and ruffians ·belonging to Alvez' caravan who
hoped by this means to pick up slaves.

I tried my hardest to persuade him to give me
canoes that I might go down the Lomâmi and thus
get back to the Kongo. But it was of no avail
and I had to remain inactive day after day.

Thus April passed without any signs of the
return of the Kanyoka party or any events worth
recording.

Some of my men, dreading the road in front,
deserted and made their escape to Jumah Merikani's camp. Hearing of this he sent them back
to·me with a message for the guidance of others
similarly chicken-hearted, that all deserters would
be immediately returned to me, if possible, or be

kept in chains until he arrived at Zanzibar, where he would hand them over to the English consul for punishment. But for this threat I believe very many would have deserted.

The time passed most heavily during this long delay, and I found it necessary to make employment to prevent becoming desperate through vexation and *ennui*.

Many otherwise tedious hours were occupied in writing, drawing, taking lunars and working them out, and in copying itineraries and meteorological observations for my journals. In the evenings I frequently went out with my gun, and the guinea-fowl and wood-pigeons I brought in were a welcome addition to my larder. And an occasional visit from Fumé a Kenna also somewhat

I also busied myself in collecting a vocabulary of Kirua and in enquiring into the manners and customs of the people, and by this means became acquainted with the ceremonies observed at the burial of a chief of Urua, which are probably unequalled in their savagery.

The first proceeding is to divert the course of a stream and in its bed to dig an enormous pit, the bottom of which is then covered with living women. At one end a woman is placed on her hands and knees, and upon her back the dead chief, covered with his beads and other treasures, is seated, being supported on either side by one of his wives, while his second wife sits at his feet.

The earth is then shovelled in on them, and all the women are buried alive with the exception of the second wife. To her custom is more merciful than to her companions, and grants her the privilege of being killed before the huge grave is filled in.

This being completed, a number of male slaves —sometimes forty or fifty—are slaughtered and their blood poured over the grave; after which the river is allowed to resume its course.

Stories were rife that no fewer than a hundred women were buried alive with Bambarré, Kasongo's father; but let us hope that this may be an exaggeration.

Smaller chiefs are buried with two or three wives, and a few slaves only are killed that their blood

may be shed on the grave ; whilst one of the common herd has to be content with solitary burial,
being placed in a sitting posture with the right
forefinger pointing heavenwards, just level with the
top of the mound over his grave.

In the beginning of May I sent another search-
party two or three days' march along the Kanyoka
road to seek some intelligence of the people for
whom we were waiting ; but they returned unsuccessful and reported that all the country they
passed through had been desolated by Kasongo,
Coimbra, and those with them.

No village is secure against destruction under
Kasongo's rule, as the following instance will
prove. A chief having presented himself and paid
the customary tribute, Kasongo professed to be
perfectly satisfied and told him that he would
return with him and visit his village. But scarcely
had they approached the place when it was surrounded by a cordon. The chief was seized and
compelled by a party of armed men to set fire to
the village with his own hands when darkness
closed in, after which he was cruelly put to
death.

The wretched fugitives, rushing from the flames
into the jungle in the hope of finding safety, were
captured by people lying in ambush. The men
were slaughtered, and the women sent to recruit
the ranks of Kasongo's harem.

Under the combined influence of immoderate

drinking and smoking bhang, Kasongo acts like a demon, ordering death and mutilation indiscriminately and behaving in the most barbarous manner to any who may be near him.

Soon after my search-party returned some people of Lovalé who had been engaged in robbing provision grounds on the road to Kanyoka arrived in camp with the information that those men I first sent to that place had reached it and were staying there instead of setting out on the homeward journey. This first party had already been absent more than two months and the second over a month, and I was daily becoming more impatient to be moving.

I dared not make any excursions from the camp into the surrounding country, for had' I left my stores for one moment I should have been robbed; and even now there was barely enough for the journey to Bihé, and Alvez I knew trusted almost entirely to theft and selling slaves as a means of provisioning his men on the road.

At last I persuaded him to send Moenooti, the principal of his own immediate followers, to bring in the fellows who were detaining us; and this time our messages were attended to and on the 26th of May the first party made its appearance.

Coimbra, who had been backwards and forwards with Kasongo, now left the caravan to plunder and obtain a batch of slaves to take to Bihé. I protested against this; but Alvez declared that

May, 1875.

if he had not returned in time we should start without him, and with this reply I had to be content.

Before we started, however, a terrible misfortune occurred owing to one of my men having lighted a fire inside his hut and smoked himself stupid with bhang. It was in the evening of the 28th of May that I heard an alarm of fire and found this man's hut in a blaze, and being right to windward of our camp the wave of fire seemed to roll along like lightning.

All the huts had been heavily thatched during the rains, and, as usual when remaining any time in camp, the men had built cooking and smoking places, which were all as dry as tinder now the rains had ceased, and added intensity to the flames.

Jumah, my servant, who was standing by me when the cry was raised, ran to his own hut, which was already burning, being only a few yards from the one where the conflagration originated. He first seized his rifle and cartridges, and then, seeing the rapidly spreading flames, left everything he possessed to be destroyed and rushed to my tent to endeavour to save as much as possible.

The books were bundled into my blankets, and although the tent had ignited before we were all out its contents were saved. The tent itself was burnt, but my precious journals, books, and instruments, were rescued, thanks to the presence of mind and exertions of Jumah, Hamees Ferhan, and one or two others. Whilst we were clearing out the tent I asked Jumah if his kit was safe. He replied, "Potelea mbali, ponya mabooku" (Let it be d——d, save the books).

In twenty minutes the whole affair was over, and

JUMAH.

then Bombay turned up with a piteous story of having his rifle and pistol burnt. The old sinner only looked after his own kit and really did nothing himself, but actually appropriated men to his service who should have been assisting at rescuing my tent and its contents.

Alvez' people took advantage of the confusion to commit many robberies for which no redress was ever offered or received, whilst for the destruction of a few of their huts I had a tremendous bill to pay, and doubtless many things alleged to have been burnt in them never had any existence.

Fumé a Kenna sent the next morning to condole

KASONGO'S HOUSE.

with me, and as a number of my men had lost their clothes she kindly presented me with a bale of grass cloth for them.

Kasongo, hearing of the return of the Kanyoka party, came back to renew his begging before we started, and Alvez sold him the snider he received from me and also, as I afterwards heard, a quantity of cartridges which were stolen during the fire. He had done nothing for me although I had made him presents and built his house, so I refused to give him anything further.

This fire delayed us considerably as the consequent claims against me had to be settled; but at last the start was made on the 10th of June.

CHAPTER VII.

MAKING "MEDICINE" AGAINST FIRE. — AN ELABORATE OPERATION. — KASONGO'S IMPORTUNATE BEGGING.—DISGRACEFUL CONDUCT OF ALVEZ' PEOPLE.—NO MERCY FOR THE WEAK.—CRINGING TO THE STRONG.—JUMAH MERIKANI'S GENEROSITY.—THE "FIEND STREAM."—STRANGE TREES.—MY MEN MISTAKE POMBÉ FOR WATER.—SWAMPS AND BOGS.—MANY SLIPS.— "SLOUGHS OF DESPOND."—ENORMOUS ANT-HILLS.—A MONARCH DREADED BY HIS PEOPLE.—SURPASSING HIS PREDECESSORS IN CRUELTY.—THE BITER BIT.—A WELCOME PRESENT.—PLAYING WITH FIREARMS—I FRIGHTEN A CHIEF OUT OF HIS VILLAGE.—ALVEZ' TACTICS.—A NEW ARRIVAL.— ENDEAVOURS TO OBTAIN ALLIES.—DRIVEN TO DESPERATION.—I DETERMINE TO MARCH ALONE.—RESULT OF FIRMNESS.

BEFORE Alvez and his people would consent to march they declared that "medicine" must be made as a precaution against fire, since it was now the dry season and the danger from this cause was great, as we had good reason to remember.

June, 1875.

Alvez, though nominally a Christian, appeared to be a firm believer in divination and incantation and had engaged a fetish man at Bihé to do this service for the whole journey at the same rate of pay as a porter, with additional perquisites and fees.

The ceremony was commenced just before sunset, and I carefully watched the proceedings and noted them as they occurred.

I was much amused in the first instance by hearing orders given for the purchase of the cheapest and smallest goat that was to be found, that animal and a fowl, being necessary for the performance.

*. The place chosen was as near às possible to the spot where the late fire broke out. The Mganga and his boy then arrived on the scene with their materials, which consisted of the goat and fowl, a large pot of water, a bark trough with a stick fastened across the middle, a basket containing clay, a ball made of shreds of bark, mud, and filth, a wooden bowl, some roots and small pieces of stick, a leafless branch, a hoe, knives, an axe, and some Urua pipe-clay.

The boy was adorned with a streak of pipe-clay down his nose and the middle of his chest, and across his upper lip.

He took his seat on the trough, turning his back to the north, the man sitting opposite to him; they then rubbed each other's arms up and down whilst the man mumbled some mystic words, after which the boy arose and laid the leafless branch upon the trough. Scraping the bark off the roots and sticks, they placed it in the wooden bowl 'and reduced it to powder, and chopped the sticks into very small fragments.

A cross, with one arm pointing to the setting sun, was made on the ground by the man with his foot, and then he took up a handful of the powdered bark and blew some towards the sun and the re-mainder in the opposite direction. Where the cross had been drawn, a hole was now made, into which the trough was put and a small quantity of water poured into it. A few drops were also sprinkled on the ground, first to the north and then to the south.

The Mganga next took two of the scraped roots, and, spitting on them, placed one at each end of the trough, and standing to the south of it picked up some of the fragments of sticks and dropped them in. In this operation he so crossed his hands that those fragments in his left should fall to the eastward of the stick fastened across the centre of the trough, and those in his right on the other side.

These motions were strictly followed by the boy, who stood at the north end of the trough.

Both again sat down, the man this time at the east end and the boy facing him. The fowl was then seized, the boy holding it by the wings and legs whilst the man grasped its head with his left hand and cut its throat, having first rubbed it with pipe-clay and being careful that the blood should fall into the trough and on the stick across it. When dead the fowl was laid upon the spot on the south side of the trough where water had been poured, with its head to the east.

The same performance was then gone through with the goat, a couple of bystanders assisting in holding it during its struggles, and its carcase was placed on the opposite side of the trough with its head to the west.

After washing his face with the blood and water, the man took a little of it in his mouth and blew some first towards the sun, and then to the eastward. He afterwards took some of the powdered bark from the bowl and rubbed his chest and hands with it and the blood and water, the boy again following his motions.

More water being poured into the trough, Alvez and many of his men washed their faces in it and rubbed their hands with the powdered bark; and a few of my people, although reputed Mohammedans, followed their example. Some of the water was then thrown into the bowl and the remainder, together with the balls of filthy clay and pieces of stick, into the hole in which the trough had been, which was finally covered by the trough, while the branch was planted at its east end.

The Mganga completed the performance by taking the bowl of water round and sprinkling the huts; and he received the remains of the goat and fowl as his perquisites.

Throughout the whole ceremony an idea evidently prevailed that the sun was to be propitiated, possibly on account of its being recognised as the source of light and heat.

I flattered myself that I had quite rid myself of Kasongo by my refusal to listen to his begging; but in the middle of the night I was aroused, and found him in camp trading with Alvez, who sold

him the rifle he had obtained from me for two
tusks of ivory. When he saw me he asked for
cartridges; but taking no notice of his request I
re-entered my hut and turned in.

Soon I heard him outside exclaiming, "Bwana
Cameroni, Vissonghi, Vissonghi" (Mr. Cameron,
cartridges, cartridges).

I laughed at him and replied, "Kasongo, Kasongo,
Vissonghi, Vissonghi;" but he continued begging
until he even asked for one only.

We were off betimes on the morning of the 10th,
and made for the direction of the village of Lunga
Mândi, a Kilolo or governor of Kasongo's, reported
to be ten marches distant and close to the western
boundary of Urua where supplies of food for crossing Ussambi were to be procured.

For the first four days we passed over hilly
and wooded country with a large number of
villages, chiefly fortified. Many of them we were
not allowed to enter, as the people were friendly
with Daiyi and feared we had come from Kasongo
to attack them.

The conduct of Alvez' people on the road was
disgraceful. They attacked any small parties of
natives whom they chanced to meet and plundered
their loads, though these consisted chiefly of dried
fish and corn which were being carried as tribute
to Kasongo.

Any cultivated spot they at once fell on like a
swarm of locusts, and, throwing down their loads,

rooted up ground-nuts and sweet potatoes, and laid
waste fields of unripe corn out of sheer wantonness.
In the villages where they camped they cut down
bananas and stripped oil-palms of their fronds for
building their huts, thus doing irreparable injury to
the unfortunate inhabitants.

On remonstrating I was informed that they had
permission from Kasongo to take whatever they
required.   But had they not been armed with guns
they would never have dared to act thus, for on
entering countries where the people carried firearms these truculent ruffians became mild as suck-
ing doves and yielded to any demands made upon
them by the natives.

The consequences of this system of living upon
the country was to be seen in the entire absence
of women and children, goats, pigs, and fowls,
from the open villages.   Only a few men remained
in them in the hope of guarding their huts against
being plundered ; but their presence was of little
avail.

While this plundering and looting was carried
on in the open, none ventured to separate themselves from the caravan when passing through the
jungle, for it was reported to be full of armed men
who would cut off stragglers, and, according to
rumour, kill and eat them.

I kept my men in hand as much as possible, and
prevented them from following the bad example
set by the rest of the caravan.   Yet this only

resulted in their being obliged to purchase food from Alvez' thieves; and I should have suffered hunger times without number had it not been for the rice and flour so generously given me by Jumah Merikani. Even to the very moment of my leaving Totéla he kept me supplied, four men arriving with bags of rice and flour and a bundle of tobacco as we were actually starting.

A number of rivers were crossed during these four days, and for some distance we marched by the banks of the Kiluilui, or "fiend stream," a name it well merited.

It rushed along the bottom of a deep chasm in the sandstone rocks only about twenty yards wide, from which light was excluded by the inter-laced branches of the trees growing on both banks forming a canopy impenetrable to the rays of the sun. Peering down from above, all seemed dark as Erebus. For the first few feet the sides were covered with ferns, and then they went sheer down for some fifty feet to the dark and roaring torrent, marked by flashing foam where rocks checked its impetuous course towards the Lovoi.

In the forests there were numerous very fine trees, amongst which the mpafu stood pre-eminent in its great size and beauty.

Some trees had four or five large buttress-like projections, measuring about six feet at the base and gradually tapering off to about twenty feet from the ground, above which the trunk ran up

in a clean cylindrical form to the height of seventy
or eighty feet before branching out.

Owing to our lengthy halt my men were entirely
unfit for much marching. Ten soon became unable
to bear their loads and one was so ill that he was
obliged to be carried.

They ascribed their illness to the impure water at
Totéla. I imagine, however, that very little water
was drunk by them whilst there; for pombé and
palm wine were plentiful, and nearly every one had
friends amongst the natives who gave them any
amount of liquor. Curiously enough the whole of
those I had sent to Kanyoka were amongst the sick.

Leaving the hill country we came to a succession
of level plains, which must be almost impassable
swamps in the rainy season and were still damp
and oozy and marked with large pits caused by
the passage of elephants. In some places their
tracks were quite fresh, and to judge from the
amount of damage done to trees and shrubs and
the manner in which the country was trampled
about—all footpaths being obliterated—the herds
must sometimes have numbered over five hundred
beasts.

We had to cross many streams flowing through
small undulations between the plains, often bordered by swamps a mile wide.

Of these the Njivi was especially difficult. Wood
grew on each side, and the river-banks were lined
with fallen trunks of trees. between which we

waded through mud often waist-deep. It was useless to trust to the delusive help of the slippery footing these trunks afforded ; for on attempting to balance oneself on one of them it would turn slowly round and precipitate the unfortunate individual into stagnant water full of rotting vegetation.

One or two such awkward experiences taught us that it was wiser to wade along the swampy ground,

NJIVI MARSH.

with the penalty of being wet to the waist, rather than to purchase a temporary immunity at the risk of a ducking from head to foot.

Beyond this was a fairly dry tract of grass, and then the morass itself. The path was knee-deep in sticky mud, and quaking bog lay on either side.

Some endeavoured to avoid the muddy path by springing from tuft to tuft of long wiry grass

which grew abundantly. But they soon came
to grief, for the tufts were merely floating on the
mixture of slime and mud and capsized directly
they were stepped upon, throwing the wretched
being who had been deceived by their apparent
stability into the treacherous bog, from which he
had to be extricated by more prudent companions
who patiently toiled along the path instead of
seeking ease at the risk of safety. Many men
were reported to have been lost in similar bogs.

Through the centre of the morass was a stream
of beautifully clear water, ten feet wide and six
deep, with an apparently firm bed of yellow sand.
But the sand was only a few inches deep, and
beneath was quaking mud.

At intervals in the expanse of swamp there were
island-like clumps of tall, slender trees, growing as
closely together as possible and rising from the
green surface without any fringe of scrub or undergrowth. They formed a dense mass owing to the
luxurious growth of various creepers netting them
together into an impenetrable thicket.

Viewed at a short distance, these swamps had
the appearance of verdant meadows, the clumps
of trees greatly enhancing their beauty; and not
until arriving at them did sad experience of these
veritable "sloughs of despond" dispel the pleasant
deception. The scene, as one looked across them,
with the caravan in Indian file winding along like
some huge black snake, was most striking.

About fifteen miles before reaching Lunga Mândi's village I was shown the place where the first white trader from Bihé · who penetrated Urua had pitched his camp. From the account given by the natives he conducted his caravan on the same principles as Alvez, and I believe the people did not appreciate his visit.

As we journeyed onward my invalids began to recruit their health and all had recovered on arrival at Lunga Mândi's.

This village was situated in a valley amongst flat-topped hills of sandstone, well wooded and with many bright streams; and here for the first time I saw ant-hills similar to those in South Africa.

I had previously met with many ten feet in height, but now suddenly came upon some of gigantic size, measuring from forty to .fifty feet; and comparing means with results, these ant-hills are more wonderful than the pyramids. It is as though a nation had set to work and built Mount Everest.

Camping a short distance from Lunga Mândi's, we were soon surrounded by natives; some coming to stare and some to sell their wares, whilst others were looking out for any small pickings they might find. Our first visitors were men only, the women and live stock having been sent across the Lovoi on a rumour reaching them that Kasongo and Coimbra were with us.

The people evidently viewed a visit from thei
sovereign as the greatest disaster that could befa
them.

At the mention of Kasongo's name there wa
immediately much lively pantomimic action as a
cutting off ears, noses, and hands, and all declare
that on his approach they would secrete themselve
in the jungle. Lunga Mândi or a deputy take

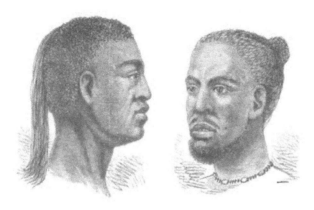

the customary tribute to him periodically to avoi
the catastrophe of a visit, and returning in safet
is looked upon as especial good-fortune.

Soon after we had settled down in camp Lung
Mândi called on us. He was very old, but excep
being half-blind from age he showed no signs o
decay, but walked with a step as light and spring
as any of the young men by whom he was sur
rounded. In the time of Kasongo's grandfather h

June,
1875.

was chief of this district, and said that Kasongo surpassed all his predecessors in cruelty and barbarism.

He remarked that he was certain I was a very good man, for he had heard that I neither allowed my people to steal nor make slaves, but made them pay for their provisions.

Alvez now experienced the unpleasant situation of "the biter bit," for he discovered that a nephew whom he had left at this place in charge of three bags of beads intended to purchase food on the return journey had appropriated most of them. Loud and bitter were his lamentations and deep his curses about these "Tre saccos — per gustare cominho."

But I was rather rejoiced on hearing that, in consequence of this most improper conduct of his kinsman, we should be obliged to hurry along on our road.

. The day after camping here, great was my astonishment at the arrival of some of Jumah Merikani's people bringing me a grass-cloth tent, sent off by him directly on receiving intelligence of mine being burnt, thus adding to the debt of gratitude I already owed him for his many and great kindnesses. The men said their orders were to follow until they found me, as it was not to be heard of that an Englishman should travel without a tent.

Lunga Mândi seemed inclined to be very

June,
1875.
friendly and presented me with one good sheep and sold me another, and in return I made him presents with which he professed himself well satisfied..

After a time he begged to be allowed to see the effects of firearms, and I fired at a target, to give him an idea of the accuracy of the rifle, at which he was much astonished. Unfortunately some one told him about the wonderfully destructive properties of the shell, and he would not be satisfied until I fired one into a tree, when the result so frightened him that he hastily left the camp and nothing could persuade him to return. I heard afterwards that he hid himself in the jungle, under the firm impression that I had been commissioned by Kasongo to take his life.

Alvez and his people encouraged him in this notion, being rather jealous at his previous friendliness towards me, and I never saw him again, although his sons often came into my hut. They said that owing to their father's age he was easily frightened; but assured me that when the caravan was gone they would persuade him that I had not the slightest intention of harming him.

On the eve of the intended start I heard that some people who had been left behind would not arrive until the following day, when another day was to be allowed for buying food. At the expiration of this time Alvez told me all was ready for starting and that we should leave at daybreak.

But when morning came a large number declined to move without Coimbra who was still engaged in slave-hunting in conjunction with Kasongo.

In vain did I represent to Alvez that when Coimbra left Totéla on this errand he had been

LUNGA MÁNDI'S SON.

warned that the caravan would not be detained for him; yet the only explanation or excuse he offered for breaking faith with me by these continued delays was that he did not wait for Coimbra but for the men with him, as their friends refused to march without them. If he persisted in going

on, he declared they would rob him of his ivory
and slaves.

Hearing that a small party which had just
arrived was independent of Alvez, I endeavoured
to induce the leader to go forward with me.

I found that he was the slave of a Portuguese trader
named Francisco Cima da Rosa, living at Mandonga,
not far from Dondo on the river Kwanza. His name
was Bastian José Perez, and he spoke Portuguese.
He had been away from home three years, having
started with some Lovalé men to hunt for ivory,
and had worked his way by degrees to Urua. When
he reached there, not being sufficiently strong to
return alone, he had been obliged to wait for Alvez'
caravan before attempting to pass through Ussambi
and Ulûnda.

He said that the threats of Alvez, who feared I
should take him for a guide, had deterred him from
coming to me before, and he assured me of his
willingness to go with me; but as Alvez would
surely march almost immediately he thought it
better to cross Ussambi in his company.

I pressed him to wait not a moment longer; but
he adhered to his view of the matter and nothing
remained but to try further persuasion with Alvez.

In the caravan there was, I knew, a large party
altogether weary of waiting but afraid to start by
themselves, and these I incited to complain. Palaver
after palaver resulted from this, and days passed
away, but still no move was made.

I then determined to march by myself at all hazards, on hearing which Bastian and the discontented part of Alvez' men promised to follow me.

This gave rise to much stormy discussion, for Alvez was furious at the idea of my slipping through his fingers. He temporised by declaring that if I would only remain three days longer he would positively start whether the people behind arrived or not; again asserting that it was not Coimbra but the natives of Bihé for whom he detained the caravan, since their relatives at that place would seize his ivory if he returned without these men.

However, I stood firm, and marched on the 7th of July, true to my decision, Alvez and Bastian accompanying me.

CHAPTER VIII.

ANOTHER FIRE.—"MEDICINE" A DELUSION.—HAVOC AND DESOLATION.—
COIMBRA'S CAPTURES.—UNMERCIFUL TREATMENT OF WOMEN.—HE CALLS
HIMSELF A CHRISTIAN.—MISERY AND LOSS OF LIFE.—ABUSE OF THE
PORTUGUESE FLAG.—ALVEZ SHARES THE FLESH AND BLOOD.—THE LOVOI.
—LIMIT OF OIL-PALMS.—COMPOSITION OF THE CARAVAN.—FIRE AGAIN.—
FORTIFICATION OF MSOA.—MSHIRI.—"A VERY BAD MAN."—HIS POWER.—
HIS FOLLOWERS.—TRADE IN SLAVES INCREASING.—ITS RESULT.—FATE OF
THE WOMEN SLAVES. — PROBABLE EXPORT. — OODS OF WAR. — EXCESSIVE
HEAT.—OUR COLDEST NIGHT.—ALVEZ LOSES SLAVES.—HIS LAMENTATIONS.
—AM TAKEN FOR A DEVIL.—MOURNFUL PROCESSION OF SLAVES.—A WEIRD
GROVE.—MATA YAFA.—VIVISECTION PRACTISED ON A WOMAN.—REBELLION
OF HIS SISTER-WIFE. — MARSHES. — A SUMPTUOUS MEAL. — BURNING A
ROADWAY.—LAGOONS.—BEE-KEEPING.

July. 1875.

AT the termination of our first march we camped by a clump of trees near a village ; but scarcely were the huts built and tents pitched before the country near us was fired, and it taxed all our vigilance and energy to prevent our camp being burnt.

The elaborate ceremonial observed in "making medicine" against fire would therefore have been of little value had we not taken effective measures to prevent the flames from reaching us.

The march had been a pleasant one as far as the country was concerned, but it was exasperating to witness the havoc and desolation caused by the thieving and destructive scoundrels belonging to the caravan.

When I was ready to pack up the next morning I was informed that no move would be made, a number of slaves having run during the night—small blame to them—and their owners having started in pursuit. This annoyed me much and I was delighted to hear that none were recaptured and no further search was to be made.

During the night some others attempted to bolt, but their masters, rendered more watchful by their previous losses, were awake and detected them before they could effect their escape. For some hours the camp was ringing with the distressing yells of these poor creatures, whose savage masters were cruelly maltreating them.

In the morning I received from Alvez an impertinent message that I was to come to him, and although this rather ruffled my temper I thought it better to go at once and ascertain the meaning of this strange conduct. On meeting he complacently told me that he had received news of Coimbra being in the vicinity, and that therefore we should wait for him.

My remonstrance and objection on the ground that we had already wasted too much time, and that so small a party could easily overtake us, passed unheeded. Alvez merely turned on his heel, saying he was master of the caravan and not my servant, and should travel or stop as he pleased.

I felt a strong inclination to shake the filthy old

rascal out of his rags, but considered it better not
to soil my fingers by touching him.

Coimbra arrived in the afternoon with a gang of
fifty-two women tied together in lots of seventeen
or eighteen.

Some had children in arms, others were far
advanced in pregnancy, and all were laden with

SCENE ON THE ROAD.

huge bundles of grass cloth and other plunder.
These poor weary and footsore creatures were
covered with weals and scars showing how un-
mercifully cruel had been the treatment received
at the hands of the savage who called himself their
owner.

Besides these unfortunate women, the party—

which had been escorted from Totéla by sóme of Kasongo's people—consisted only of two men belonging to Coimbra; two wives, given him by Kasongo, who proved quite equal to looking after the slaves; and three children, one of whom carried an idol presented by Kasongo to Coimbra, which worthy thought it as good a god as any other though he professed to be a Christian.

His Christianity, like that of the majority of the half-breeds of Bihé, consisted in having been baptized by some rogue calling himself a priest, but who, being far too bad to be endured either at Loanda or Benguella, had retired into the interior, and managed to subsist on fees given him for going through the form of baptizing any children that might be brought to him.

The misery and loss of life entailed by the capture of these women is far greater than can be imagined except by those who have witnessed some such heart-rending scenes.

Indeed, the cruelties perpetrated in the heart of Africa by men calling themselves Christians and carrying the Portuguese flag can scarcely be credited by those living in a civilised land; and the Government of Portugal cannot be cognizant of the atrocities committed by men claiming to be her subjects.

To obtain these fifty-two women, at least ten villages had been destroyed, each having a population of from one to two hundred or about fifteen hundred in all. Some may, perchance, have escaped to neighbouring villages; but the greater portion were undoubtedly burnt when their villages were surprised, shot whilst attempting to save. their wives and families, or doomed to die of starvation in the jungle unless some wild beast put a more speedy end to their miseries.

When Coimbra arrived with so rich a harvest Alvez was equal to the occasion and demanded a number of the slaves to meet the expenses incurred in having detained him.

With this additional amount of misery imported into the caravan we marched the next day and crossed the Lovoi, some by a fishing-weir bridge and others by wading where it was mid-thigh deep and a hundred and twenty feet wide. The river had evidently fallen considerably since the cessation of the rains, as there were signs of its having been treble its present width and fully twelve feet in depth. The banks were fringed with the beautiful feathery date-palm growing on a grassy strip, whilst a background of fine timber gave a charming effect to the whole.

The Lovoi here forms the boundary between Urua and Ussambi. Beyond it I observed no oil-palms, the height above the sea now being over 2,600 feet, which appears to be the general limit of their growth. In a few instances they may be met with at 2,800 feet, and, according to Dr. Livingstone, at Ma Kazembé's they grow at three thousand feet above the sea, that being undoubtedly a very exceptional case.

Three miles of a steep ascent from the river brought us to camp near the heavily stockaded village of Msoa.

The different parties of which the caravan consisted were as follows: my own party formed one camp; Alvez and his people with their slaves formed another; Coimbra, his wives and slave gang, a third; and Bastian a fourth; besides which there were two camps of independent parties from Bihé; another of Kibokwé people; and yet one more of Lovalé men, or, as they were usually called, Kinyama men, after a chief of that country.

Fire again came upon us shortly after we arrived, one of these small camps being burnt, and the whole country, which was covered with long grass, was soon in flames. The other camps were fortunately pitched where the grass was short, and thus escaped.

Some slaves wisely took advantage of the excitement and regained their liberty.

Around Msoa the country was pretty and prosperous, the districts being populous and the villages protected by stockades and large dry ditches encircling them.

The trenches were ten or twelve feet deep and of the same width, and the excavated earth was used to form a bank on the outside of the stockade so as to render it perfectly musket-proof. These

unusual fortifications were intended as a protection
against the raids of Mshiri, the chief of Katanga.

Of Mshiri I had before heard and he was
reputed to be a " very bad man " (*mtu mbaya
sana*); but I had no idea that he extended his
depredations as far as Ussambi.   He· is one of
the Wakalaganza, the principal tribe among the
Wanyamwési, and many years ago he penetrated
with a·strong party as far as Katanga in search
of ivory.   When there he saw that his party,
having the advantage of possessing guns, could
easily conquer the native ruler.   And this he
forthwith proceeded to do and established himself
as an independent chief though Katanga is properly
in the dominions of Kasongo.

As such, Kasongo and his father, Bambarré, had
frequently sent parties to demand tribute from
Mshiri; but they had always returned from their
mission with anything but success, and neither
Kasongo nor his father thought it advisable to risk
their prestige by proceeding against him in person.

Mshiri has collected around him large numbers
of Wanyamwési and malcontents from amongst the
lower order of traders from the East Coast, and
obtains supplies of powder and guns by trading
both to Benguella and Unyanyembé.

Caravans commanded by half-caste Portuguese
and slaves of Portuguese traders have visited him
for over twenty years and furnish numerous
recruits to his ranks.   Ivory being scarce, his

principal trade is in slaves and copper. The latter is procured on the spot from the mines at Katanga; but for slaves he has to send far and wide.

In consideration of a small payment he allows parties of his adherents to accompany slave-trading caravans on their raids, and on returning to his head-quarters the slaves are divided between the traders and himself in proportion to the number of guns furnished by his people.

His trade with Bihé and the West Coast is rapidly increasing, and large tracts of country are being depopulated in consequence.

Only a small proportion of the slaves taken by the caravans from Bihé and the West Coast reach Benguella, the greater part, more especially the women, being forwarded to Sekélétu's country in exchange for ivory. And it is not improbable that some of these eventually find their way to the diamond fields amongst the gangs of labourers taken there by the Kaffirs.

Nevertheless I am convinced that more are taken to the coast near Benguella than can be absorbed there, and that an outlet for them must exist. I am strongly of opinion that, in spite of the unremitting vigilance of the commanders of our men-of-war, and of the lives and treasure that England has expended in the suppression of this inhuman traffic, many slaves are still smuggled away, possibly to South America or the West Indies.

July,
1875.

Outside the stockaded village large collections
of horns and jaw-bones of wild beasts were
placed in front of small fetish huts, as offerings to
induce the African gods of war and hunting to
continue favourable to their votaries.

From these villages the road led through woods
and open savannahs and across a wide swamp
drained by the Luvwa, running in several small
channels to the southward and ultimately falling
into the Luburi, an affluent of the Lufupa.

We camped on a large open plain destitute
of trees or shade, and where the grass had lately
been burnt.

The excessive heat of the baked ground, combined with that of the rays of the unclouded sun,
was almost unbearable. And this burning day
was followed by the coldest night we had yet
experienced in Africa, owing to the clearness of
the sky and the consequent excessive radiation,
the thermometer only marking 46°·5 Fahr. in my
tent in the morning.

At this camp the nephew of Alvez and the
slaves who had appropriated the beads at Lunga
Mândi's took the opportunity of running away.
They had all been flogged and kept in chains
until the caravan started, when they were released
and given loads to carry with the utterance of
many dire threats as to what should happen to
them at Bihé; so, finding themselves unwatched,
they evidently thought it wise to decamp.

Alvez, thus baffled, halted to search for the objects of his wrath; but as Coimbra was going foraging for provisions at a village which was to be our next station I took the .opportunity of accompanying him and looking for better quarters than the roasting spot we were then occupying.

On the road we met with several streams and

VILLAGE OF KAWALA.

small swampy places—" bad steps," as Paddy would call them—but at the end of our march were re- warded by finding a delightful camping-ground close to Kawala.

This was another entrenched village, and Poporla, the chief, said that some of Mshiri's people had lately passed leaving him unmolested owing to the strength of his fortifications.

Excepting a little corn, no food was procurable; but the people were so delighted with the extraordinary circumstance of a caravan being ready to pay for what was required that they allowed us to buy at most moderate prices.

From Poporla's wife, who accompanied her husband to the camp, I managed to obtain half-a-dozen eggs, which were a great treat. But Poporla was horrified at the idea of a "great man" being reduced to eating eggs, and brought me a basket of beans-and a piece of charred meat. It was, I believe, the only flesh they had in the village, and on close examination it proved to be the windpipe of some wild animal.

With some difficulty I avoided being almost compelled to eat this in the chief's presence, he was so anxious that I should begin and not mind his being there. But, under the pretence of extreme politeness, I escaped the delicious morsel. After he had left my servant exchanged it with one of Coimbra's people for a head of Indian corn.

Alvez arrived the following day not only having failed to find the runaways, but having lost two or three more slaves. With many lamentations over the hardness of his fate, he came to me expressing a hope that I should remember him and his losses.

This I could, with a clear conscience, promise to do; for, to my dying day he will ever be present to my mind as one of the most loathsome productions of a spurious civilisation.

It pleased me to hear that, in his opinion, the slaves ran owing to the opportunities offered by short marches and numerous halts, and therefore he should press on to the utmost. I was selfish enough to hope that in consequence of this we might go forward without any more vexatious halts.

From Kawala we marched by Angolo, and the inhabitants came to us eager to sell flour and corn for beads.

I now found that Alvez and his people had, in a great measure, made arrangements for providing themselves with stores for the downward journey by obtaining a particular sort of bead. It is not imported from the West Coast, but they had stolen large quantities from the Warua, who are particularly fond of them and buy them from the Arabs.

Camping for that night in the jungle, we next marched to Lupanda, three days being occupied on the road. The route was well watered and the villages were embanked and stockaded; and although the inhabitants of some would have no communication whatever with the caravan, others came freely into camp with corn for sale. The matama harvest had just been gathered, and it was cheap and plentiful.

Just outside a village I saw a dead python thirteen feet eight inches in length, but not of great girth.

At none of these villages were we allowed to
enter, but while I was waiting near one for the
caravan to come up two of my men managed to
get inside with the intention of trying to buy
the rarity of a fowl or goat for me. Directly
they were discovered a shout was raised, and all
the people retreated into an inner palisade and
closed the entrances.

The inhabitants then began threatening my men
with spears from this inner fortification, and they
judged it advisable to withdraw. But after a time
the people gained confidence, and seeing only myself
and three followers ventured out to satisfy their
curiosity by staring at us from a distance.

At last I induced one of the natives to come
near me, but after having a good look he covered
his face with his hands and rushed away with a
yell.

He had never before seen a white man, and I
really believe he thought I was a devil.

A boy about ten years of age then approached
me and I gave him a few beads and a little tobacco ;
and on observing that no injury befell the youngster
other people surrounded me with much laughing
and staring, and a good-natured old woman even
consented to sell me a fowl.

Whilst we were engaged in a lively conversation
—by signs—Alvez' caravan appeared, and the
natives immediately bolted into the village and
closed the entrances.

The place I had chosen for my cámp was near
the path, and the whole of the caravan passed on
in front, the mournful procession lasting for more
than two hours. Women and children, footsore
and over-burthened, were urged on unremittingly
by their barbarous masters; and even when they

SLAVE GANG.

reached their camp it was no haven of rest for the
poor creatures.

They were compelled to fetch water, cook, build
huts, and collect firewood for those who owned them;
and were comparatively favoured if they had contrived some sort of shelter for themselves before
night set in.

The loss of labour entailed by working gangs
of slaves tied together is monstrous; for if one

pot of water is wanted twenty people are obliged
to fetch it from the stream, and for one bundle
of grass to thatch a hut the whole string must
be employed. On the road, too, if one of a
gang requires to halt the whole must follow
motions, and when one falls. five or six are
dragged down.

The whole country was well wooded and the
streams were almost innumerable. Groves of
gigantic trees sprang up without undergrowth,
and a weird feeling of awe stole over me as
I wandered in my loneliness amongst their huge
trunks, and looked up at their towering heads
whose outspreading branches obscured the light of
the mid-day sun.

At Lupanda the chief brought a tusk of ivory
for sale, and the caravan was halted a day that
Alvez might bargain about the price. And even
then he did not purchase it.   •

I had some conversation with these people and
also with a chief, named Mazonda, whose village
we had passed the day before. They told me that
Mata Yafa, who had been deposed by his sister,
was stealing through the country about eight miles
north of us, being on his way to solicit the assistance of his friend and kinsman Kasongo to rein-
state him in his government.   •

In addition to cutting off noses, lips, and ears,
the morbid curiosity of this wretched creature led
him, on one occasion, to extend his studies in vivi-

section even to sacrificing an unfortunate woman who was about to become a mother.

To this his sister—who was also his principal wife—objected, being prompted by the instinct of self-preservation; for she urged that, being herself a woman, she might some day be chosen as a subject by Mata Yafa in his search for knowledge. So gathering together a strong party she attempted to surprise and kill him in his hut at night.

Rumour of these intentions having reached him, he escaped with a mere handful of men, and his sister proclaimed a brother the ruler in his stead.

A quantity of copper—principally obtained from mines about fifty miles south of this place—was brought into camp here as an exchange for slaves. It was cast in pieces shaped like St. Andrew's cross, as before described, and was carried in loads of nine or ten slung at each end of a pole, weighing altogether from fifty to sixty pounds.

Upon my picking up a half-load consisting of ten pieces and holding it out at arm's-length the people were greatly astonished and declared I had made a "great medicine" to be enabled to do this. Some of the villagers and several of Alvez' and my own people put their powers to the test, and one of my men managed to hold out six pieces, but the average was four or five.

It must be remembered that none of these people had ever before attempted this, and many of them could, doubtless, have far excelled me in other trials of strength; but I am of opinion that the average muscular power of the native is decidedly less than that of the white man.

On leaving Lupanda an entire day was occupied in crossing a marsh of deep mud and frequent streams covered with tingi-tingi, over which we struggled from island to island and ultimately camped on one covered with fine timber.

At this marsh both the Lomâmi and Luwembi have their source, and unite after the Luwembi has passed through Lake Iki.

On the march I saw a herd of small antelope and succeeded in shooting one after much patient stalking. I directed my men to skin and cut it up whilst I went after the remainder of the herd, in the hope of getting another shot.

When I returned a squabble had arisen between my men and some of the Bihé people, as the latter asserted a claim to half the buck because the herd had first been noticed by one of them. I settled the dispute by saying that he who first saw the herd should receive a small portion of meat, but as for the rest they might go and be hanged.

To Alvez I sent some as a present, and the ungrateful old rascal immediately demanded more on the plea that the caravan was his and therefore all game shot ought to be brought to him for distribution. It is probable that the message I sent in reply was not entirely satisfactory nor

altogether polite, but I proceeded at once to appropriate the haunch and the kidneys for myself and
divided the rest amongst my own men.

Besides the buck I bagged some doves, and
consequently had quite a sumptuous meal consisting of roast haunch of venison, broiled dove,
and the tender shoots of young ferns boiled for
asparagus.

The next march was through country once very
fertile but now deserted, and after seven miles we
were completely stopped by long grass. We were
consequently obliged to return to the opposite bank
of a stream we had just crossed and fire the grass
in front in order to clear a road.

When the flames had travelled a short distance
I followed in the expectation of shooting some
game, but only saw small birds and numerous
hawks and kites, which swooped into the smoke
and flame in pursuit of their prey and sometimes
fell victims themselves.

We now appeared to be exactly on the watershed between the rivers running to the Lualaba
below Nyangwé; and those falling into it above
that and Kassali. We passed grass-grown lagoons,
giving rise to many streams, near one of which we
camped.

The chief of a neighbouring village visited us,
and from him I ascertained the names of rivers
we had crossed; but when I enquired the name
of himself and his village he at once went away

July, 1875.

without answering, fearing that I should work magic against him. From this place we marched to the village of Fundalanga, nearly the last in Ussambi, and halted there three days to purchase provisions. On the road there were enormous bamboo brakes extending for a distance of about eight miles.

At Fundalanga's bees were kept in hives and beeswax was collected for trading purposes, as caravans returning from Katanga usually passed this place and bought large amounts of wax with the copper they had obtained at Katanga.

One march further brought us to the Lubiranzi, which we crossed, and entered Ulúnda, on the 27th of July, 1875.

HUT IN ULÚNDA.

CHAPTER IX.

ULÛNDA.—BORN IN SLAVERY.—ELEPHANT RAGOÛT.—ALVEZ DODGES ME.
—COMPELLED TO FOLLOW HIM.—THE WALÛNDA.—A DIRTY RACE.—CURIOUS
FARE.—RETURNING THANKS.—REMARKABLY SMALL HUTS.—I DROP INTO A
PITFALL.—MY RIFLE GIVES SATISFACTION.—ZEBRA.—A COLD DIP.—ICE
IN AUGUST.—LOVALÉ PEOPLE PUSHING EASTWARD.—COWARDLY DEMEANOUR
OF BIHÉ MEN.—KAFUNDANGO.—ESCAPE OF A SLAVE GANG.—THEIR CRUEL
TREATMENT.—MATERNAL AFFECTION.—SAVAGE MANNERS OF LOVALÉ MEN.
—EXTORTION.—RUDENESS OF DRESS.—CLEVER IRON WORKERS.—ARROW-
HEADS AND HATCHETS.—BEEF ONCE AGAIN: BUT NOT FOR ME.—NUMEROUS
FETISHES.—THE ZAMBÉSI AND KASSABÉ.—INTERLOCKING OF THEIR SYSTEMS.
—AVAILABLE FOR TRAFFIC.—MODE OF FISHING.—KATENDÉ IN STATE.—
RECOLLECTION OF LIVINGSTONE.—THE LEGEND OF LAKE DILOLO.

ULÛNDA is a long and narrow strip of country —about a hundred miles wide at the point where we entered it—lying between the fifth and twelfth degrees of south latitude. The principal portion of the inhabitants are Walûnda, but Mata Yafa, his immediate retainers, and some of the governors of districts are Warua. The villages are small and few and far between, and the greater part of the country is still primeval forest.

After one march we halted for the sake of some women who gave promise of an immediate addition to the numbers of the caravan.

I went out with my gun all day but returned unsuccessful, not having seen either hoof or feather. Some of Alvez' people were more fortunate and shot two small elephants, on which account we remained another day that the meat might be divided.

I procured a piece of the trunk, for knowing it was considered a great delicacy I had rather a curiosity to taste it ; but whether Sambo's cookery did not do justice to this choice morsel, or it required some one better versed in gastronomy than I to appreciate its peculiar flavour, certain it was that I never again ventured on another mouth-. ful of elephant ragoût.

The process of cutting up the elephants' carcases was a scene of disgusting confusion. All Alvez' people were upon and about them, hacking and tearing them to pieces and fighting and squabbling among themselves like a pack of pariah dogs.

Encouraged by the sight of this big game, I went out the next day for about six hours and beat up every bit of cover I came across, and just before returning a large eland bounded out of a thicket. I knocked him over with a shell but he regained his feet, and I then sent a bullet into him from my second barrel. I found that the bullet had gone through heart and lungs, but the shell, striking the thick part of the bone of the shoulder, had burst without penetrating far. The base of the shell was flattened out like a wafer.

One of my men also brought in an eland, and my party was then as well provided with meat as Alvez' people, who kept the elephants entirely to themselves. They would not give us any, though I had endeavoured to buy some portion for my men; and even the small piece of trunk which I obtained to gratify my curiosity I paid highly for.

The meat having been packed we continued our journey, and after only two hours' marching through jungle came upon some villages from which the inhabitants had fled.

Alvez' people instantly stopped and declared they would camp there, as any amount of food was to be obtained for nothing.

Thoroughly disgusted, I went on in the proper direction with a few of my followers, leaving orders for Bombay to come after me with the remaining men and their loads. After walking an hour I sat under a tree to wait for Bombay. He shortly appeared with half-a-dozen men and no loads, for Alvez having taken another road my people had followed him. It was useless to send after him, so nothing remained but to return and follow him up.

Passing through a village which had been pillaged, I flushed a large flock of guinea-fowl feeding on corn scattered about by the plunderers, and bagged one fine fellow, which put me in better humour before I reached camp.

For some considerable time before overtaking Alvez the stench arising from the loads of putrid elephant, which having been hastily prepared had already turned bad, afforded us ample proof that we were in the track of his caravan.

I spoke to him concerning the direction of hi
road, and asked his object for marching S.S.E.
when Bihé was about W.S.W. He replied tha
it was a very good road and the only one he knew.

My men were too frightened about the country
in front to follow me alone, and said that not on

VILLAGE IN ULÚNDA.

• amongst them knew where to find provisions o
water, or could speak the languages of the people
we should meet. There was certainly much truth
in this, and knowing that if I left Alvez the greater
part of my men would desert me and follow him
I was driven to submit to his guidance.

July, 1876.

first Walûnda I had seen, and a dirty, wild-looking race they appeared.

The clothing of the men consisted of skin aprons whilst the women contented themselves with wearing a few shreds of bark cloth.

Their wool was not worked up into any fashion but simply matted with dirt and grease, and they were remarkable for the entire absence of ornament.

There was nothing to show that they ever had dealings with caravans, for not one person possessed a bead or piece of cloth. I gave a few beads to a man from whom I tried unsuccessfully to extract a little information, and he was greatly delighted with the present.

Our next march was most tiresome and troublesome, for the paths being all " gone dead," as the people said, and the only huts we saw being deserted, we frequently missed our way. But late in the afternoon we reached the place we were making for, when I had the doubtful satisfaction of learning that the road I wished to follow the day before would have brought us here direct.

We were now close to the village of Moéné Kula, a sub-chief of Ulûnda, and on the main road between Mata Yafa's capital and the copper mines and salt-pans near Kwijila.

These were passed by the Pombeiros, Pedro Joās Baptista and Anastacio José, when they journeyed from Mata Yafa's capital to Ma Kazembé; the forty days' desert which they were informed lay between the two places evidently being the country of the predecessor of Kasongo. No doubt that Mata Yafa was jealous of him, and consequently sent the travellers round, instead of through, his dominions. No parties had, however, been past for some time, on account of the disturbed state of affairs at headquarters.

From the people here I heard that a former Mata Yafa died about a year previously, and he of whom we heard in Ussambi had succeeded him. But being even more cruel than the generality, he had been supplanted by one of his brothers aided by the sister of whom we had been told.

Some people from Moéné Kula brought Alvez and myself a small pot of pombé, some charred buffalo's flesh, and a hind leg of a buffalo approaching a state of putrefaction; and although it was impossible to eat this meat we found it useful to exchange for corn.

On giving them beads in return, the headman rubbed earth on his chest and arms, and then the entire party knelt down and clapped their hands together three times, commencing very loudly and then growing fainter. This was repeated three times.

Early the next morning we passed near Moéné Kula's village, an irregularly built collection of small hamlets, some being enclosed by rough fences of thorny bushes and others open. The huts were

CROSSING THE LUKOJI.

neatly built but remarkably small, the walls not being above three feet high.

Beyond the village were provision grounds, supposed to be protected by fetishes consisting of small enclosures in which was planted a dead tree with numerous gourds and earthen pots hanging on its branches.

During this march I had the misfortune to sprain my ankle so badly that I was obliged to rig up a hammock and be carried for some days.

The winding road passed many small hamlets consisting only of a few huts in the centre of a patch of cleared and cultivated ground. They were surrounded by fences about four feet high, constructed of tree-trunks piled one upon the other and kept in position by stakes planted at intervals.

The huts were all small, and while some were circular with conical roofs and walls of stakes with the interstices filled in with grass, others were oblong with sloping roofs, and were lined with mats.

A few open plains in the intervals amongst the forest of which the country was chiefly composed were even now muddy although the dry season had so far advanced. In the rains they must be swamps.

On the 5th of August we crossed the Lukoji— the principal eastern affluent of the Lulua—a large river receiving most of the smaller streams we had lately passed. A few miles from this place was the village of a Kazembé, the second ruler of Ulûnda, but he was absent, having gone to pay his respects to the new Mata Yafa.

Two days later we reached a village of about twenty huts in the middle of a large enclosure; and whilst climbing over the fence at what appeared to be a proper entrance I heard people call out, "Take care! there's a hole." I looked at the ground most carefully and, avoiding a small hole, placed my foot on what seemed a remarkably sound spot.

Immediately the surface gave way and I made a rapid descent into a pitfall for game, but saved myself from reaching the bottom by spreading out my arms as I fell, and thus escaped without any more serious injury than a severe shaking.

Kisenga, situated just between the sources of the Lulua and Liambai or Zambési, was arrived at the next day, and being the last station in Ulûnda we remained here a few days to procure corn and make flour for a reported march of five days between this and Lovalé.

The moon served well for taking lunars, and in three nights I managed to get a hundred and eighty-seven distances, and thus fixed this important position accurately.

Here we met a small party of Lovalé people looking for ivory and beeswax. They were armed with guns, and as was always the case with those possessing them were far more curious with regard

[Page]

VILLAGE OF SONA BAZII.

to mine than people who had never before seen any
firearms. My heavy rifle was examined with much
admiration but they did not consider it sufficiently
long, their own weapons being lengthy Portuguese
flint-locks. But when one of them consented to
shoot at a tree distant about fifty yards I followed
with shell, putting the one from the second barrel
into the hole made by that from the first. They
were then quite satisfied as to the power and
accuracy of my firearms.

After leaving Kisenga, three days' marching
through alternate jungle and large plains brought
us to the village of Sona Bazh, lately built by some
Lovalé people. On the road we saw many tracks
of large game and also a herd of zebra. The
pretty beasts were playing and feeding wholly un-
conscious of our being so near, and I took a long
look at them through my field-glasses.

From Sona Bazh could be seen the heavy timber
fringing the banks of the Zambési, about ten or
twelve miles south of us, the river at this point
running W.S.W. We were now on the watershed
between that river and the Kassabé, constantly
crossing streams running either towards one or
towards the other river.

The road first led into a dip through which the
river Luvua drained to the Zambési. In my tent
the minimum thermometer had stood at 38° Fahr.,
but on descending into the dip the ground was
frozen and the pools covered with ice.

August,
1875.
To me it was quite delightful to feel the crisp
ground crunching under my feet, but possibly my
unshod and half-naked followers did not regard
the change in temperature with the same pleasure.

Until the 18th of August we continued marching through many swamps and crossing rivers
chiefly flowing to the Zambési. The few villages
on the way had been recently established by Lovalé
people, who are rapidly pushing further east.

The inhabitants carried guns, and the Bihé
men, so brave and bold amongst the natives of
Urua who had no better weapons than bows and
arrows and spears, were here extremely mild and
frightened to say or do anything which might
offend, and submitted to the most unreasonable
demands without a murmur.

The escape of a gang of slaves detained us, much
to my annoyance, within one march of Kafundango,
the first district in Lovalé proper.

I had nothing but rice and beans to eat, and I
was told that at Kafundango food was most plentiful, which was a trifle tantalising to a hungry man.

We arrived there the following day, and found
it a district with numerous small villages. The
huts were well built and of various shapes, the
strips of bark tying the bundles of grass which
formed the walls being so disposed as to form
patterns.

For a piece of salt I obtained one fowl; but
the people would not even look at my remaining

beads, being very eager for cloth, of which I had none for trading. My only stores were a few beads and seven or eight viongwa, or shell ornaments from the East Coast. But these I was

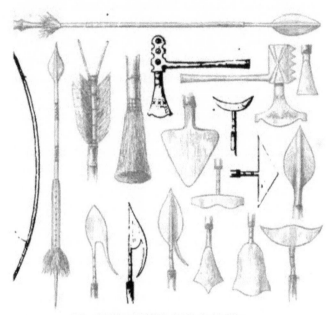

BOW, SPEARS, HATCHETS, AND ARROW-HEADS.

obliged to retain for the purpose of buying fish, with which to pay our way to Bihé.

During this halt another string of twenty slaves belonging to Coimbra ran away, and a day was lost in waiting whilst he looked for them; but the search, I am happy to say, was fruitless.

I had noticed the bad condition of this gang
several times on the road, the poor wretches being
travel-worn and half-starved, and having large
sores caused by their loads and the blows and
cuts they received. The ropes that confined them
were also, in some instances, eating into their flesh.
And I saw one woman still carrying the infant
that had died in her arms of starvation.

How keenly, in the midst of these heart-rending
scenes, I felt my utter powerlessness to assist these
poor suffering creatures in the smallest degree, may
well be imagined.

That so many had escaped was a relief to me;
although there was reason to fear that numbers
of them died of starvation in their endeavours to
reach home, or fell into the hands of Lovalé men,
who are reputed to be harsh task-masters.

The people of Lovalé are very savage in their
manners and habits, and being armed with guns
are much feared by passing caravans.

No tribute is demanded as in Ugogo, except by
one or two chiefs, but they invent many claims as
a means of extorting goods from those passing
through their villages.

Everything in their mode of living is regulated
by the magicians or fetish men, and they cleverly
lay traps for the unwary traveller. Thus, should
a stranger chance to rest his gun or spear against
a hut in their villages, it is instantly seized and
not returned unless a heavy fine is paid, the

excuse being that it is an act of magic intended to cause the death of the owner of the hut. If a tree which has been marked with fire should be cut down for building in camp, similar demands are made; and so on through an unlimited category.

Their dress is rude in the extreme, the men wearing leather aprons, and the women a few small thongs like the Nubian dress, or a tiny scrap of cloth.

Their hair is plaited into a kind of pattern and plastered with mud and oil and looks almost as though their head-dress were carved out of wood.

HEAD-DRESS.

They import iron in large quantities from Kibokwé and work it cunningly into arrow-heads of various fantastic forms and very prettily ornamented hatchets. The hatchets are also very ingeniously contrived, the upper part of the blade or tang being round, and it may be placed in the handle to serve either as an adze or axe.

At the moment of starting from Kafundango I heard from Bastian that he intended leaving the caravan and marching towards Kassanci.

By this time we were so far south that to have accompanied him would have added greatly to the distance, and being short of stores I dared not risk making my journey longer than was absolutely necessary. I therefore contented myself with giving him letters addressed to the English consul

at Loanda with particulars of my movements, in the event of Bastian being able to send them there.

These letters were never delivered, and Bastian either failed to reach his master, or the master thought it advisable to suppress an Englishman's

On this march we once again had the satisfaction of seeing some cows, the first specimens of the bovine race that we had met since leaving Ujiji. But my men and myself frequently suffered severely from hunger, the people only consenting to sell provisions for slaves, cloth, and gunpowder, none of which I could give them.

VILLAGE IN LOVALÉ.

Throughout the first part of Lovalé the country consisted of a continuation of large open plains, patches of forest and jungle and many neatly built villages. The huts were square, round, and oval, having high roofs, in some instances running into two and three points.

Our manner of marching was free from any

variety. Sometimes we were delayed by runaway slaves; at others by the chiefs desiring Alvez to halt for a day, which he most obediently did although it usually cost him some slaves, and he even supplied the requirements of one chief by a draft from his own harem.

Innumerable old camps along the road bore testimony to the large traffic, principally in slaves, which now exists between Bihé and the centre of the continent.

Fetishes were numerous in all the villages. They were usually clay figures spotted with red and white and intended to represent leopards and other wild beasts, or rude wooden figures of men and women.

Some of the plains we crossed are flooded to a depth of two or three feet during the rainy season, when the water extends completely across the watershed between the Zambési and the Kassabé.

Indeed the systems of the Kongo and Zambési lock into each other in such a manner that, by some improvement in the existing condition of the rivers and by cutting a canal of about twenty miles through level country, they might be connected, and internal navigation be established from the West to the East Coast. It would, of course, be necessary to arrange for passing some of the more important rapids by easy portages, or, hereafter, by locks.

When flooded these plains are overspread by

numerous fish, consisting principally of a sort of mud-fish and a small minnow-like fry.

The natives, taking advantage of small inequalities of surface, dam in large expanses which become shallow ponds when the floods subside. Holes are then made in the dams and the water is drained off through wicker-work placed in the gaps, when the surface of the ground which formed the bottom of the pond is found to be covered with fish. They are roughly dried and exported to the neighbouring countries or sold to passing caravans.

On the 28th of August we arrived at the village of Katendé, the principal chief of a large portion of Lovalé, which now consists of two or three divisions although it was formerly under one ruler.

Dried fish was reported to be plentiful here, and especially on the Zambési, about fourteen miles south of our camp. We therefore decided on halting whilst men were despatched to procure a sufficient quantity of fish to pay our way through Kibokwé. I sent a party on this errand with all my long-hoarded viongwa but two. And they were now the only remaining stores I had to depend upon after the fish should be expended.

Together with Alvez I visited Katendé, and found him sitting in state under a large tree, surrounded by his councillors.

On either side was a fetish hut, one containing two nondescript figures of animals and the other caricatures of the human form divine, whilst from

August, a branch of the tree a goat's horn was suspended
1873. by a rope of creepers, as a charm, and dangled
within a few feet of the sable potentate's nose.

He was dressed for the occasion in a coloured
shirt, felt hat, and a long petticoat made of
coloured pocket-handkerchiefs, and he smoked un-

FETISH HUT.

remittingly the whole time, for he was an ardent
votary of the soothing weed.

As it happened that his stock of tobacco was
nearly exhausted, I gained his esteem by making
him a present of a little, in return for which I received a fowl and some eggs.

I questioned him about Livingstone, whom he
remembered as having passed by his village ; but

respecting the great traveller, except that he rode August, 1875. an ox, a circumstance which seemed to have imprinted itself indelibly on Katendé's memory. Since Livingstone's time he had changed the position of his village twice.

In the afternoon a number of natives came into camp, and from one of them I heard the following story or legend of Lake Dilolo, which well merits being related here as I received it.

" Once upon a time, where Lake Dilolo now is, stood a large and prosperous village. The inhabitants were all rich and well-to-do, possessing large flocks of goats, many fowls and pigs, and plantations of corn and cassava far exceeding anything that is now granted to mortals.

" They passed their time merrily in eating and drinking, and never thought of the morrow.

"' One day an old and decrepit man came into this happy village, and asked the inhabitants to take pity on him, as he was tired and hungry, and had a long journey to travel.

" No one took any notice of his requests; but he was instead pursued with scoffs and jeers, and the children were encouraged to throw dirt and mud at the unfortunate beggar and drive him out of the place.

" Hungry and footsore, he was going on his way when a man, more charitable than his neighbours, accosted him and asked what he wanted. He said all he wanted was a drink of water, a little food, and somewhere to rest his weary head. The man took him into his hut, gave him water to drink, killed a goat, and soon set a plentiful mess of meat and porridge before him, and when he was satisfied gave him his own hut to sleep in.

" In the middle of the night the poor beggar got up and aroused the charitable man, saying, ' You

GAME TRAPS.

have done me a good turn, and now I will do the same for you ; but what I tell you none of your neighbours must know.'

" The charitable man promised to be as secret as the grave, on which the old man told him that in a few nights he would hear a great storm of wind and rain, and that when it commenced he must arise and fly with all his belongings.

"Having uttered this warning the beggar de-
rted.

"Two days afterwards the charitable man heard
n and wind such as he had never before heard,
d said, 'The words that the old man spoke are
ie.' He got up in haste, and with his wives,
ats, slaves, fowls, and all his property, left the
omed place safely.

"Next morning where the village had stood was
ke Dilolo; and to the present day people camp-
5 on its banks or crossing in canoes on still
ghts can hear the sound of pounding corn, the
igs of women, the crowing of cocks, and the
eating of goats."

Such is the true and veracious legend of Lake
lolo.

CHAPTER X.

JOÃO THE WHITE TRADER.—PUTRID FISH.—DISHONESTY OF THE NOBLE
SAVAGE.—FESTIVE NATIVES.—SCANTY APPAREL.—ELABORATE HAIR-DRESS-
ING.—CATARACTS.—SHA KÉLEMBÉ.—ALVEZ PROVES PICKLE.—EXCHANGING
A WIFE FOR A COW.—AN ATTEMPTED BURGLARY.—BAFFLED.—THE THIEF'S
COMPLAINT.—UNPARALLELED AUDACITY.—REVENGEFUL THREATS.—SMELTING
FURNACE.—HIGH FLAVOURED PROVISIONS.—SAMBO CHAFFS A CHIEF.—FOREST.
—A WELL-DRESSED CARAVAN.—WANTED, A DAIRY MAID.—FRIENDLINESS OF
MONA PÉHO.—A WELL-VENTILATED SUIT OF CLOTHES.—"SHAM DEVILS."—
BLACKSMITHS. — AM BELIEVED TO BE A LUNATIC. — ALVEZ' REPUTATION
AMONGST TRADERS.—I SELL MY SHIRTS FOR FOOD.—A VILLAGE EATEN UP
BY A SERPENT.—AN ECLIPSE.—KANYUMBA'S CIVILITY.—ALVEZ TRIES TO
ROB THE STARVING.—NATURAL HATS.—FALSE RUMOURS OF FIGHTING ON
THE ROAD.

September,
1876.

DURING our stay at Katendé's, Alvez received information that João, the white trader who had been to Urua, had lately returned from Jenjé, and was now at Bihé fitting out a new expedition, and we might therefore expect to meet him.

Jenjé, as far as I could learn, is the country of the Kaffirs over whom Sékélétu was king when Livingstone passed in that direction.

The men whom we sent to procure fish returned with only a few baskets full, and we had to continue our march with this small supply, trusting to the chance of obtaining more as we proceeded. Happily we were not disappointed, but were enabled to buy as much as we required.

The means of paying my way now consisted of two viongwa and about a dozen baskets of fish.

That these fish should be used as an article of diet is most remarkable, for being only partially sun-dried and then packed in baskets weighing about forty or fifty pounds, they soon become a mass of putrefaction. There can be no difference of opinion as to their unfitness for human food, yet the people seem to thrive on them.

The art of cheating is very well understood by the native fishmongers, for in the centre of some of the baskets I found earth, stones, broken pottery, and gourds so stowed as to make up the proper weight and bulk. Indeed, as far as my experience goes, the noble savage is not one whit behind his civilised brethren in adulterating food and giving short measure, the only difference being in the clumsiness of his method.

We were spared any further halts until the 7th of September, when we arrived at the village of Sha Kélembé, chief of the last district in Lovalé.

Our road lay across enormous plains—which are flooded in the rains—intersected by streams having trees growing along their banks; but on the last two days of the march we entered a country more thickly wooded and broken into small hills.

Here we had our first view of the Lumeji, a noble stream over fifty yards wide and more than ten feet deep, with a swift current running in a very tortuous course through a broad valley bounded on either side by wooded hills.

On this portion of the route the people came into camp freely, and continued dancing, drumming, and singing all night long, thus effectually banishing sleep. And in the morning they added insult to injury by expecting payment for their unwelcome serenading. Their demands, however, were not exorbitant as they were well satisfied with a handful of fish.

Fishing baskets exactly similar to those in Manyuéma were used here, and the women carried their loads in the same manner as those at Nyangwé, viz. in a basket secured on the back with a band across the forehead.

The women were so scantily dressed that a stick of tape would have clothed the female population of half-a-dozen villages.

But though they neglected to dress themselves they devoted much time to their hair, which was evidently considered the most important part of their toilette. It was arranged most elaborately, and when finished was plastered with grease and clay and made smooth and shiny.

Some formed it into a number of small lumps like berries; others into twisted loops which were differently disposed, being sometimes separate from each other, and occasionally intermingled in apparently inextricable confusion. In some instances the hair was twisted into a mass of stout strings

rojecting an inch or two beyond the poll, the
nds being worked into a kind of raised pattern. __
As a rule the hair was brought down to the
yebrows and round to the nape of the neck, so
s to entirely conceal the ears.

Many further adorned their heads with a piece
f sheet tin or copper punched and cut into fanci-
ul patterns, and some wore a couple of small locks
anging down on each side of the face.   There

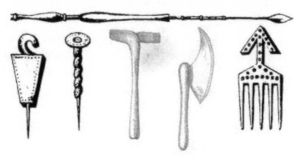

ARMS AND ORNAMENTS.

vere numerous varieties in working out these
ashions according to individual taste, but all had a
:ertain likeness to those here described.

On approaching Sha Kélembé's the roaring of
ome cataracts of the Luméji was heard, but I had
10 opportunity of seeing them, as the road led us
iway from the banks of the river.

To reach the village we passed what might well
1ave been mistaken in England for an ornamental

shrubbery with bushes like laurels and laurestinus, while jasmine and other sweet-scented plants and creepers rendered the air heavy with their odour. I thought I distinguished the smell of vanilla, but could not discover from what plant it proceeded.

Alvez was evidently on good terms with Sha Kélembé, and managed to make excuses to delay us till the 12th of September. But notwithstanding this friendship, Sha Kélembé mulcted him heavily during his stay and compelled him to pay two slaves and a gun to Mata Yafa—the paramount chief of the western portion of Lovalé, and not to be confounded with the Mata Yafa in Ulûnda.

One of the slaves thus sent away was a woman who I had reason to suppose was the favourite concubine of Alvez; and another of his harem was bartered away for a bullock, so fickle in his attachments and utterly heartless and unfeeling was he.

Amongst other excuses for stopping here, Alvez expressed his opinion that João's caravan was just in front, and by starting we should miss meeting him.

Whilst we were thus detained a plot to rob me came to light, and had it not been frustrated I should have been altogether deprived of the means of buying the fish upon which we had now to depend as an exchange for food.

It appeared that Coimbra and some other men, including two of Alvez' slaves, having heard that

I possessed some viongwa, determined to make an
attempt at stealing them. They induced one of
my people to enter into the plot, and rewarded him
for his complicity by paying him about one-third
of their value in beads, on the understanding that
he would commit the theft.

But fortunately my faithful Jumah, well knowing how valuable the viongwa were, had locked
them up securely in a box with my books and thus
prevented their being stolen.

Coimbra and his limited company now heard
that I had only two left, and when they saw one
of these expended in the purchase of a goat it
awakened them to the rottenness of their specu-
lation and convinced them that there was little
prospect of getting any return for the beads they
had expended in bribing my man.

Feeling no shame whatever in declaring themselves thieves, and being abetted by Alvez, they
brought forward a claim not only for the value
of the beads used to encourage my man to rob
me, but also, with an effrontery almost past belief,
for the value of the fish they would have purchased
with the viongwa had the intended robbery been
completed. Of course I objected to this prepos-
terous claim with indignation; but Coimbra and
the others openly declared that they would seize
as a slave the man who had been bribed, if their
demand was not settled.

I told Alvez in unmistakable language my

opinion of those making this unheard-of claim, as also of others supporting them and thus aiding and abetting barefaced thieving. He replied that if it were not settled he would probably be robbed, and impressed upon me that we were not in a civilised country. Coimbra and the rest were, he said, "Gentes bravos," and would either kill or steal the man if deprived of their anticipated plunder.

In order to save this man, who though he had proved himself a most shameless thief was otherwise worth half-a-dozen of the ruck of the caravan, I consented to satisfy the demand; but, having no means of paying the scoundrels myself, was obliged to ask Alvez to settle the matter on the promise of recouping him at some future time.

Perhaps some who do not weigh the whole circumstances and surroundings of this affair may possibly think that I erred in yielding; but I could not fail to see, much as it annoyed me, that this course was absolutely necessary to prevent the wreck of the expedition.

The idea of having to pay men because they had failed in their attempt to plunder me was so entirely novel that I confess there appeared to me something about it almost ludicrous. I should imagine that these are about the only people in the world who would put forward and seriously maintain such a claim without expressing shame in the slightest degree.

Near the camp was a small and peculiarly shaped

furnace for smelting iron, and I was told that the greater portion of the iron worked in Lovalé was smelted at this place. The ore is found in the form of large nodules in the river-beds, whence it is dredged up at the termination of the dry season.

Sha Kélembé's was left on the 12th of September, a large proportion of fish having been expended during the halt; and, as it was impossible to keep such high-flavoured stores in my tent on account of the effluvia, some of the remainder was stolen, leaving me with only one viongwa to cover expenses on the journey to Bihé.

The prospect was extremely disheartening, and already I had commenced to tear up and dispose of such clothes as I could possibly spare from my scanty kit.

Marching up the valley of the Luméji we turned to the right by the advice of Alvez, to avoid Mona Pého, chief of one of the three districts into which Kibokwé is divided. We passed many villages and camped at the head of a valley drained by one of the numerous affluents of the Luméji.

A number of natives came to my camp, which was an hour in advance of that of Alvez, and I had just succeeded in opening a conversation, when I heard a disturbance suddenly arise and found that Sambo, who was always skylarking and in some sort of innocent mischief, had caused it by chaffing an old chief who averred that he had been grievously insulted.

I enquired into the matter at once with due
gravity, although it was difficult to avoid laughing
outright at Sambo's comical account of the affair.
But the old man could not see the joke and was so
deeply offended that before his pacification could
be accomplished I had to part with my viongwa as
a present. I owned a small private stock of flour
only sufficient for three or four days and rice
enough for two more, and the men were just as
well, or badly, off as myself, and it therefore
seemed extremely probable that we should pass
some hungry hours before reaching Bihé.

The marching of the next day was through
forest intersected by long glades with streams
running through them, those passed on the latter
part of the march falling into the Kassabé. The
forests were very fine, with a scanty undergrowth
of jasmine and other sweet-scented and flowering
shrubs, whilst the ferns and mosses were exceed-
ingly beautiful.

On camping we were soon surrounded by the
people of a caravan from Bihé which had halted
here. They seemed to look with disdain upon us
who were travel-worn, thin, and mostly clothed in
rags of grass cloth, whilst they were fat and sleek,
and decked out in print shirts, jackets and red
nightcaps or felt hats.

This caravan was out buying beeswax, so I
borrowed some from Alvez to exchange with them
for cloth. João, they said, was at Bihé pre-

ιring for another journey to Kasongo's country,
ιving been down to Jenjé whilst Alvez had been
vay.

I endeavoured to gather some items of news of

CROSSING A STREAM.

the outside world from these.people, but they knew
nothing of it, rarely going to the sea coast; the
porters for the track between Bihé and Benguella
are Bailunda who never go east of Bihé, and the
people of that place only engage for the interior.

Three more marches, the latter part being in a hilly country, brought us to the valley of the Luméji. We crossed the river where it was fourteen feet wide and six deep, on a rickety bridge, and camped at the village of Chikumbi, a sub-chief of Mona Pého's.

Here we remained one day that Alvez' caravan might procure provisions for themselves; but for my men and myself it entailed the endurance of a little extra starvation.

There were many cattle about, principally black and white, without humps and of moderate size; and although the people had long possessed them the art of milking had been allowed to remain a mystery. Goats and fowls were plentiful, but, being far too poor to buy any, I contented myself with honey and farinha, the meal made of cassava.

Chikumbi gave us a most astounding account of the road between Bihé and the coast. He declared it was closed, as also was that to Loanda. Six thousand people under four traders were reported to have banded together to attempt to break through, but had been unsuccessful.

Alvez asserted that he had heard the same story from the Bihé caravan we had met, and said it was perfectly true. He was so very positive in this statement that I at once concluded it must be false; especially as there is a considerable trade in beeswax between Bihé and Benguella, and where there is traffic there must be roads.

September, 1875.

Mona Pého's was near here, but Alvez decided not to visit him as he would surely detain us for two or three days. There were also some Bihé people there as prisoners, and if it were known that Alvez visited Pého. without procuring their liberation their friends would, he said, plunder his settlement in revenge. Yet after this declaration we marched straight for Mona Pého's.

When we had been two hours on the road we were stopped at a large village governed by a chief named Mona Lamba, who informed us that we must halt there and not proceed until he had apprised his suzerain, Mona Pého, of our approach.

Mona Lamba was a good-looking young fellow, dressed in a blue jean coat with corporal's stripes on the arm, and a petticoat of red broadcloth; and, although interfering with our progress, he was very civil and invited me and a few others into his hut to have some refreshment. When we had seated ourselves he produced a huge gourd of mead and filled a pint mug for me. Being very thirsty I emptied it at one draught, not knowing its strength; and I heard that Mona Lamba entertained a great admiration for me on account of my feeling no ill effects, as a pint is usually sufficient to make the natives intoxicated.

This mead is a mixture of honey and water made to ferment by malted grain. It is quite clear, and has the taste of strong sweet beer.

Mona Lamba brought a further supply of this

liquor into our camp in the afternoon, but I refused his pressing invitation to drink, not wishing to forfeit the high opinion he held of my sobriety.

He very much wanted my Austrian blanket, but I named five bullocks as its price, for I could not possibly spare it. Then he wished to exchange coats as a token of friendship, and though I should have been the gainer I had no inclination to assume corporal's stripes, so made him some small present to satisfy him that I reciprocated his friendly feeling.

Before we started on the following day he was again in camp with more mead which he warmed over the fire, and the morning being chilly I found this stirrup-cup very comforting.

A short march brought us to a valley through which a small stream ran. On one side was Mona Pého's village hidden amongst the trees, and on the other we made our camp, having to exercise the greatest care in felling trees for building not to touch any with bee-hives on them.

A very large party from Bihé was here engaged in collecting beeswax, and I found that the account given by Alvez of their being forcibly detained was a gratuitous and uncalled-for falsehood.

Alvez bought cloth from these people, and I endeavoured to obtain some from him. He promised to give it me on my note-of-hand, and then only supplied me with about a dozen yards instead of the forty or fifty agreed upon.

In the afternoon Mona Pého called on us, being escorted by about twenty men firing guns and shouting and yelling as they drew near. He was dressed in an old uniform coat, a kilt of print, and a greasy cotton nightcap, and immediately behind him were some men bearing huge calabashes of mead. He insisted on my hobnobbing with him over this liquor, but as my men were around us and joined in draining the flowing bowl it was all consumed without any disastrous results.

As a present he brought me a little flour and a pig which was in an expiring condition and died a natural death immediately it reached the camp; and, apologising for having such a small supply of food, gave me cloth to buy something for my men.

Having to make him a return present I was sorely puzzled, but managed to satisfy him with a flannel sleeping suit. With this cloth in addition to what I had screwed out of Alvez I was enabled to serve out sufficient to provide my men with some rations, but it left me destitute.

From Alvez, Mona Pého wanted a slave with which the former was very loth to part as he averred he could obtain fifty or sixty dollars for him in Benguella. The dispute thus arising delayed us a day, although it ended in the slave being given.

Whilst we were here a man came into camp dressed in a suit of network of native manufacture covering every part of his body except his head, over which he wore a carved and painted mask. The net suit was striped horizontally with black and white, the gloves and feet pieces being laced to the sleeves and legs, and the join between the body and drawers being concealed by a kilt of grass.

The mask was painted to resemble an old man's face with enormous spectacles, and some grey fur covered the back part. In one hand he held a long staff, and in the other a bell which he constantly tinkled. He was followed by a little boy with a bag to receive such alms as might be bestowed upon him.

SHAM DEVIL.

I enquired what this strange individual was supposed to be, and was informed he was a "sham devil," and afterwards ascertained that his functions were to frighten away the devils who haunted the woods.

Those haunting the woods of Kibokwé are reputed to be both numerous and powerful, and each possesses its own particular district. They are supposed to be very jealous of each other, and should ic meet an opposition demon in its district its moyance is so great that it goes away to seek me place over which it may hold undisputed sway. Sham devils " are supposed to closely resemble al devils, and by showing themselves in their ported haunts, make them move to some other cality. In consequence, icy are well paid by the ihabitants, and being so the fetish men of ic tribe they enjoy a mfortable income.

On the 21st of Septem- r we left Mona Pého's, id before starting I was iformed that we should eet a European trader i the road, but who he as nobody knew. I was f course very anxious see this strange trader : traveller and solve the ystery.

SHAM DEVIL.

We passed through jungle with many villages, -in one of which smiths were using hammers with indles, the first I had seen in Africa except those r making bark cloth—and then proceeded along a illey by the source of the Luméji, which wells up in circular basin about sixty feet in diameter, and is at

Climbing a steep hill we found ourselves on a large plain, and shortly afterwards saw a caravan approaching. I pressed on, anxious to ascertain whether this was the party of the reported white trader, but found that it was a caravan journeying to Katanga under charge of a slave of Silva Porto, a merchant at Benguella who is known to geographers by his travels in company with Syde ibn Habib in 1852-54.

The slave in charge spoke Portuguese but could give me no news. He was greatly astonished at seeing me and asked where I had come from, when some of Alvez' people replied that they had discovered me " walking about in Urua."

He then enquired what I was doing. " Did I trade in ivory ? " " No." " In slaves ? " " No." " In wax ? " " No." " In indiarubber ? " " No." " Then what the devil did I do ? " " Collect information about the country."

He looked at me a moment as if fully convinced that I was a lunatic and then went on his way in amazement.

From the next camp Alvez despatched people to his settlement at Bihé to fetch cloth to pay the ferry across the Kwanza, and I took the opportunity to forward maps and letters, hoping they might reach the coast before me.

We had five very stiff marches before reaching the village of Kanyumba, the chief of Kimbandi, a small country lying between Kibokwé and Bihé.

On our journey we met many small parties of Bihé people buying beeswax, and a large caravan, commanded by two more .slaves of Silva Porto, on its way to Katanga to purchase slaves.

The principal of the two was a stout old negro about fifty years of age, dressed in a long blue. frock-coat with brass· buttons, blue trousers, and broad-brimmed straw hat. He and his companion voluntarily informed me that I could not have travelled with a worse caravan than that of Alvez, an opinion in which I fully concurred.

On seeing the respectable appearance of the leader of this caravan, I hoped that I might obtain some tea or biscuits from him. But not a thing could I get, and I had to sell my shirts in order to keep us from actual starvation, and also to tear up my greatcoat and dispose of it in small pieces.

During these five days' marching we entered the basin of the Kwanza and crossed two of its principal affluents, the Vindika and Kwiba, both considerable streams.

I noticed a most curious hole in the side of a hill close to the source of a small stream, and thinking I saw a clear space in the jungle I left the path to go towards it. After walking a few yards I was greatly surprised to find myself standing on the edge of a cliff thirty feet high, overlooking a sunken space about forty acres in extent, the whole, except for about twenty yards, being surrounded by these cliff-like sides.

The bottom of the hollow was level and of red soil with dry watercourses full of white sand, and numerous curious-looking hillocks of red clay were scattered over its surface. It seemed as though this cavity had been cut in the hill, and numerous model mountains placed there. Some natives told me that a village had once stood there, but the people were very wicked, and a great snake came one night and destroyed them all as a punishment, and left the place as I had seen it. And this they evidently believed.

At Kanyumba's I took the opportunity of observing an eclipse of the sun to determine longitude. I fitted the dark eye-piece of my sextant to one tube of my field-glasses and put a handkerchief in the other, and managed to time all four contacts. The only notice taken of the eclipse by the people was that they ran to their huts. There were no groups of awe-stricken natives expecting to see a snake eating the sun, or supposing that the end of the world was come, though the diminution of light was very considerable.

Kanyumba was very civil and sent me a calf as a free gift, for I had nothing whatever to present him with in return. This was the first meat I had tasted, with the exception of a dove I shot, since leaving Sha Kélembé's.

When the old man heard I had walked from the other side of the continent and intended to go home by sea, he earnestly tried to dissuade

ιe, promising that if I returned his way he would
.o everything he coûld to assist me. If I went
·y῀water, he said I should be certain to lose
ιy way, as there would be no marks whatever to
·uide me.

Alvez, ever ready for any dishonest action, tried
ο cheat me out of the calf Kanyumba had given
ιe, asserting that he had paid for it; but from
ome of his followers who were on anything but
;ood terms with him I
earnt that this was entirely
aĺse, and therefore refused
ο surrender the veal.

The people of Kimbandi
·ress their hair very taste-
ully, sometimes wearing it
n one side of the head, in
he form of a small cocked
at trimmed with cowries,
·hilst the hair on the other
ide hangs down in long
inglets. Others made their hair resemble a low-
·rowned hat, the brim being trimmed with beads
·r cowries.

We left our hospitable friend Kanyumba on the
·0th of September and camped close to the banks
f the Kwanza, where we were rejoined by men
·ho had been to Alvez' settlement to obtain cloth
ο pay our passage across the river.

From them I heard that João—João Baptista

Ferreira, as I now found he was called—was still
at Bihé with another white man, Guilhermé
Gonçalves, who had lately arrived from Europe. I
was also informed that the letter sent by me had
been despatched to João for forwarding to the coast.
My endeavours to gain any news of European
affairs were unsuccessful, for no one had any ideas
of anything beyond Bihé and Benguella. They
were entirely wrapped up in the affairs of their
own little world, though, to judge from the sensa-
tional and untrue stories of dangers on the road
so frequently circulated, there was evidently a
demand for news of some sort.

The following day we crossed the Kwanza, and
were then only one march from Alvez' settlement.
It was therefore plain that the accounts given of
fighting on the road were utterly unfounded.

These stories as they travelled from mouth to
mouth had been greatly magnified, and it was
said that no fewer than six thousand men on
their way to Bihé from the coast, had been driven
back after four days' hard fighting. One leader
of a caravan was reported to have lost all his
stores and about two hundred men in the struggle.

This and similar canards had been recounted to
me with every detail, the narrators evidently being
blessed with the most fertile imaginations, and it
was impossible to arrive at any certainty as to
their truth or otherwise. I need hardly remark
that they were fully believed by my people, who

l become very gloomy at the prospect of a
gthened delay at Bihé. But now they were
portionately rejoiced, and all were in excel-
t spirits.

SHAM DEVILS.

CHAPTER XI.

THE KWANZA.—ITS NAVIGATION.—NEAT VILLAGES.—CONVIVIAL GATHER-
ING.—A HEAD OF HAIR.—CATTLE PLAGUE.—THE KOKÉMA.—FILTHY VIL-
LAGES.—A LIVELY CHASE.— RECEPTION OF ALVEZ.—PAYMENT OF. HIS
PORTERS.—SOAP AND ONIONS.—MY RAGGED CREW.—ALVEZ CHEATS ME AT
PARTING.—A MAN IN TEARS.—AN ARCHERY MEETING.—A TORNADO.—THE
TOWN OF KAGNOMBÉ.—ITS SIZE.—KAGNOMBÉ'S OFFICIALS.— A SECRETARY
UNABLE TO WRITE.—MSHIRI'S MEN.— THEIR JOURNEYS FROM COAST TO
COAST.—KAGNOMBÉ'S LEVÉE.—MY SEAT OF HONOUR.—KAGNOMBÉ'S BEST
CLOTHES.—HIS FULL STYLE AND TITLE.—STRONG DRINK.—FETISH PLACE.
—SKULLS.—GRAVES.—HIS GUARDS,—HIS HAT.—SENHOR GONALVES.—HIS
HOUSE.—BREAKFAST.—HE TELLS ME HIS HISTORY.—HIS KINDNESS AND
HOSPITALITY.—THE INFLUENCE OF MEN OF HIS TYPE.

October,
1875.

EARLY on the 2nd of October we broke up our
camp, and, descending a bank twenty-five feet
in height, came upon a dead level a mile and a half
across. On the further side of this flowed the
Kwanza, which floods the whole of this plain in
the rainy season.

Before reaching the river we passed several
small pools and swampy places where numerous
water-fowl were disporting themselves, and I shot
a small but very pretty snow-white heron. The
river was sixty yards wide, and more than three
fathoms deep in the middle, with a current of
barely three-quarters of a knot.

On the opposite side were two villages situated
on a bank similar to that near our last camp.

They were inhabited by the ferry-people, who owned numerous canoes, but they were very miserable rickety constructions, from sixteen to eighteen feet long with only eighteen inches beam.

Instead of entrusting my box of journals and instruments to them, I put my indiarubber boat into working order and ferried my people and stores across in her, much to the astonishment of the natives. It was fortunate I adopted this course, for several canoes capsized, and some slaves narrowly escaped drowning. Two who were tied together and were unable to swim would undoubtedly have been drowned had not some of my men been with me sufficiently near at hand to render assistance.

The Kwanza, so far as I could learn, is navigable for some distance above the point at which we crossed. And since the vessels of the Kwanza Steamship Company trade regularly to the falls just above Dondo, it would appear that a moderate expenditure of capital and labour would enable small steamers to be put on its upper waters, thus to intercept the greater portion of the trade between Benguella and the interior, and assist materially in opening up the country to European enterprise.

Leaving the river, we soon entered a wooded and hilly country with many villages situated in large groves, in some instances surrounded by stockades. The huts were large and well built, being usually square, with walls about eight feet high and thatched pointed roofs. The walls were plastered with white or light red mud, and often decorated with rough sketches of men carrying hammocks, pigs, horses, &c.

There were also numerous granaries built on platforms raised about three feet from the ground. They stood eight to ten feet high, were circular in form, with a diameter of six or seven feet, and were covered by a movable conical roof of grass, the only means of access being by its removal.

Pigs and fowls were in great plenty, but the people, being satiated with cloth owing to their constant intercourse with the coast, would sell us nothing, or asked higher prices than we could afford.

After some hours' marching we arrived at a village which seemed far more prosperous and civilised than the rest, and on entering were accosted by two very respectable-looking mulattoes who were the proprietors. They invited me to stay and drink with them, but hearing that the Kokéma was close in front I pressed onwards, and arrived early in the afternoon at a village named Kapéka, near the river.

Here I halted under some large trees to await Alvez' arrival, but he did not make his appearance until nearly sunset. He was then accompanied by the two mulattoes and a number of their wives, all drest in their best, and some carrying small kegs of pombé.

The chief of Kapéka also came with a large pot
' pombé as his share of the debauch, and a
neral drink round then commenced.

The hair of the chief wife of the principal
ulatto was frizzed to such an enormous extent
at her head would scarcely have gone into a
ishel basket. She, as well as her husband,
rancisco Domingo Camoen, was a light mulatto.

At the village there was a herd of about forty
ittle belonging to the chief, but although they
ere imported from the Kaffir countries, where
iey are commonly milked, no milk was obtained
om them here as the natives declared that they
ere much too fierce to allow of any attempt being
iade. Formerly the herds about Bihé were more
umerous, but some years since a cattle plague

October, 1876.

or murrain swept them entirely away, and those in the country at this time had been brought from Jenjé.

Nearly two hours were occupied the following morning in ferrying the caravan across the Kokéma, about forty yards wide and two fathoms deep at this point.

Shortly afterwards a disturbance arose between some of my people and the natives, owing to one of my men who retired into a patch of cultivated ground having been discovered there by the owner. He demanded compensation for his land having been defiled and had to be appeased by a present of cloth.

If they were only half as particular about their dwellings as their fields, it would be a good thing, for their villages are filthy in the extreme and would be even worse but for the presence of large numbers of pigs which act as scavengers.

Our road led through very charming country with steep hills, with scars and landslips exposing the red sandstone in vivid contrast to the bright greens of the grass and foliage.

Some of Alvez' porters here attempted to bolt with their loads of ivory, and this gave rise to a lively chase, terminating in their capture after a hard run.

Alvez having friends at several villages, accordingly stopped to drink with them, much to the delay of our march, but in the afternoon we arrived near his settlement and halted for stragglers to close up, so that we might make our entry in due form; and powder was served out that a salute might be fired when we marched in.

We then entered the village, and were immediately surrounded by a horde of yelling women and children who had assembled from far and near to welcome the return of the porters.

In front of Alvez' house half-a-dozen men were keeping up a rapid fire in response to the guns of our party. Amongst them were two of Alvez' assistants, one a civilised black man named Manoel, who, like his master, was a native of Dondo; the other a white man commonly known as Chiko, who had escaped from a penal settlement on the coast. Manoel at once came forward and conducted me to a very decent hut, which he informed me was to be my quarters during my stay.

On Alvez making his entry he was mobbed by women who shrieked and yelled in honour of the event and pelted him with flour; and we learnt that his long absence had almost persuaded his people to believe him to be lost, and could they have mustered sufficient men and stores they would have despatched a party in search of him.

Unlimited pombé was served out, and when comparative quiet had been restored those who carried ivory gave up their loads and others in charge of slaves delivered them over to the care of the women.

October, 1875.
The porters were then paid from eight to twelve yards of cloth each, and a few charges of powder. This, together with the twelve yards every man had received before starting, made in all about twenty yards of cloth as pay, and a few .charges of powder as a gift, for upwards of two years' service.

Of course men would not engage for such ridiculous rates of pay were it not that they' profited by rapine and robbery in passing through countries where the people did not possess guns.

However, they were well satisfied with the result of their journey and announced their intention of starting, when the approaching rains were over, with as many of their friends as 'they could muster, to revisit Kasongo for the purpose of obtaining more slaves from that enlightened ruler.

This to me was a day of luxuries, as Alvez, for a consideration, supplied me with some coffee, onions, and soap.

This last commodity I had been without for nearly a year, with the exception of a piece about a couple of inches square which Jumah Merikani gave me, and I now thoroughly enjoyed its unsparing application.

Alvez' settlement differed only from Komananté, a native village adjoining it, in the larger dimensions of some of his huts; and, although he had according to his own account been settled in Bihé for more than thirty years, he had made no

ttempt at cultivation or rendering himself com-
rtable.

In order to procure this clothing it was necessary to buy ivory and beeswax from Alvez to
exchange, as he assured me it was utterly impossible for me to get any credit. But I afterwards found that he had misled me in order to
seize another opportunity of fleecing me by charging
a high price for the wax and ivory ; for on meeting
Senhor Gonçalves he told me he would readily
have sold cloth to me at Benguella prices, adding
only the cost of porterage.

Further delay also arose through waiting for a
guide. Alvez wished to send Chiko ; but he refused fearing he might be recognised, and Manoel
was told off for the duty.

I had also to await the arrival of some Bailunda
—who act as porters between Bihé and the coast—
who were to carry thither some wax for Alvez, to
be exchanged for stores which would enable him to
proceed to Jenjé with the view of selling his slaves.

At last, on the 10th of October, I started. I
selected a small number to accompany me on a
visit to Kagnombé the chief of Bihé, and Senhor
Gonçalves, leaving the remainder to follow and re-
join me at the settlement of João Baptista Ferreira.

At the moment of marching one of those whom
I had directed to come on afterwards commenced
crying because his chum was going with me. He
declared I had sold him to Alvez for a slave, and
altogether made such a hullabaloo over the matter
that I felt obliged to allow him to join my little

arty. This man was a specimen of some whom
ombay engaged at Zanzibar, and I had to drag
cross Africa.

We then marched through fertile and well-
ooded country intersected by many streams.
he villages were surrounded by plantations,
bacco being grown in small enclosed plots close

VILLAGE IN BIHÉ.

) every hut, and I also noticed a very seedy-
oking European cabbage. In the woods I fre-
uently detected a scent like vanilla, but was
nable to find the plant that emitted it. Guavas
rew wild in great profusion.

In a clear space outside one of the villages some

The target was made of a root found in the
jungle and cut into circular form about one foot in
diameter. It was rolled slowly across the open
space at about forty yards from the marksmen, and
on an average one arrow in ten struck it. This
was the only occasion on which I saw shooting
practised as an amusement in Africa.

After losing our way three or four times we
arrived at a village of considerable size belonging
to Senhor Gonçalves, and I was lodged in the
large hut used by him on his visits.

The whole population were his slaves, but the
greater number were now absent on a journey to
Jenjé under the command of one of his sons. He
possesses some half-dozen of these villages, the
population of each forming the nucleus of a caravan, the remainder being composed of hired natives
of the neighbourhood.

We were fortunate in gaining the village when
we did, for almost directly we had obtained shelter
a heavy tornado came on accompanied by torrents
of rain. It had been preceded by a peculiar lurid
light, which, as the sun had set some little time,
must have been electrical.

Three hours' march from here was the town of
Kagnombé, the largest I came across during my
whole journey, being more than three miles in
circumference.

It contained a number of separate enclosures
belonging to different chiefs, who used them

when visiting the place to pay their respects to Kagnombé. October, 1875. Much space was occupied by cattle and pig pens and tobacco gardens, besides which there were three large gullies—the sources of streams flowing to the Kokéma—so that the population, though large, was not nearly so numerous as the size of the town had led me to expect.

On arrival I was met by Kagnombé's secretary, chamberlain, and captain of the guard, who wore red waistcoats as sign of their dignity. The secretary was more ornamental than useful, being unable to write, but a subordinate, a black man and native of Dondo, was better educated and conducted the trade of Kagnombé with the coast.

These officials conducted me to a hut which had been prepared for my reception, and immediately, without allowing me any time for refreshments, commenced bothering me with questions as to what I intended to offer their chief as a present.

A snider rifle and a little cloth which I obtained for the purpose whilst at Komananté were all I could well give. But with this they assured me he would be anything but satisfied, and I was obliged to part with a large leopard-skin presented to me by Jumah Merikani, and which had been most useful as a rug.

Throughout the day crowds came to stare at me, and when driven by heavy showers to take refuge in my hut the people did not scruple to follow me uninvited and it was needful to keep a sharp look-out for pilferers.

Amongst the crowd were some men attached to a caravan belonging to Mshiri, on the return journey from Benguella. They all had the Unyamwési tribal marks, and the majority could speak Kinyamwési. One asserted that he was a Mnyamwési, but on cross-examination I found he was really a native of Katanga but had once been to Unyanyembé.

I have no doubt that many of Mshiri's men have visited both coasts, and that a message might be sent by means of these people from Benguella to Zanzibar.

Mshiri has issued an edict compelling all his subjects to adopt the tribal marks of the Wanyam-wési, and many natives of Bihé visiting Katanga have also complied with this order to curry favour with him.

About nine o'clock the next morning a messenger informed me that Kagnombé was ready to receive me. Making myself as tidy and present-able as the scantiness of my kit would allow, and taking with me half-a-dozen of my men, I went to one of the gulleys on the side of which Kagnombé's private compound was situated.

The gate was guarded by men wearing red waistcoats and carrying spears and knives, and on entry I found a double row of small stools placed for the accommodation of the audience, while at the ar end was the large arm-chair of the great man umself standing on my leopard-skin.

Seeing no particular place assigned to me, and lot feeling disposed to occupy a stool on a level vith my men, I sent for my chair.

This proceeding was at first most warmly esisted by the officials on the ground that no erson was ever allowed to sit on a chair in the resence of Kagnombé. I therefore should not be

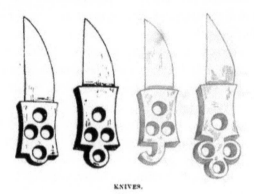

KNIVES.

permitted to introduce such a fashion. In reply I assured them that it did not matter, for I should simply withdraw from the levée and not wait to see Kagnombé, upon which my chair was admitted, and I took my seat.

When all was ready the door of an inner enclosure was opened and the chief appeared. He wore an ancient suit of black bundled on anyhow, and a large grey plaid thrown over his shoulders, the ends being held up behind by a naked little boy.

On his head was a dirty old wide-awake hat, and, notwithstanding the earliness of the hour, he was already about three-parts drunk.

No sooner was he seated than he commenced informing us of his power, saying that he was a greater man than any other king in Africa, for besides his African name he had a European one. His full style and title was King Antonio Kagnombé, and his picture, the picture of Antonio Kagnombé, had been sent to Lisbon.

Further he informed us that we were not to judge of his mightiness by the seedy appearance of his present attire, as very grand clothes had been given him by the Portuguese authorities when he was at Loanda.

He had passed some years at that place and was supposed to have been educated, but the sole effect of this education seemed to have been the blending of the vices of semi-civilisation with those proper to the savage.

Having heard that I had been a long time on the road he was graciously pleased to express his satisfaction at the presents I had made him, but desired me to remember that if ever I passed his town again I must bring gifts more suitable to his greatness.

The oration being concluded we moved into the inner compound, overshadowed by an enormous banyan-tree, and where some huge female bananas, producing seed but no fruit, were growing. When the seats were rearranged Kagnombé entered one of the huts within the enclosure, and shortly re-appeared with a bottle of aguardienté and a tin pannikin.

He served out a "nip" all round, and then putting the bottle to his lips took such a deep draught that I expected to see him fall down in-sensible. But the only effect was an increase in his liveliness, and he commenced swaggering and dancing about in the most extraordinary manner, occupying intervals in his performance by further pulls at the bottle. When it was finished we were free to take our departure.

I rambled about the town and neighbourhood and visited the great fetish place. Here the skulls of all the chiefs whom Kagnombé had conquered were kept spiked on poles surrounded by the heads of leopards, dogs, and jackals.

Not far from this was the burial-ground of his family, the graves in which all lay east and west. Broken pots and crockery were scattered on each, and in the centre was a fetish hut where offerings of food and drink were placed for the manes of the departed.

Outside Kagnombé's compound a large tree was pointed out to me as being the usual reception place for the Portuguese. Here his chair is brought and put upon the summit of a small mound, the visitors having to sit on stones or roots at its foot. I was assured that my being allowed to enter his private enclosures was a mark of high honour, no white man having ever before been admitted.

Of the two enclosures, the outer one is really his main guard, and all night long men are stationed there on sentry. These guards are also employed to lead the van when Kagnombé engages in war, the duty of carrying his hat, which plays an important part in action, devolving upon the captain of the guard.

When a village which it is intended to capture is approached the hat is thrown over the palisades and a tremendous rush is made to recover it; for he who is fortunate in the attempt and brings it back is considered the hero of the day, and is rewarded with gifts of concubines and liquor.

The following morning, after having despatched Manoel with farewell messages to Kagnombé, I started for the settlement of Senhor Gonçalves and arrived there after a pleasant walk of a few hours.

Drawing near to the settlement, I was much impressed by its appearance of neatness and good order, and on entering found myself in a well-kept courtyard. In this there were a large store-house and two small dwellings, whilst a palisade in front divided them from the principal house, which was flanked on one side by a magnificent grove of orange-trees covered with fruit.

THE HOSPITABLE SETTLEMENT OF SENHOR GONÇALVES. BIIIE.

A Spanish mulatto met me and led the way into October, 1875. the sitting-room, where Senhor Gonçalves' two sons and a white man who had formerly been boatswain of a Portuguese man-of-war, were at breakfast.

This room quite astonished me. The floor was planked, the windows had green jalousies, the ceiling was of white cloth, and the walls were plastered and painted in a neat pattern. And upon the table, which was covered with a clean white cloth, all manner of good things were spread.

Senhor Gonçalves, an old gentleman of charming manners, welcomed me warmly, and, telling me not to stand on ceremony, bade me fall to. This I was nothing loth to do, and thoroughly enjoyed the best meal I had tasted for many a long day. Everything was well cooked, and good biscuits, butter, and other "canned' delicacies" helped to form the solids which were washed down by *vinho tinto* followed by coffee.'

. After breakfast Senhor Gonçalves told me of himself and his doings here, and conducted me round his establishment.

He had at one time been master of a ship, but, tiring of the sea, settled at Bihé thirty-three years ago. When he had been thirty years in Africa he returned to Lisbon with the idea of ending his days there in peace. But his friends of former times being dead, and he being too old to make new ones, he never felt comfortable there and after three years' absence determined to return to Bihé. He had only arrived about three weeks when I paid him this visit.

Before leaving for Lisbon he had a capital garden with European vegetables, and grew vines and wheat which flourished marvellously. But during his absence everything was neglected, and the only things remaining were his oranges—which were finer than any I had ever seen—and a hedge of roses thirty feet high, now in full bloom.

His principal trading was with Jenjé for ivory, and Kibokwé for beeswax, and altogether trade was fairly profitable. Twice he was burnt out and lost everything and was obliged to recommence business on borrowed capital, the high interest on which had nearly swallowed all his profits for a time, but now he was free and unembarrassed.

Each of the six villages he owned supplied a caravan. One was now travelling under the charge of a son, and another under a servant; and two more were about to start.

His sons had lately returned from Jenjé and said they met English traders there with bullock-waggons, and had been most friendly with them.

We sat a long time yarning and smoking good English birds'-eye after dinner, and then I was given a comfortable bedroom, and for the first time since spending a night on board the *Punjáb* I experienced the pleasure of sleeping between sheets.

Tempting as the hospitality and many comforts of

vided those coming to him were prepared to pay October, 1875. in advance for his predictions.

The principal instrument for reading the decrees of fate consisted of a basket trimmed with small skins, the bottom being formed of a piece of gourd. This was filled with shells, small figures of men, tiny baskets and packets containing .amulets, and a heterogeneous collection of rubbish.

. The method of divining was something after the manner adopted by ancient dames in more civilised parts of the globe, who imagine they can look into the future by gazing intently at the dregs in the bottom of a tea-cup.

On being consulted the basket was emptied of its contents, and as the queries to which answers were desired were put to the magician he selected such things to be returned to the basket as he considered appropriate. He then gave it a dexterous twist, and after carefully inspecting the manner in which its contents had arranged themselves delivered the all-important answer to the anxious dupe.

Besides telling fortunes he also did a lively amount of trade in charms and amulets, without which no African would consider himself safe on a journey. One charm I noticed was in very large demand, as it was supposed to prevent slaves from running away. It was composed of a large horn filled with mud and bark, and having three very small horns projecting from its lower end.

October,
1875.
I had often seen these charms in the possession of Alvez' people, who placed them in the ground close to the owner's quarters in camp, and constantly anointed them with red earth and oil in order to propitiate the spirit believed to exist within them. Alvez had one of these horns lashed to his flag-staff; but I believe he used the anointing oil more for his own purposes than those of the devil's.

When the fetish man found no more buyers of charms he offered to cure any disease with which any person present might be afflicted. To some he gave charms as a remedy, but to the majority he administered draughts made from various roots and herbs. He also showed himself an adept at shampooing.

João's principal stock for trading with Kasongo consisted of flint-lock muskets and powder; and when possessed of a sufficient number of firearms I have no doubt he will try his hand at robbing caravans; for when I passed through his country he had every inclination to take to highway robbery, but lacked the necessary power.

After a day's halt at João's we started for the coast, accompanied by a gang of Bailunda carrying gear belonging to Alvez and intended for sale at Benguella. It was arranged that the headman of this party should act as my guide, Manoel being interpreter between him and me.

We passed Belmont—somewhat inappropriately named, being situated in a hollow—and then over

large down-like hills with very little wood, excepting around the villages, which were all shaded by
groves of fine trees.

Belmont is the settlement of Silva Porto—a name
well known to African geographers—which had
once equalled, if not surpassed, that of Senhor
Gonçalves; but its owner having discontinued
travelling and settled at Benguella, it was placed
under the care of slaves, and had consequently
greatly deteriorated. Its orange-trees had run
wild and were unpruned, and that which had
formerly been a carefully kept garden was no better
than a tangled waste.

The rains were now beginning to set in regularly, and at our first camp we passed a most
miserable night. There was scarcely any grass or
brushwood with which the men could hut themselves, and they were consequently exposed to one
continued downpour of cold rain.

I fared equally badly, for my grass-cloth tent
was so thoroughly worn out and full of holes that
the water came through it freely. There was not
a dry corner where I could sleep, so I coiled
myself up in a space about two feet square with
a piece of mackintosh over my head.

As day broke the rain ceased and we managed
to light a fire and I then gave each man a small
nip of the brandy which had been given me by
Gonçalves. After this we started, and, though wet
and miserable, my men were fairly light-hearted.

Gradually we entered more broken and wooded country, with stony hills showing out here and there. On these villages were built and encircled by stone walls and palisades, while others on the bare hills were surrounded by heavy groves of trees, and reminded me much of farms on the Wiltshire downs.

Whilst crossing a level tableland I saw enormous flocks of birds, and what was supposed to be an extraordinarily large one in rapid motion was pointed out to me. The object had so curious an appearance that I used my field-glasses to obtain a better view, and then discovered that the dark cloud was caused by the dust and steam rising from a large herd of buffalo galloping madly to the eastward.

On the road we met many up parties of Bihé people who had been trading with the Bailunda. They were usually rather drunk and abusive, and in some instances attempted to rob my stragglers, so that it required great forbearance and some tact to avoid getting into serious collision with them.

They asserted that we had no right to be travelling in their country, as we should be the means of opening up the road to other strangers and traders and deprive them of their monopoly.

Although these people were thus unfriendly towards us, the chiefs of the villages were kind and civil, and invariably brought us pots of pombé.

'o have refused this proffered hospitality would
lave been a dangerous policy and have lessened
he good feeling which existed; but much time
vas· sometimes wasted owing to these halts for
·efreshment.

PORTERS FROM BIBÉ.

The nights were now constantly rainy and we
had some wretched experiences; but being near the
end of my journey I felt inclined to make light of
every trouble.

And in addition to being continually wet we

owing to their constant intercourse with the coast, were overwhelmed with cloth and wanted only powder or aguardienté in exchange for provisions. We had neither of these articles of commerce, and consequently were frequently compelled to go hungry.

On the 18th of October we passed the Kutato, a most extraordinary river forming the boundary between Bailunda and Bihé.

We crossed by a bridge then under water, the strength of the current being so great that some men were washed off and only saved themselves by catching at bushes on the bank. On reaching the other side we found ourselves upon an island, situated amongst numerous rapids and cascades breaking out from a rocky hillside. The difficulty of getting across seemed at first sight almost insuperable; but after a time we discovered that there were, however, places where it was possible to jump from rock to rock, and then to wade through the rapids themselves on narrow shelves, holding on meanwhile by ropes of creepers stretched from side to side for that purpose. A single false step or the snapping of the creeper-rope at these points would have been fatal, for nothing could have saved one from being dashed to pieces amongst the rocks beneath.

The stream below this was about sixty yards wide, very deep, and running like a sluice. I afterwards heard that we were considered most

fortunate in crossing without mishap; for at that
season of the year people had frequently been lost
in making the attempt, and it was often necessary
to wait a week or fortnight before the passage was
practicable.

Looking back from the other side, a most striking
sight was presented by this mass of water bursting
out of the precipitous hillside, and broken by the
rocks and little bushy islands into foaming cascades.

Many small streams were passed which occasionally flowed for some distance in subterranean
channels. They worked in amongst loose stones
which were covered with soil and vegetation, the
underground portion of their course being sometimes only some forty yards in length; but in
other instances they seemed to have disappeared
altogether and no doubt helped to supply the
water which formed the " burst of the Kutato."

The following day we arrived at the village of
Lungi, the dwelling-place of the head of the
Bailunda who were accompanying me, and halted
to enable them to prepare food for the road to
Benguella. I was told this would occupy three
days, so I decided to have a hut built instead of
remaining that time in my leaky tent. The men
also managed to make themselves comfortable, wood
and grass for building a camp being plentiful.

The wife of the headman was now taken ill,
and he, with an amount of marital affection which

was very creditable, would not hear of leaving her
until she recovered.

This arrangement being particularly inconveni-
ent, I tried to reason with him against adhering to
his resolve, and to my surprise I afterwards found
I was suspected of the evil eye, and was accused
of having bewitched the woman by looking at her
husband.

Although this would seem rather an indirect
method of bringing about so dire a calamity, yet
it was thoroughly believed in, and a fetish man
was brought to give his opinion of my optics.
Fortunately he declared that there was nothing
evil about my eyesight, and informed the headman that it behoved him to assist me in everything, and that on arriving at Benguella he would
find I possessed an open hand.

This covert appeal to my generosity was not to
be resisted, and I could not feel otherwise than
grateful for his favourable opinion of me when
under suspicion; so I gave him a piece of cloth
out of my scanty stock, bringing my store down
to four yards.

The brother of the guide who had expressed
his determination to remain behind to nurse his
wife now volunteered to conduct us to Benguella,
but had to prepare his food before starting.

The chief of Lungi, Menyi Hombo by name,
had been a Pombeiro of Senhor Gonçâlves; and
although he was well aware of my inability to

make any return for kindness shown, was very October, 1875. hospitable, bringing us pombé daily and presenting a goat to me, besides one to my men.

Here I received the unwelcome intelligence that the letters and map I forwarded before reaching Bihé were barely ahead of me now. It appeared that when they arrived at Komananté, Manoel at once sent them to João, who entrusted them to two runners to take to the coast. These worthies arrived at a village close to Lungi about a fortnight before me, but, meeting some chums just returned from Benguella with a large stock of aguardienté, remained there with them. In their opinion such an opportunity was not to be neglected, and from the moment of their arrival they had spent their time in one continued state of drunkenness.

I immediately sent for the letters and was fortunate in getting them; and after this experience I concluded it would be better to become my own postman.

Little worthy of record occurred during the stay at Lungi. The principal employment of the men was making clothes of a somewhat uniform pattern for entry into Benguella, and I had to look sharply after them, for they were much inclined to shirk their work and expend the material I had given them in drink.

Whilst writing in my hut one day I was astonished at hearing that a white man had come to the camp and desired to see me. Who it might be I could not imagine, having been told that no white traders were in the country excepting João and Gonçalves.

I found that my visitor was a young Portuguese who, together with two companions, had come here to trade, having obtained a few stores on credit at Benguella.

His partners, however, quarrelled so grievously that words came to blows, and one, after knifing and killing the other, ran off with all the goods and left this young fellow destitute.

He was now in pawn to the chief of the village where he was staying and was prevented from leaving, as the merchant who advanced the stores for the first venture refused to supply him with anything further until he was paid. This forced detention did not trouble him greatly, for he was very comfortable and well looked after by the natives and did not appear to have any desire to be taken out of pledge.

At last the Bailunda had their food ready, but the chief of Lungi having told them that the following day was an important festival, they refused to start, being anxious to share in the customary bout of pombé-drinking.

I went to witness the performance, and under a huge banyan-tree in the outer portion of the village, found singing, dancing, and drinking proceeding in great force. The men and women danced together, their suggestive motions being accompanied by ribald songs, and the scene was one of licentious- ness almost beyond belief.

The chief, who was comparatively sober, re- mained in an inner compound shaded by large trees and barren bananas like those at Kagnombé's. One part of this compound reached to the summit of an almost precipitous ascent, from which a charming view was obtained.

He informed me that in consequence of having been in the service of Gonçalves he had no desire to join in orgies such as the one I had witnessed; but added that he was powerless to prevent them, for if the people were deprived of their drink and dancing they would rebel and murder their rulers.

I had much trouble on leaving here, owing to many of my people having rheumatism and swollen limbs caused by the wet and cold. Poor little Jacko and a man named Yacooti were unable to walk, and it was necessary to contrive litters for carrying them.

Almost directly after starting we came upon rocky hills with brawling burns rushing along their rugged courses, and here and there falls from twenty to thirty feet in height, the crystal water sparkling in the sunlight as it dashed from crag to crag. Large tree-ferns grew on the banks, and amongst the bushes were myrtle, jasmine, and other flowering shrubs, whilst a variety of beautiful ferns similar to maiden-hair and other delicate kinds, flourished in the damp crevices of the rocks.

As we went forward the scenery increased in beauty, and at last I was constrained to halt and surrender myself to the enjoyment of the view which lay before me.

I will content myself with asserting that nothing could be more lovely than this entrancing scene, this glimpse of paradise. To describe it would be impossible. Neither poet, with all the wealth of word-imagery, nor painter with almost supernatural genius, could by pen or pencil do full justice to the country of Bailunda.

In the foreground were glades in the woodland, varied with knolls crowned by groves of large, English-looking trees, sheltering villages with yellow thatched roofs ; shambas, or plantations, with the fresh green of young crops and bright red of newly hoed ground in vivid contrast, and running streams flashing in the sunlight ; whilst in the far distance were mountains of endless and pleasing variety of form, gradually fading away until they blended with the blue of the sky. Overhead there drifted fleecy white clouds ; and the hum of bees, the bleating of goats, and crowing of cocks broke the stillness of the air.

As I lay beneath a tree in indolent contemplation of the beauties of nature in this most favoured spot, all thought of the work still before me vanished from my mind ; but I was rudely awakened from

MOUNTAINS BETWEEN BAILUNDA AND COAST.

my pleasant reverie by the appearance of the loaded caravan, with the men grunting, yelling, and labouring under their burdens. Thus the dream of fairyland was dispelled and the realities of my work with its toil and trouble returned.

That evening we camped in a wood, a clear space having literally to be cut out of the masses of sweet-scented creepers which festooned the trees.

Here I again divided the caravan into two parts as it was necessary for me to visit Kongo, the chief of the Bailunda, at Kambala, and I had been informed that it would be impolitic to be accompanied by all my men on the occasion.

I therefore selected four of my own people including Jumah, Manoel, and the chief of the Bailunda porters, and three of their immediate followers, leaving the remainder of the party to proceed by the direct road to the next camp, thus giving the invalids, who were steadily increasing in number, two short marches and a good rest.

Kambala is situated on a rocky hill in the centre of a wooded plain surrounded by ranges of hills. The entrance to the village was over a smooth sheet of granite, and then, passing through two or three palisades, we were conducted into a small division containing four huts which we were invited to make use of.

The huts clustered about the rocks in a most extraordinary manner, advantage being taken of every shelf and projection capable of being built upon. Thus a next-door neighbour was generally either almost above your head or below your feet. · Trees of fair proportions grew out of the crevices, tobacco was planted close to the huts, and the palisades were covered with flowering creepers.

Some of Kongo's principal councillors welcomed us on arrival, but the task of entertaining us

KAMBALA.

fell chiefly upon the shoulders of the wife of the prime minister, he being absent on important duty. Our hostess brought a large supply of porridge and dried locusts for my people, and several inhabitants paid us visits, each bringing with him a pot of pombé.

My anxiety was to gain an early audience with

present. I had brought a rifle for him, but his
people wisely preferred an old flint-lock carried
by Manoel, for which I gave him the snider.
It was arranged by the court officials that I should
see the king the following day, but I managed
to overrule this delay, and our interview was then
appointed to take place in the afternoon.

The hour for our reception having arrived, we
were taken to the very summit of the hill, where
the king's hut and that of his principal wife were
situated on a small level surface.

This position was inaccessible on all sides save
the one by which we approached and was surrounded by a heavy palisade. On our way to it
no fewer than thirteen separate lines of stockading
were passed, while the path was in some places so
steep that we were obliged to use our hands to
clamber up.

Just before reaching the royal compound we
halted by an open hut containing a large bell
which was tolled by men stationed on guard to give
notice of our arrival, and there we waited until
permission to proceed was obtained from Kongo.
Watch and ward was kept at this post both day
and night, to prevent any one approaching without due warning being given ; and this also was
the chosen scene of executions, which I heard
were rather frequent, though the barbarous practice
of mutilation was unknown.

After a time we received permission to enter the

royal precincts, and found a few stools placed round an antiquated arm-chair which served as King Kongo's throne. Amongst this group my seat was placed.

Kongo then entered, dressed in a much faded and dilapidated uniform, with a huge battered

VISIT TO KING KONGO.

cocked-hat on his head; and being very aged and much under the influence of drink, he had to be helped along and placed upon his throne. I advanced and shook hands with him, but doubt very much whether he had a clear conception of who his visitor might be.

Some officials commenced a conversation with me, remarking that everything they said was to be understood as the king's own words, but he had really very little voice in the matter. As usual they asserted that Kongo was the greatest chief in the world. Taking me to a gap in the palisade they pointed to the surrounding country as being under his rule, and showed me the position of several villages scattered about in the plain that lay at our feet, as being those that supplied the inhabitants of Kambala with food.

The gun was then presented in due form, and we took our leave.

On returning to my hut I passed a party of women pounding corn. They did not use pestles and mortars as elsewhere, but pounded the grain on the polished surface of a granite rock, kneeling to their work and using small mallets formed of a piece of hard curved wood.

When we reached our quarters the prime minister's wife was there with more porridge and locusts for my men and a fowl for myself. After sunset we were left to our own devices, and, notwithstanding heavy rain, passed a comfortable night as the huts proved quite weathertight.

In the morning our hostess again waited upon us with our breakfast, and wished us all farewell. In return for her hospitality she asked me to send her a small brass bell from Benguella, a modest request which I gratified by forwarding half-a-dozen, together with a piece of good cloth sufficient to make her happy for a long time. From her features and appearance, which were decidedly prepossessing, I believe she had some amount of white blood in her veins, being too as light as a mulatto.

Much curiosity was excited here respecting my beard, and some strange stories were circulated by people who had seen me and considered this appendage a noteworthy peculiarity.

We left Kambala by the same gateway as we entered—which I believe to be the only means of getting in or out of the place, so jealously guarded is the rocky fortress of King Kongo—and soon afterwards sighted an extraordinary peak standing up amongst the hills, more inaccessible than Pieter Bot's mountain at the Mauritius.

It took the form of an enormous prism of granite, and its native name *Temba Lui*, meaning "devil's finger," was in keeping with its appearance.

Several villages on the road had cattle feeding near them, and the people looked in comfortable circumstances. Drink was offered to us at all, but flour was not forthcoming except for barter, and the want of this necessary food compelled me to begin to tighten up my belt.

In the afternoon we fell in with the rest of our party and found Jacko and Yacooti able to walk again, though several other men were ill. According to Bombay, Yacooti died while on the march and was thrown into the jungle by way of burial,

pon which he came to life again and was imme-
iately able to walk.

At this camp we were joined by many Bailunda
ound for Benguella with flour to exchange for
guardienté. One of them I noticed with a
umber of large cocoons in a basket, and on en-
uiring what they were for he cut one open,

TEMBA LUI (THE "DEVIL'S FINGER").

lowed the caterpillar still moving inside, and,
utting it into his mouth, swallowed it, smacking
is lips with great gusto. Caterpillars in this
articular stage were, I was told, considered a
reat delicacy.

The whole caravan being now assembled, I trusted
e might reach the coast without further delays:

for in consequence of our halt at Lungi the men had already expended much of their cloth, and unless we pushed onwards it was probable we should have a hungry time on the road. I hoped under these circumstances that the men would see the necessity for marching, if only for their own sakes; but I was doomed to disappointment.

POUNDING CORN AT KAMBALA.

CHAPTER XIII.

MY DISPIRITED CREW.—NATIVE BRIDGES.—BAD WEATHER.—SECURE DWELL-
INGS.—BREAKDOWN OF MY MEN.—A MAN MISSING.—FALLEN OUT BY THE
ROADSIDE.—A FEARFUL NIGHT.—SEARCHING FOR THE STRAGGLER.—DELAY
DANGEROUS.—THE STRAGGLER ARRIVES.—PAST RECOVERY.—HIS DEATH AND
BURIAL.—LOCUSTS.—THE SLAVE-TRADE ON THE COAST.—MODE OF EMBARKA-
TION.—FAILING STRENGTH OF MY CARRIERS.—I THROW AWAY TENT, BOAT,
BED, ETC.—A RUSH FOR THE COAST.—OUR HIGHEST CAMP.—GAY UMBRELLAS.
—A MULATTO SETTLEMENT.—CASCADES.—NUMEROUS UP CARAVANS.—THEIR
TRADE.—NO FOOD LEFT.—SEARCH FOR A CAMP.—DEAD BEAT.—A TEDIOUS
MARCH.—SKELETONS OF SLAVERS' VICTIMS.—STARVATION AND EXHAUSTION.
—THE SEA.—LEAVING THE WORN-OUT MEN BEHIND.—THE FINAL EFFORT.
—SCURVY ATTACKS ME.—HELP.—A GOOD SAMARITAN.—A HAVEN OF REST.

ANOTHER wretchedly wet and rainy night November, 1875. seemed to deprive my people of the little energy they possessed, and the drag of the march was indeed painful.

Instead of being as men who had nearly accomplished a difficult task, they looked and moved more like a funeral procession. The distance was not great, but the time occupied was dreadfully long, and on arriving at our camping-place the men were too dispirited to hut themselves properly, though rain was threatening. Others who had lagged behind did not reach camp till after dark.

On the road we passed the Kukéwi, a large stream falling into the sea at Nova Dondo, and also one of its affluents, the Kuléli, besides numerous rills and streams.

Both these rivers were crossed on bridges constructed of poles planted in the bed of the stream; and upon others lashed at the top smaller poles and branches were laid to form the footway. When first laid down these were secured to the cross-pieces by lashings; but they had rotted away, and consequently the bridges afforded a very precarious footing. That over the Kukéwi was more than a hundred feet long and twelve feet wide, and was a most creditable specimen of construction by uneducated natives.

The threatenings of the weather were not belied by the night, and in the morning more men professed themselves unable to bear their loads. One man was too unwell to walk and it was with great difficulty I managed to find carriers for him.

Much of this illness was undoubtedly caused by want of shelter, so I resolved to remain in the rear of the caravan to prevent any straggling and staying about on the road instead of hastening into camp. And a wearisome time I had on this march, occupying nine hours and a half, for more than four hours were wasted in driving the men along.

We passed through a break in a range of wooded mountains with villages perched on their summits or nestled among the trees on the steepest

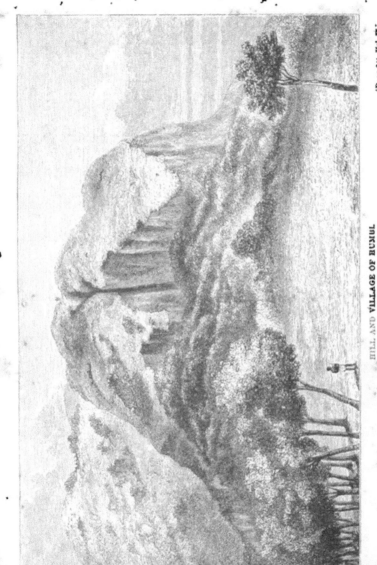

HILL AND VILLAGE OF BUKUL

slopes so as to be easily defended, while in the _{November,} valleys there were large plantations of cassava and _{1875.} Indian corn.

The natives seemed very industrious and put more energy into their work than I had seen for some time. Men and women were busy preparing their fields for new crops, and others, in couples, were carrying up to the villages at a smart trot enormous baskets of cassava slung upon poles. Amongst them was a man who spoke Portuguese. He came to enquire who we were, and gave the men some roots of sweet cassava.

Other hills, in every variety of shape and form imaginable, were now seen directly in front of us, while on the right of our road a portion of the range we had passed ended abruptly. Its appearance reminded me of the north front of the rock of Gibraltar, and on the summit was the village of the chief of the district, to which no stranger had ever been admitted.

At the foot of this hill, named Humbi, the carriers of the sick man came to a dead stop and declared themselves altogether incapable of taking him any further, although I had detailed seven men for this duty in order that they might constantly relieve each other. The camp was fortunately near at hand; so I allowed the carriers and their burthen to remain here, and, pressing forward myself, sent other and fresher men to assist them.

Notwithstanding my care in bringing up the rear of the caravan, a man named Majuto was missing.

It appeared that he proposed to another that they should leave the road and hide in the jungle in order to rest and sleep, remarking that if I saw them lying down on the road I should compel them to move forward. The other fellow refused, but let Majuto go without telling any one about it until camp was reached.

When I heard of his absence it was becoming dark and heavy rain had set in, rendering it useless to think of sending people to seek for him; but I determined to halt the next day and send out a search-party if he did not put in an appearance by the morning.

Of all the wretched nights I have passed this was the worst. It rained so heavily that the ground was converted into semi-liquid mud, and my tent seemed to have given up all idea of keeping out the wet. I was also very anxious about the unfortunate Majuto; for knowing him to be ill I much feared that such a night, without food, fire, or shelter, would kill him.

As soon as day dawned I persuaded some of the Bailunda, and the freshest of my men to go in search of the poor fellow, whilst others went foraging for food.

My experiences of the night made me resolve that, if possible, more comfort should be provided

for all of us before turning in again, and accordingly built a hut for myself and saw that the men
sheltered themselves properly. The appearance of
the sun also gave us an opportunity of drying our
limited belongings, and before long we managed
to give the camp a somewhat habitable appearance.

Several swarms of locusts passed during the day,
some so thick as to obscure the sun, and my men
gladly seized the opportunity of securing some for
food.

Both parties sent out in the morning returned
during the afternoon. The foragers had obtained a
small quantity of food, including a fowl, for which
two yards of cloth out of the four I possessed had
been given. But those who had been searching
for Majuto came in without having seen or heard
anything of him, though they had been back to the
place where he quitted the road and had made
enquiries of every native they met.

It was then four o'clock and heavy rain had again
set in, and no further search could be made that
day. But I decided that, if nothing was heard of
him meanwhile, I would myself have a thorough
hunt the next day with men who had been resting
in camp. If that should prove unsuccessful I
intended to make arrangements with the chief of a
neighbouring village to forward Majuto to the
coast should he be found.

Further delay in marching threatened to end in
disaster, for every day the men became more feeble,

November,
1875. and I was afraid of losing many if I lingered on the road.

All anxiety as to the fate of the straggler was put at rest at seven o'clock by his arrival, wet and wretched and more dead than alive, having eaten nothing since leaving the caravan. I placed him under the charge of some of his chums, and saw him dried and shampooed and made as comfortable as the circumstances of our case allowed; but the poor fellow was past recovery and died a few hours later.

Manoel told me that if the Bailunda, who fortunately were in another camp, heard of the death of Majuto, we should be required to pay a heavy fine to the chiefs near before burying him. We therefore set to work cautiously and quietly by firelight, and digging a grave in one of the huts scattered the earth about by the handful.

Then we buried the poor fellow according to Mohammedan rites, prayers being said by one of his co-religionists, and piled the earth over the grave so as to represent a sleeping-place covered with grass, and one of the carriers lay upon it for an hour or two to give it the appearance of having been used.

It was well that we took these precautions, for visitors came to our camp before we started, and had there been any visible signs of a grave we should have had some trouble.

Soon after leaving camp we found a swarm of

locusts which had settled the night before and were now so torpid from the cold that they could be shaken from the trees and gathered up in any quantity. Of this circumstance my hungry people were not slow to take advantage.

The manner in which the locusts covered the trees was most extraordinary, every twig and branch and the trunk a short distance above the ground being entirely enveloped by them. In many places they were two and even three deep. As the sun became more powerful they began to work their wings without leaving the trees, making a noise like rushing water. Then the stronger ones commenced to move, and in less than half an hour they all had flown.

Many natives were busily engaged in collecting them, and actually cut down trees of fair size which were thickly covered in order to secure this delicacy.

Only two hours and a half were spent on the march this day although we were six hours on the road, and one man, heedless of the sad fate of Majuto, straggled away and hid himself and remained absent until the evening.

Up caravans were now rather frequently met, but being principally composed of and owned by natives no news could be gathered from them.

A small party of Senhor Gonçalves' men also met us in the morning and stated that slaves were no longer allowed to be taken into Benguella, and

that all brought there lately had been liberated and
the importers punished.   This was unexpected and
unwelcome news for Manoel and the Bailunda
accompanying me, whose faces at once lengthened
considerably.

Manoel had informed me only the day previous
that slaves were still exported from the coast, especially from Massomédés. He said they were held
in readiness for embarkation, although scattered
about the town in small parties instead of being
kept in barracoons as formerly, and a steamer came
in for an hour or two, shipped the slaves, and was
off again immediately.

I enquired their destination, but he could give
me no information on that point, and indeed was
too ignorant to know much of the outside world.

After this day's exhibition I saw that the
marching powers of my men had gone from bad
to worse, and that some decisive steps must be
taken or the caravan would never reach the coast,
now only one hundred and twenty-six geographical
miles distant.

Upwards of twenty men complained of being
unable to walk far or to carry anything; swelled
legs, stiff necks, aching backs, and empty stomachs
being the universal cry.

Taking my pipe to my assistance, I sat down for
half an hour's reflection, and then resolved on the
action to be taken. It came to this : throw away
tent, boat, bed, and everything but instruments,

journals, and books; and then, taking a few picked men, make a forced march to the coast, sending thence assistance to the main body. And this was no sooner decided than acted upon, for no time was to be lost.

Manoel appropriated my abandoned tent, bed, and boat, and lodged them with a friend in a village near by; and early on the following morning I started—with five of my own men, Manoel and two of his, and the Bailunda, who said they could go at any pace—to make a rush for the coast, leaving three of Manoel's people to act as guides to the caravan.

Jumah, Sambo, Hamees Ferhan, Marijani, Ali ibn Mshangama were the men who volunteered to accompany me.

My kit consisted of what I stood up in, and a spare shirt, a pair of slippers, a blanket, frying-pan, tin cup, sextant, artificial horizon, and writing materials; making in all a load of about twenty pounds, which was shifted from man to man on the journey.

My personal stock of food and stores for the road was composed of half the fowl obtained at Lungi, a little flour, and my last two yards of cloth.

The men were rather better off, as the cloth I had given them on leaving Bihé was not ex-pended, and Marijani, who being able to speak Portuguese had acted as interpreter, had been presented with three pieces of cloth. Two of these I bought to leave with Bombay for the use of the caravan.

We set out at a good speed across rough and broken country, but about noon the Bailunda, who had boasted about their pace, gave in, saying that they did not calculate upon going at such a rate.

About three o'clock we halted at a small camp situated upon a large open upland, and made ourselves as comfortable as might be and took advantage of the stream running at the foot of the hills to enjoy a bathe. I felt rather stiff after the sharp march, but Jumah was an adept at shampooing and took some of the kinks out of my muscles.

This camp was the highest point throughout the whole journey, being 5,800 feet above the sea, and the adjoining hills might have been eight hundred feet higher.

A large up caravan of Bailunda passed us here. Many of them had umbrellas which might have rivalled Joseph's coat for variety of colour, each gore being a different tint. Red, pink, green, yellow, blue, violet, and white were sometimes to be found in one umbrella. Empty paraffin tins were carried by a number of porters, and I was much puzzled as to their use.

The next day we rose with the lark, and I was so hungry that I could not resist finishing the remains of my fowl, although well aware I could scarcely hope for another taste of flesh between this and the coast.

Leaving camp we made a gradual ascent, and, passing through a gap, found before us a steep and almost precipitous descent, down which we went like goats, jumping from stone to stone.

Hamees Ferhan, my gunbearer, now began to complain of fatigue and I had to relieve him of my heavy rifle and cartridges, giving him my fowling-piece in exchange.

Another caravan with gay umbrellas and empty paraffin tins met us at the bottom of this descent, and the leaders expressed great astonishment at finding a white man with so few followers, and on foot. Their wonderment was still greater when told whence we had started the day before, and they declared they had never before heard of people getting over so much ground in a day. But harder marches were yet in store for us.

No sooner had we reached this valley than we had to commence the ascent of other hills, and on arriving at their summit found ourselves overlooking other ranges in front of us, their crests piercing the clouds which hung at our feet.

Away to the south was a village situated on a small conical mount, and this was the settlement of a colony of mulattoes springing from the intercourse between whites and natives.

These mulattoes generally possessed some small property, but being unable to hold any position amongst whites at the coast and being too proud to mix freely with pure blacks, they had settled here. I was told they lived in peace and comfort, and having large numbers of slaves, occasionally despatched trading caravans.

Descending again, we went through a deep gorge with its sides clothed with trees, the graceful form and light foliage of the wild date-palm contrasting well with the darker and heavier shades of the acacias.

From amid this mass of tangled wood a cascade burst forth and fell in an unbroken sheet into a rocky basin seventy or eighty feet below, whence clouds of spray were scattered over the trees and ferns around. And then the waters, by a series of smaller leaps, joined a stream rushing through the centre of the gorge.

We were now upon a level plain covered with open forest, and as we were about to enter the wood I noticed a grave composed of a pile of loose blocks of granite with a rough and massive wooden cross reared at its head. This, I was told, was the grave of a daughter of Major Coimbra (Coimbra's father), who married Syde ibn Habib and died here in childbirth. After her death Syde ibn Habib returned to her father's settlement at Boa Vista and married her sister, evidently determined to have a better-half with some European blood in her veins. This second wife he took with him to Zanzibar.

On this march we met no fewer than ten up caravans, numbering seventy to eighty men each. They were principally laden with small bags of salt, and bottles and kegs of aguardienté which they had purchased at Benguella.

A stream running through a muddy swamp which we reached about noon, affording an opportunity for bathing, we halted to enjoy a dip and rest and a bit of damper to appease our hunger. On resuming our march we entered well-wooded but broken ground with numerous torrents and rills, and outcrops and vast sheets of granite.

From a high hill we descried ranges of mountains still lying in front, while at our feet there was a decent camping-place where we decided to halt. Before us was the river Balomba, eighty feet wide and waist-deep, flowing fast towards the north-west, and ultimately falling into the sea as an independent stream some little distance north of Benguella.

Caravans continued to pass us, bound up country, and nearly the whole number seen by us during the day traded only between Bailunda and the coast. They carry thither the flour of Indian corn and cassava on which the slaves at Benguella are fed, and receive in exchange salt, aguardienté, and sometimes cloth.

Their loads are light and they travel fast, being no more than about three weeks absent from their homes in Bailunda.

During these journeys the men live almost entirely on drink, never eating more than a handful or two of porridge daily. Yet they seem to work well and thrive wonderfully. No women travel with these caravans, for owing to the short time they are on the road it is possible to manage domestic affairs without their aid.

This day we had eleven hours' hard walking and were very glad indeed to camp. The height of the camp was 3,870 feet above the sea, nearly 2,000 feet lower than our halting-place of the previous night and considerably more than 2,000 below the highest level we had crossed on this day's march.

After a good shampooing from Jumah ("Man Friday," as I called him, Jumah being the Kisuahili for Friday), I turned in to enjoy my well-earned sleep.

Five o'clock the next morning saw us on the move again. Crossing the Balomba we passed some cultivated ground and villages perched upon small rocky hills, the huts corresponding so exactly with the colour of the red sandstone rocks that I should not have noticed them but for curls of smoke rising into the morning air. On through jungle, across torrent beds and streams, up and down we went' until we reached a level lying between two mountains.

Here there was much cultivation, the bottom being very fertile, and sugar-cane, Indian corn, and

tobacco grew in profusion. We endeavoured to
persuade some people working in the fields to _____
supply us with food, but they refused to enter into
any commercial transactions with us.

Going empty away from these unsociable natives,
we soon afterwards met a large caravan carrying
two apologies for flags, and bringing up the rear
were some men wearing hats and coats. ·

They had a large stock of aguardienté, and some
had evidently been engaged in lightening their
loads that morning, being very overbearing and
quarrelsome. First they attempted to hustle us
out of the road, and then behaved toward us
generally in a very objectionable manner. One
fellow knocked up against me purposely, upon
which I tripped just as purposely, though seemingly by accident, and sent him sprawling with
his load by way of a hint that he could not expect
to have his own way in everything.

We continued on the march until about two
o'clock, when Manoel asserted that as we were
close by the village of a chief whom he knew we
must stop to obtain flour, our stock being well-
nigh exhausted.

The exact locality of this village being unknown, I was thinking of despatching scouring
parties in every direction to search for it, when
a child was heard crying about a hundred yards
away, and on approaching the sound the village
was discovered. Although immediately beside us,

it was entirely hidden from the path by trees and rocks.

We succeeded in getting a small quantity of flour, and the chief brought me as a present a little Indian corn and a gourd of the sourest pombé possible. He expressed regret at not having heard of my intended visit as he would then have given me something respectable, but now he had nothing prepared.

Marching on again and passing some huge blocks of granite, we reached more level ground well wooded and watered. We overtook two down caravans and even managed to pass them after a considerable amount of racing, for they did not at all appreciate being beaten by a white man upon their own ground.

Just before sunset we found ourselves amidst a swarm of locusts on the point of settling, and my people were anxious to collect them; but camp was still some distance ahead, and I knew we were much too tired and weary to make another start that night if once we halted. The camp we had decided to occupy was situated on a large open plain broken by occasional blocks of granite, named Kutwé-ya-Ombwa—the dog's head—but when we arrived we found it already occupied by a caravan. Thus we were compelled to search for another in the dark.

After a while we stumbled upon a wretched little place with which we were inclined to be satisfied being thoroughly tired out; but it hap- pened that one of the men engaged in picking sticks for our fire discovered a larger and better spot, to which we immediately removed.

I was almost dead beat by this day's work; for, including all halts, we had been travelling for thirteen hours over rough and difficult country. But I knew that the first signs of fatigue betrayed by me would be the signal for the breakdown of the whole party, so I struggled to keep up appearances. I managed my stars, and boiled my thermometer to ascertain our height above the sea.

When day dawned I saw on the other side of the plain a range of sterile-looking mountains, which we reached after two hours' marching across the broken level.

On the right of the entrance to a pass there was a precipitous bluff with great masses of rock—balanced like the Cornish rocking-stones— perched upon its summit. On the left, on the opposite side of a deep ravine with a rapid stream flowing through it, were enormous dome-like mounts apparently formed of single masses of smooth granite. Their surface was washed clean by the rains and they were devoid of vegetation, excepting a few cacti which had taken root in slight fissures near the summit. Further down the pass were other masses, many of which had the appearance of bastions of some Titan forts.

Our path was along the northern side of this

pass, over sheets of steep and slippery granite divided from each other by patches of thorny scrub, with rills draining down to join the stream we heard murmuring in the depths of the gorge hundreds of feet below us.

At times we were obliged to clamber over huge masses of stone on our hands and knees; at others to descend into the gorge to avoid some giant block jutting out beyond the path; and then to clamber again to our old level with the assistance of the creepers which grew in the crevices.

Graves and numerous skeletons testified to the numbers whose lives had been sacrificed on this trying march, whilst slave clogs and forks still attached to some bleached bones or lying by their sides, gave only too convincing a proof that the demon of the slave-trade still exerted his influence in this part of Africa.

Clogs and forks were also hanging on trees, some being so slightly affected by the weather that it was evident they had not been there longer than a month or two. Doubtless they had been removed from some flagging wretches in the belief that weakness of body had extinguished all idea of escape, and in the hope that the strength which was insufficient to bear the weight of the clog might still prove enough to drag the unfortunate human chattel to the coast.

We halted here to bathe in the stream and gather fresh energy for the afternoon.

Fearfully hard work was now beginning seriously to tell on me, but I was wonderfully buoyed up by the knowledge that every step was taking me nearer to the coast and to rest. My head and legs, more especially the ankle I had sprained in Ulûnda, gave me much pain.

After more hours of wearying clambering we entered upon an open plain, and to my sorrow I noticed that it was surrounded by mountains which gave promise of hard labour on the morrow.

Shortly before sunset we were near a village in the small district of Kisanji, and here made our arrangements for sleeping under some baobabs of which we had seen the first in the pass. I was so exhausted that when the men took the opportunity of having another bathe it was impossible for me to do the same, being only fit to lie under the shade of a baobab-tree.

Soon after settling down a few men and women gathered around to stare at us, and I was surprised at their small pretensions to anything approaching civilised appearance although they were not far from the coast.

A small and greasy cloth round their waists, and a mass of strings of beads—almost looking like a bolster—around their necks, constituted their dress. One woman wore in addition a small square of cloth intended to hide her breasts; but it was a failure.

I tried to persuade the women to give me some milk for the cloth I had carefully hoarded up to this time; but they set a light value on my little store, and I had to borrow more from Marijani before I could procure about a quart; and very

PEOPLE OF KISANJI.

sour stuff it was, fresh milk being altogether un-attainable.

We were off by half-past four the following morning and soon came upon a number of up caravans just starting on their march. Now the mystery of the empty paraffin tins was explained, fo

November,
1875.

and they certainly served the purpose of kettle-
drums admirably.

Scrambling along a steep and rocky ridge of
hills intersected by several watercourses and ravines with almost perpendicular sides, and then up
a path not unlike a broken-down flight of steep
steps, we reached the summit of the range.

What was that distant line upon the sky ?

We all gazed at it with a strange mingling of
hope and fear, scarcely daring to believe it was
the sea. But looking more intently at that streak
happily left no room for doubt.

It was the sea, and Xenophon and his ten
thousand could not have welcomed its view
more heartily when they exclaimed, " ὁ θαλάττα ! ὁ
θαλάττα !" than did I and my handful of way-worn
followers.

There was little "go" left in me now. I was
very nearly broken down ; for though my head and
legs had ceased to ache so acutely I was suffering
excruciating pain in my back.

At almost every step I feared I should be
compelled to lie down and wait for some assistance from the coast ; but I thought of the poor
exhausted fellows behind who were trusting to me
to send them aid, and being sustained by the near
approach of the end of my journey I still managed
to keep on my legs.

The remainder of this day was spent in crawling
over rocks and dragging through pools, waist-

deep, dammed up in hollows since the last rains
and now slimy and stagnant. I confess that it was
a relief when about four o'clock I heard some of
my men declare they could march no further; for
though I was fully aware of the vital importance
of pushing on and should have hesitated to suggest a halt, yet I was very weak and glad indeed
to rest.

One of my people and another of Manoel's being
still able and ready to march, we despatched them
with the letters I had recovered at Lungi, and a
note begging any charitably disposed person to
send a little food to meet us on the road. I then
ate my last morsel of damper and turned in, in-
tending the next day to make the final effort.

Somewhat refreshed by the night's rest, we continued our way through the pass until noon—
the rays of the sun reverberating from the rocks
making one feel as though in a furnace—and on
emerging from it made our mid-day halt at an
angle of the Supa, which drains the pass and falls
into the sea at Katombéla.

On going to this stream to bathe I was greatly
surprised at my curious appearance, being covered
with purple spots; and I noticed that a slight
bruise on my ankle had developed into a large
and angry-looking place.

I was still more astonished on lighting my pipe
by way of breakfast—for my pipe was now my
only food—to find my mouth bleeding. Of the

cause I was ignorant, for I did not then know that I was attacked with scurvy.

From some passing caravans we heard that our two messengers had been seen that morning, and would by this time have arrived at Katombéla.

On again, across a rough and waterless plain lying between us and the hills behind Katombéla and Benguella, and then over precipitous hills formed of limestone, with many huge ammonites and other fossils and having the appearance of cliffs which might once have faced a sea. They were intersected by ravines and dry water-courses, up and down the sides of which we clambered in the dark, slipping about and bruising ourselves.

But what did it matter? The next morning would see us at Katombéla.

At the bottom of a ravine we found water, which was a godsend to me, for my mouth was still bleeding and I had already used that brought by us from our mid-day halting-place.

Another steep climb brought us almost to the summit of the last ridge, where it was somewhat level. And numerous fires dotted about denoted the camps of caravans that had started that evening from Katombéla and were halted here, ready to commence their march early in the morning without being delayed by the attractions of the grog-shops.

One of my men, a short way in advance of me,

now shouted, "Here's our camp-master," and
hastening on I saw Manoel's messenger.

He had with him a basket containing wine,
bread, tins of sardines, and a sausage; and
although my mouth would not admit of my eating
without pain I managed to take some supper, for
I had tasted nothing since the previous evening.
From a note, in English, from Mr. Seruia, a
trader at Katombéla who had kindly sent out
these provisions, I learnt that my letters had
been forwarded to Benguella. My messenger, it
appeared, was too tired to return, so Mr. Seruia
had sent one of his own people back with Manoel's
man.

This was my last night outside the pale of civilisation, and though thoroughly tired I was much
too excited to sleep.

Long before the rising of the sun we were all
on the move, and, quickly finishing the remains of
the supper, started on our last march. Twenty
minutes brought us within sight of the sea, and
I then noticed the position of Katombéla and
Benguella with regard to each other. I had
been puzzled on hearing that the former was
passed before reaching Benguella and could not
understand the course of the last march; but now
I found Katombéla situated on the seashore
instead of ten or twelve miles inland, as I had
imagined from the description given me.

A man engaged in searching for runaway slaves

told me that rumours respecting an Englishman coming from the interior had been rife for some time, but no one had believed them.

I ran down the slope towards Katombéla swinging my rifle round my head, which I believe was almost "turned" for very joy; and the men, carried away with the same sense of relief, joined in the running till we approached nearer the town. Then I unfurled my colours and went forward more quietly.

Coming towards us I saw a couple of hammocks with awnings, followed by three men carrying baskets; and on meeting this party a jolly-looking little Frenchman jumped out, seized the baskets and instantly opened a bottle to drink "to the honour of the first European who had ever succeeded in crossing tropical Africa from east to west."

For this hearty welcome I found I was indebted to Monsieur Cauchoix, an old officer of the French navy who had settled as a merchant at Benguella. Hearing of my approach between ten and eleven o'clock the night before, he had immediately started off to meet me.

His other baskets were also full of provisions, which he distributed to my men, throwing loaves of bread at the hungry mortals; after which we moved on, and in a few minutes arrived at a house which he owned in Katombéla.

I need not say how greatly I have been grieved

at receiving the sad intelligence of the death of this
kind-hearted Frenchman while on his passage home
to Europe. He intended to have visited England,
and I had been looking forward to the pleasure of
renewing the acquaintance of one who had so
readily shown me the greatest kindness and attention when I was sorely in need of succour.

MINE ON ROAD.

CHAPTER XIV.

PEACE AND PLENTY.—KATOMBÉLA.—MY ILLNESS INCREASES.—CARRIED TO
BENGUELLA.—MEDICAL ADVICE AND GOOD NURSING.—MY RECOVERY.—
ARRIVAL OF MY STRAGGLERS.—DEATH OF ANOTHER MAN.—BOMBAY'S OB-
JECTIONABLE BEHAVIOUR.—AN ORIGINAL CHARACTER.—BENGUELLA.—ITS
TUMBLEDOWN FORT.—CONVICT SOLDIERS.—THEIR LOYALTY.—MY MEN
INDULGE TOO FREELY.—ARRIVAL AT LOANDA.—RECEPTION BY THE CONSUL.
—COURTESY OF THE GOVERNOR.—AN AMUSING INCIDENT.—MY MEN OBJECT
TO THEIR QUARTERS.—PREPARING TO SEND THEM HOME.—LIBERAL OFFERS.
—PURCHASE OF A SCHOONER.—FITTING HER OUT.—VISIT TO KISEMBO.—NO
CHARTS OBTAINABLE.—A WINDFALL.—DEPARTURE OF MY CREW IN THE
FRANCES CAMERON.—LEAVING MY LOANDA FRIENDS.—HOMEWARD BOUND.—
MEETING OLD FACES.—SAFE AT HOME.

A T the house of Monsieur Cauchoix my men were November, provided with quarters and an unlimited 1875. supply of food; while I was conducted to a comfortable bedroom and was given some new clothing. And it was well that I obtained this fresh kit, for my old flannel shirt was so rotten that in pulling it off rather hurriedly my head went through the back of it.

Having bathed and dressed, feeling the most thorough enjoyment at being once more restored to civilisation,, I received visits from Dr. Aguia, the judge at Benguella; Monsieur Leroux, the Katombéla agent of my host; Mr. Seruia, and others.

I lost no time in requesting that arrangements might be made ·for sending men and food to the assistance of my people who remained behind, and Cauchoix kindly undertook to manage everything for them. He consulted with the *chéfe*—as the Portuguese officer in charge of a small settlement is called—and the native chief; and that evening twenty men with hammocks, vegetables and other food, and cloth with which to buy a bullock at Kisanji, were started off to meet my worn-out stragglers.

The great soreness of my mouth had now increased, and on looking at it Cauchoix at once saw that I was attacked with scurvy, but assured me that with good diet I should soon get well.

My men were thoroughly enjoying themselves and there was certainly some excuse for their indulging rather freely; but I was not prepared to find all, except Jumah, drunk within an hour after their arrival.

In the afternoon I went round Katombéla. It is a small place consisting of about a dozen houses belonging to Benguella merchants, a square fort with a few honeycombed guns propped upon stones, a market-place, and some smaller buildings such as grog-stores.

The only stone house was that in which I was being entertained, and during a recent rising of the natives all the Europeans had taken refuge there. The other buildings were of *adobes*, and white-washed.

Although Cauchoix applied carbolic acid to my

MAISON CAUCHOIX.

(Page 208, Vol. II.

mouth while we were visiting the *chêfe*, I found it impossible to eat anything when we returned to our quarters.

From this time I rapidly grew worse. My tongue became so swollen as to project beyond my teeth, and blood ran from my mouth. About two o'clock in the morning, Cauchoix, who was sleeping in the same room, seeing how ill I was and that no time was to be lost in applying proper remedies, roused his men, and, laying me in a hammock, hurried me away to Benguella to obtain the advice of the medical officer there.

When we arrived I was unable to speak or swallow and my body was covered with blotches with a variety of shades of purple, blue, black, and green, the rest of my skin being a deadly white. Dr. Calasso, in charge of the hospital, came immediately to see me and ordered poultices to be placed on my throat and some solution to be injected into my mouth every ten minutes, while the clotted blood which threatened to choke me was extracted by means of pincers.

My kind host Monsieur Cauchoix and the doctor watched by me, never leaving me alone for eight-and-forty hours. At the end of that time, thanks to those who treated me with such skill and care, I was able to swallow a little milk, and the disease had been conquered. Had it attacked me a day or two earlier, when out of the reach of medical advice, nothing could have saved my life.

Now that I could swallow I began to pick up, and progressed so rapidly towards convalescence that on the fourth day I was able to take an airing in a maxilla and called on the governor, Major Brito, who had constantly been to see me.

He had also most kindly furnished my people with quarters in a Government building, and had directed the commissariat department to supply them with rations.

The next day, the 11th of November, the remainder of the men arrived, excepting Ferhan Mhéhé who died after I parted from them. A few had been robbed of their clothes by the natives whilst straggling behind the caravan.

Bombay celebrated his return to civilisation by getting exceptionally drunk and behaving in a most insolent and abusive manner to several people, including the kind-hearted Monsieur Cauchoix when he was engaged in seeing the men properly lodged and the sick sent to hospital. I would have punished him for his blackguardism had not those against whom he offended begged that it might be overlooked.

In the employ of Cauchoix there was rather an original character who amused me much. He was an American and had served in an English brig, but having taken upon himself to give the captain and mate a severe thrashing, he was landed here and sent to prison. He was curious to know whether I had " been on my own hook," or had been "working for a company," and remarked that he should have liked being with me, except that "he didn't care about the darned walking." Amongst other callings he had been master of an American barque and traded in snakes which he obtained up some African river. He was so pleased with this line of business that he •enquired whether I could tell him of any big snakes, as if so he would be off in search of them at once.

Benguella is second·in importance amongst the Portuguese towns on the West Coast and carries on a considerable trade with the interior in bees-·wax and ivory, and some of the merchants possess fishing stations along the coast. The town is laid out in wide streets, and, the houses being white-washed and the doors and windows painted in bright colours, had a very clean appearance. In a central position in the town is a tastefully arranged public garden, where a band performs on Sunday evenings. The only public buildings are a well-constructed custom-house, a very good hospital, the house of the governor, a court-house, and a church which is never opened except for baptisms and burials.

There is also a large fort constructed in the form of a parallelogram and having a sufficiently imposing appearance from the sea; but its armament consists only of honeycombed old guns of various calibres, either mounted on rotten, broken-down wooden carriages, or propped up on piles of stones so as to show their muzzles above the parapets.

The garrison numbers about thirty white soldiers, chiefly convicts, and two companies of blacks. Discipline is not rigidly enforced, for I found the sentry posted outside the governor's house sitting in the middle of the road smoking a pipe and taking off his boots.

Besides the convicts serving as soldiers there are others employed on public works; and they were then engaged in constructing a causeway across a portion of the plain lying between Benguella and Katombéla, which is flooded in the rainy season.

The loyalty of the soldiers to their flag I did not expect to find very marked, but I was scarcely prepared for the proposal made to me by a white non-commissioned officer, that if I desired to take the town he would place himself and his comrades at my disposal and would give up the fort to me on condition that I should give them meat three times a week instead of only once, which was the allowance they received from the Portuguese.

The inhabitants of Benguella were all ready to show every kindness to me, and I was frequently invited to the houses of Dr. Aguia, Mr. Ben Chimol, and Dr. Calasso.

There are many good gardens where European vegetables and fruits are grown, the light and sandy soil only requiring water to make it fertile;

and that is always obtainable within six feet of the surface though near the sea it is slightly brackish.

A few horses are also kept there and the place boasts of one· carriage; but the usual means of locomotion, as no white man ever walked during the daytime, is the maxilla, which is slung from long poles over which awnings are spread and carried by two men. The bearers walk· with a peculiar step and avoid jolting; and altogether it is a very comfortable·mode of moving about.

My men, I regret to say, did not behave very well, owing to the cheapness of vile spirits; and it was necessary to deprive them of their arms to prevent bloodshed in their drunken squabbles. One fellow hacked another over the head with a sword-bayonet, for which offence I had him confined in the cells in the fort and kept on bread and water for the remainder of our stay.

On the return of the mail steamer from Mossamédés, the southernmost Portuguese settlement, the governor ordered a passage for me and my men to San Paul de Loanda. Nearly all the town came to see us off; and, as it was night before we sailed, there were fireworks in honour of the occasion.

The steamer was the *Bengo* of Hull, but sailed by Portuguese officers. under the Portuguese flag, the only Englishman on board being the chief engineer, Mr. Lindsay.

On the morning of the 21st of November, a fortnight after my arrival at Katombéla, we

anchored in the harbour of Loanda.   I was puzzled
at first how to get on shore, as none but private boats came alongside, but hearing English
spoken by a gentleman who had come on board
I introduced myself to him and he immediately
offered me the use of his boat; and added that a
maxilla, waiting at the landing-place, was at my
service to convey me to the consulate.   For
these friendly offices I was indebted to Mr.
Edward Warberg.

Arriving at the consulate, my knock was
answered by a little mulatto servant who ran away
on seeing me and left me standing at the door in
some astonishment; but another entrance on my
right was soon opened and the consul himself
appeared.

He looked rather hard at me, as though
wondering who the seedy-looking individual before
him might be.   I then said, " I have come to
report myself from Zanzibar—overland."

At the mention of " Zanzibar" he began to
stare, but at the word " overland " he stepped back
a pace, and then coming forward placed both his
hands on my shoulders and said, " Cameron !
My God !! "   The tone in which these words were
uttered made me feel that in David Hopkins, the
consul, I had found a true friend.

Bringing me some letters a year old which had
been waiting here for me, he said that on that
very morning he had been looking at them with

Carnegie, the vice-consul, remarking that I should
never turn up to get them ; and a few hours later
I stood at his door ! He lost no time in making
me comfortable at the consulate.

On calling upon the Governor-General of Angola,
Admiral Andradé, I was most warmly received,
and to him I am greatly indebted for kindness and
courtesy shown towards me during my stay.
We enquired whether quarters for my followers
could be provided in any of the Government
barracks, and by his directions Lieutenant Mello,
of the Portuguese navy, his aide-de-camp, made
the necessary arrangements and relieved me of
all, trouble, for which I was grateful, being still
very weak. This officer had served for some years
on board one of her Majesty's ships and was
considered one of the English community at
Loanda.

Rather an amusing incident occurred in the
afternoon on the arrival of H.M.S. *Cygnet*. The
commanding officer, Lieutenant Hammick, being
unwell, he deputed Sub-Lieutenant Thomas to
make an official call upon the consul, and it
so happened that he landed at the same moment
as my men. The populace of Loanda, imagin-
ing that this smart-looking officer had walked
across from Zanzibar, followed him with great
curiosity and many remarks as he came up with my
men, who were marching in a body with colours
flying.

On arriving at the fort, where quarters had been provided, the men objected to enter, saying they did not understand why they should be put in prison after having followed me across Africa — for to the Zanzibar mind fort and prison are the same, in their language they are synonymous; but after some persuasion and an assurance that the gates should remain open they settled down.

A few days afterwards the *Spiteful* arrived on her way to join Commodore Sir W. N. W. Hewett, and Captain Medlycott took a letter to him from me, asking for any assistance he might be able to render towards sending my men to Zanzibar.

However, as it was by no means certain that any of the ships at the disposal of the commodore could be spared to help me, I made every effort to find immediate means of sending them back.

MM. Papé and Pasteur, the heads of the Dutch West African Trading Company and consul and vice-consul for H.M. the King of the Netherlands, offered to lend me a steamer to take my followers to St. Helena—whence there was communication to the Cape and Zanzibar—on the condition that I should pay for coals, stores, and harbour dues, they giving the use of ship and crew gratuitously.

Although this was most kind and liberal I was obliged to decline, for on calculating the expense I found that it would cost more than buying and fitting out a vessel; so I determined either to charter or purchase some small craft that would do for the work.

The first offer I received was the charter of a schooner for £1,700, and I was to refit and provision her for the voyage. This I thought too much, and shortly afterwards her sister ship, the *San João di Ulloa* being for sale, the consul and myself bought her for £1,000 and fitted her out for the cruise.

There then seemed no prospect of finding any one to navigate her round the Cape, and I therefore made up my mind to do it myself.

Fortunately I was relieved from the necessity of this duty by Captain Carl Alexanderson, F.R.G.S.—well known to the Royal Geographical Society for his survey of the lower waters of the river Kwanza—volunteering to take the command. Knowing him to be a thoroughly good sailor I entrusted him with the command, feeling perfectly confident that the navigation of the schooner— which on transfer to the English flag I had renamed the *Frances Cameron,* after my mother— could not be in better hands.

In refitting the schooner we were assisted by men kindly lent from the Portuguese guard-ship by Admiral Andradé, and I also received help from the *Cygnet* when she was in harbour.

Some little trouble arose on a few occasions between my men and the native police, and it was amusing to see my fellows bringing a policeman's

cap or sword to the consulate to complain of
the conduct of the man to whom these belonged.
They rightly judged that the owner must reclaim
his property, and then they would be able to
identify him and state their grievance. Owing
to the great consideration and kindness of the
governor-general and Lieutenant Mello, nothing
serious came of these squabbles.

As the schooner could not be ready to leave
Loanda for some time, I went up to Kinsembo with
Mr. Tait, a merchant who had a house there, that
I might have an insight of a trader's life when
away from any settlement. We had a tedious and
disagreeable passage in a sailing boat generally
used for cargo, the bilges not being as clean as
they might have been.

Kinsembo consists of half-a-dozen establishments
belonging to different firms, and being north of
the Portuguese boundary, trade is carried on without any formalities as to custom-house, &c. I
wished much to visit a famous rock called the
column of Kinsembo, on which there are reported to
be inscriptions by Vasco de Gama and other early
Portuguese discoverers; but when I had called on
the chief, whose fetish would not allow him to
behold the sea, it was time to leave for the south-
going Portuguese mail at Ambriz in order to
return to Loanda.

Ambriz is about twelve miles south of Kinsembo,
and just north of it is a stream which the natives

will not allow the Portuguese to cross although other Europeans can pass freely. This river may be considered the real northern boundary of the province of Angola, although our Government only recognises the power of the Portuguese up to 8° S., whilst this river is in about 7° 48′ S. At Ambriz the Portuguese have a custom-house and other Government buildings, and a small garrison.

On returning to Loanda I found everything progressing satisfactorily. We were, however, at our wits' end for charts and sailing directions for the schooner, for, notwithstanding that Mello had given me all that could be found in the Government stores, I could get none for the Mozambique. But fortune favoured us most unexpectedly by the arrival of a fine schooner flying the R.Y.S. burgee and white ensign. This proved to be the *Linda* owned by Mr. F. Lee, a Royal Academician, who was returning to England from the Cape. He had visited Zanzibar the year before and was supplied with the latest local charts and directions, which he very kindly gave to us.

At last, on the 8th of February, all was ready, and Captain Alexanderson set sail with a crew of four besides my Zanzibar men, accompanied some little distance by the boats of the English residents and those of the *Cygnet*, which was then in harbour.

The next day the *Sirius* arrived, having been

ordered by the commodore to give me every
assistance and, if necessary, to take me and my
people to the Cape, from whence they could be
sent to Zanzibar by the mail steamer. As the
men had already sailed I had nothing to request
except that in case of falling in with the schooner
she might be given a tow.

My thanks are due to Messrs. Newton and
Carnegie and to Mr. George Essex, as well as to
the consul, for their hospitality and great assistance rendered in fitting out and provisioning the
vessel.

Soon after the schooner sailed, the steamship
Congo, Captain King, arrived, and in her I took a
passage for Liverpool. Our voyage home was long
and tedious, owing to the number of ports at which
we called, numbering nearly seventy.

At every place we touched I was most warmly
welcomed. At Loango, Dr. Loesche Pechel, of the
German expedition, persisted in coming off to see
me, although it was a perilous undertaking, causing
him to be capsized six times in the surf.

At the Gaboon the French authorities were most
kind and courteous. Admiral Rébourt, commanding the South Atlantic squadron, was there in
his flag-ship, and sent his barge to take me on
board to breakfast with him, and his officers vied
with each other in offering kindnesses of every
description.

At Lagos, where we stayed three days, I was the

uest of the lieutenant-governor, Captain Cameron
ees, and before leaving had the good-fortune to
eet the commodore on board the *Active*.

At Cape Coast I found Captain Strachan, C.M.G.,
s governor, who until we met had no idea that

CUSTOM-HOUSE AT BENGUELLA.

was the same Cameron whom he had known as
small midshipman on board the *Victor Emmanuel*,
hen he was aide-de-camp to Sir Henry Storks at
orfu.

While I was at Sierra Leone the *Encounter* came
, and I had a joyful meeting with Captain

Bradshaw, my old captain in the *Star* durin; the Abyssinian campaign.

Again at Madeira I met the Channel squadro: and many old friends—Admirals Beauchamp Sey mour and Phillimore (another of my old captains and Commander Fellowes among the number.

And on the 2nd of April we arrived in th Mersey, and it was with a heart full of gratitud to God for His goodness in protecting me throug! so many dangers that I recognised my mothe amongst those waiting to welcome me on my retur to England after an absence of three years an four months.

SIERRA LEONE.

FORMATION OF THE CONTINENT.—RIVER BASINS.—DESERTS.—THE WATER-SHEDS.— ZAMBÉSI.— KONGO.— PHYSICAL GEOGRAPHY.— USEGHARA MOUNTAINS.—FERTILE SOIL.—THE LUGERENGERI VALLEY.—THE KUNGWA HILLS.—GUM-COPAL.— TIMBER-TREES. — FAUNA.— SNAKES.—THE MUKONDOKWA VALLEY.— LAKE UGOMBO.— MPWAPWA.— BARREN SOIL.— THE MARENGA MKALI.—UGOGO.—A DRIED-UP COUNTRY.—ZIWAS.—XANYENYÉ.— USEKHÉ.—GRANITE.—KHOKO.—THE VALE OF MDABURU.—THE "FIERY FIELD."—THE MABUNGURU.—JIWÉ LA SINGA.—URGURU.—UNYANYEMBÉ.—A CULTIVATED COUNTRY.—UGUNDA.—UGARA.—THE KAWENDI MOUNTAINS.—UVINZA.

THE object of this and the following chapters is to discuss briefly the geography of that portion of Africa traversed by me, and its future prospects, both with regard to commerce and the abolition of the slave-trade.

Speaking roughly, tropical Africa consists of a central plateau—the lowest portion of which is the valley of the Kongo—separated from low tracts fringing the coast by lines of hills and mountains. These lines of mountains in some places approach closely to the coast, and at others recede from it, and also vary greatly in height; yet the ranges are perfectly easy to trace.

In consequence of this formation of the continent it may be broadly described as forming three divisions—the low-lying and unhealthy littoral, the mountain ranges, and the central plateau. It

is not necessary here to remind the reader that this
plateau consists of almost every sort of country,
presenting great natural diversities.   Independent
groups and ranges of mountains, great lakes and
noble rivers, abound in the heart of the "Dark
Continent."

Another way of forming the continent into geographical divisions would be by considering each
great river basin to be one, and the watersheds to
be natural lines of demarcation.

Taking this as a starting-point, with our present knowledge of Africa, the great basins would
be those of the Nile, Kongo, Zambési, Niger,
Ogowai, and the rivers draining into Lake Tchad.
The minor rivers draining the littoral and adjacent
mountains, which do not fall into any one of the
main basins and as a rule only receive the rainfall
of a small portion of the country, need not, in a
sketch like the present, be classed independently.

Besides these basins there are also the great
deserts of the Sahara and the Kalahari, which
separate fertile tropical Africa from fertile tempe-
rate Africa.

Of these the Sahara is by far the largest and
most sterile; the Kalahari during the rainy season
being covered with vegetation which affords sus-
tenance to innumerable wild animals, whilst the
Sahara, except in an oasis around an occasional
spring, always presents the same sandy and
parched appearance.

Having as yet such scanty data for our geographical knowledge of Africa, it is difficult to trace the precise watershed between any two systems, and therefore my observations on the subject must necessarily be liable to great modifications as exploration gradually opens out regions now unknown.

The basin of the Nile is probably bounded on the south-west by the watershed reached by Dr. Schweinfurth; on the south of the Albert Nyanza, by the highlands between that lake and Tanganyika, whence the watershed pursues a tortuous course to Unyanyembé (where, I believe, the basins of the Nile, Kongo, and Lufiji approach each other), and then follows a wave of high land running east till it turns up northwards along the landward slopes of the mountains dividing the littoral from the interior. Passing by Kilima Njaro and Kenia, it extends to the mountains of Abyssinia, where the sources of the Blue Nile were discovered by Bruce, and so on to the parched plains bordering the Red Sea, where no rains ever fall. The western boundary of the Nile basin is of course the eastern portion of the desert.

The basins of the Niger and the Ogowai cannot yet be defined with any degree of exactitude, and the northern boundary of the basin of the Kongo has still to be traced.

The Zambési drains that portion of the continent south of the Kongo system, and north of the

Kalahari desert and the Limpopo, the northern boundary of the Transvaal Republic; some of its affluents reaching to within two hundred and fifty miles of the West Coast.

The mighty Kongo, king of all African rivers and second only to the Amazon (and perhaps to the Yang-tse-Kiang) in the volume of its waters, occupies a belt of the continent lying on both sides of the equator, but most probably the larger area belongs to the southern hemisphere. Many of its affluents fork into those of the Zambési on a level tableland, where the watershed is so tortuous that it is hard to trace it, and where, during the rainy season, floods extend right across between the head-waters of the two streams.

The "Uellé," discovered by Dr. Schweinfurth, may possibly prove to be the Lowa, reported to me as a large affluent of the Lualaba, to the west of Nyangwé; or, if not an affluent of the Lualaba, it most probably flows either to the Ogowai or the Tchadda, an affluent of the Niger.

In the above sketch of the watersheds I but simply give my own opinion, liable to alteration, as every day may bring more accurate knowledge of the interior of Africa.

I will now endeavour to give an idea of the physical geography of the different regions on my route from coast to coast, and also to point out to what system the streams passed may be considered to belong.

On leaving Bagamoyo the first portion of the
journey was across the littoral region lying between
the Useghara mountains, the dividing range
between the lowlands and the interior ; but before
reaching them passed a range of hills, which are
off-shoots of their southern part.

These hills are drained principally by the
Kingani and its affluents, the chief of which is the
Lugerengeri, which falls into the sea close to
Bagamoyo.

Between these and the main range is the Makata
plain or swamp, drained by the Makata river—
known higher on its course as the Mukondokwa,
and as the Wami where it falls into the sea.

The first portion of this section of the route was
composed principally of rolling grassy plains with
occasional small hills and strips and patches of
jungle. It was but sparsely inhabited, and the
villages lay concealed in the jungle on the summits
of the hills.

The soil was composed of reddish sand and
water-worn pebbles covered with dark vegetable
humus, and seemed to be of inexhaustible fertility.
The country was intersected by numerous nullahs,
or temporary watercourses, which all drained to
the Kingani.

Manioc (*Jatropha*) of the sweet sort, Indian
corn, *Holcus sorghum*—the Kaffir corn of Natal
and Dourra of Egypt—ground-nuts, sem-sem, and
castor-oil were grown by the inhabitants. Their

only live stock were goats and a few wretched sheep and fowls.

Towards Msuwah the country began to rise decidedly, and outcrops of granite and quartz sometimes showed through the soft red sandstone which formed the upper stratum.

From Msuwah we continued on a fairly high level till we descended into the valley of the Lugerengeri, which is one of great beauty and fertility, and where sugar-cane was cultivated in addition to the crops previously mentioned.

Directly after crossing the Lugerengeri the Kungwa hills were entered—part of the range mentioned by Burton as the Duthumi hills—a mass of mountainous granite and quartz elevations of very confused shapes and forms, surrounding a fertile and populous tract full of small conical hills. Their summits were crowned by villages, the slopes covered with Indian and Kaffir corn, and rice was cultivated in the small valleys.

Where not under tillage, the lower levels were masses of cane-grass and bamboo growing high above the head of the traveller and only allowing occasional glimpses of the beautiful scenery around.

Emerging from this basin by a pass in the hills, the tortuous valley of the Lugerengeri was again reached, and the path led along between the stream and a range of hills to the south, the sides of which were scored by numerous torrents which, in exceptionally rainy seasons, bear ᛧdesolation to the villages in their course.

The town of Simbawéni having been passed, the Lugerengeri was again crossed, and then the road lay close under a promontory-like hill of granite with cliff-like sides to the Makata plain, a wide and open expanse of very slightly undulating ground with numerous fan-palms in some places, and on the drier spots clumps of forest trees. The wet parts are sticky clayey mud occasionally varied in the rainy season by stretches of mingled marsh and water from one to two feet in depth.

The mountains of Useghara rise abruptly in a mass of granite peaks on the western side of this plain. Here a few villages are to be seen, but the eastern part is entirely wild and the favourite haunt of herds of giraffe, zebra, and buffalo.

Close to the coast in this district the semi-fossil gum-copal is found by digging from five to seven feet below the surface, and the copal-tree still grows in some parts.

The trees are principally acacias, of which there are many varieties covered with masses of different-coloured blossoms. There are also several kinds of valuable timber-trees and a few fruit-trees. Near the sea the cocoa-palm, the mango, the mfuv—producing a sort of damson-like fruit—jack-fruit tree, oranges, sweet lemons, limes, the custard-apple, the papaw, guava and tamarind, also mzambarau—another plum-tree—are cultivated.

African teak, black-wood, *Lignum vitæ*, the mparamusi, indiarubber trees and vines, the wild date,
the *Borassus flabelliformis*, the raphia—mwalé—and
many kinds of thorns and creepers grow luxuriantly
in the woods, whilst bamboos and cane-grass fill
the swampy bottoms and the plains are covered
with a variety of grasses which attain a height of
six or eight feet in the rainy season.

The inhabitants vary greatly in their manners.
Near the coast they have mostly adopted the habits
of the Wamerima; but the grass kilt—like that of
the Papuans—is still to be seen near Simbawéni,
and people smear their heads with red-ochreish
earths and oil. In the villages at the foot of the
mountains are seen extraordinary necklaces made
of brass wire coiled horizontally—flemished, in
nautical language—and extending sometimes a foot
or more from the neck.

The rivers of these districts abound in hippopotami and crocodiles. Buffaloes, giraffes, zebras,
antelopes of various sorts, anteaters, ocelots,
occasional elephants, hyænas, leopards, wild cats,
monkeys, wild pigs, beautiful little squirrels,
jackals, the buku, a huge rat often larger than
a rabbit, mongoose, the carrion crow, guinea and
jungle fowl, a sort of francolin, numerous hawks,
goatsuckers, orioles and sunbirds, wild pigeons
and doves, form a portion of the fauna. But
though numerous in species, individuals are rare
owing to the quantities destroyed every year in

the annual burnings of the grass, when every man and boy sallies forth intent on destruction.

To these people all flesh is meat, and vast quantities of beasts and birds are therefore destroyed by their human foes whilst others perish in the flames.

Every pool and swamp swarms with frogs, and the insect world so teems with new and wonderful forms of life, that here the entomologist —as in tropical Africa generally—may find extensive fields for study and discovery.

Snakes are not numerous and the greater portion are not venomous, though the cobra capella exists and is much dreaded. There is also a snake which is said to be able to project its saliva to a distance of two or three feet, and when that saliva falls on man or beast a lingering and painful wound results. Arachnidæ are common and of several varieties, scorpions being by no means rare in the native huts, whilst the webs of gigantic spiders festoon the poles forming the roof and are sometimes seen covering whole trees in the jungles.

The next portion of the route was the passage of the Useghara mountains by the road leading from Rehenneko. The mountains are principally composed of granite and quartz, sheets of polished, wet, and slippery stone in the torrent-beds often making footing insecure. In some places red sandstone overlies the skeleton of granite, and acacias grow, wherever soil is lodged, rising above

each other "like umbrellas in a crowd;" and in
the low-lying, moist hollows the mparamusi towers
high above all its companions.

After crossing the first part of these mountains
we ·followed for some distance the valley of the
Mukondokwa, of which Burton has aptly remarked
that "the mountains seem rather formed for the
drain than the drain for the mountains." I cannot
do better than refer the reader who requires a
more detailed description of the valley of the
Mukondokwa than the nature of this book allows
me to give, to the " Lake Regions of Central
Africa," by Captain Burton, a work which, for
minuteness of detail, must ever stand foremost
amongst books of descriptive geography. The
route he followed soon after passing the village
of Muinyi Useghara diverged from ours, which
a short distance beyond the village left the
Mukondokwa and followed the valley of one of its
affluents, the Ugombo, to the lake of the same
name, in which it takes its rise.

The path on both sides was bordered by lofty
hills often surmounted by peaks and blocks of
granite and gneiss, and showing in many places
great seams of red sandstone half-grown over with
brushwood.

Lake Ugombo is a sort of natural reservoir
dammed up by small hills, and receives the
drainage of a portion of the barren tract between
it and Mpwapwa, which lies in the basin of the

Mukondokwa, and in the rainy season is a very considerable sheet of water. Late in the dry season it is merely a pool sufficiently large to shelter the small number of hippopotami which remain, for as the waters decrease the greater number go down the river Ugombo to find a refuge in the deeper reaches of the Mukondokwa.

From Lake Ugombo there is a gradual but considerable rise towards the watershed between the Mukondokwa basin and that of the Lufiji, the one lying immediately beyond it.

This portion of the route is barren and sterile, the soil composed of sand and gravel of quartz and granite overlying clay with numerous and much-weathered boulders of granite cropping out. The only vegetation consisted of wiry grasses, thorny shrubs, baobab-trees and kolquals and other members of the family of *Euphorbia*. A few dry nullahs marked the spot where in the rainy season torrents flowed to Lake Ugombo.

The watershed being crossed, a tangled network of nullahs, small rocky ridges and patches of thorny jungle, extended as far as the slopes below Mpwapwa, and then, ascending a broad watercourse, streams and pools of water were found flowing down the hills and gradually losing themselves in the sands. Near these streams was much cultivation and the people had herds of cattle.

A spur of hills stretches out to the westward from the range of the Useghara mountains. Mpwapwa

and its neighbouring villages are situated on a
terrace-like ridge half-way up the slopes of these
hills, which are almost entirely of granite, and, as
usual, clothed to their summits with acacias. The
road lies along this terrace from Mpwapwa to
Chunyo, and there descends into the Marenga
Mkali, which may be fairly considered as the commencement of the central plateau as well as of the
large country of Ugogo, though nominally Ugogo
is not entered till the Marenga Mkali is passed.

The Marenga Mkali is an open level tract for
the first fifteen miles, with numerous small hills,
chiefly composed of blocks of granite, often of a
conical form, scattered about—there being only a
scanty vegetation of thin grass and thorns—and
intersected by numerous watercourses which drain
to "the river of Maroro" in the rainy season.
Afterwards it becomes more broken and there is a
good deal of thorny jungle.

Notwithstanding the want of water experienced
in crossing the Marenga Mkali, most probably
it might easily be obtained there at any time by
sinking wells, especially those of the Abyssinian
pattern, as the rainfall during the season is very
great.

Leaving the Marenga Mkali, the aspect of Ugogo
is that of a brown dried-up country with occasional
huge masses of granite and the stiff *Euphorbia*
clinging to their sides. There are no vivid greens
or freshness of colour, the only trees to be seen

being the gigantic and grotesque baobab and a few
patches of thorny scrub.

The formation is sandstone, in some places overlaid with a stratum of clay. The water is bad,
and only *to* be obtained from pits made by the
natives to store some of the superabundant rainfall,
or by digging in the beds of the watercourses.

But in the rainy season all is different, the
whole country is then green and verdant and large
expanses are covered with matama, pumpkins
and tobacco, which form almost the only crops
cultivated by the inhabitants.

To the north of the route a wave of higher
land forms the watershed between the basin of
the Nile and that of the Ruaha (the upper course
of the Lufiji), across the latter of which it led.

A peculiar feature of Ugogo is the small ziwas
or ponds surrounded by verdure and acacias, as
refreshing to the weary traveller as an oasis in the
Sahara. Numerous water-fowl, duck, teal and
others, frequent these ponds all the year round.
These ziwas are scattered about Ugogo in many
places, and often during exceptionally dry seasons
afford the only supply of water the inhabitants
can obtain both for themselves and the large herds
of cattle they possess. Sometimes even this last
resource fails them, and then desolation and death
reign around.

From this chain of ponds a jungle march across
broken country led to the district of Kanyenyé,

a flat plain lying between two parallel ranges of
hills running north and south.   A few of the
welcome ziwas are to be found in Kanyenyé, but
generally the country is parched and arid.

Nitrous particles glisten in the watercourses and
in the beds of dried-up pools, and these the natives
collect and make into cones like sugar loaves and
export to their neighbours.

Ascending to the summit of the range of hills on
the west of Kanyenyé, another level plateau with
fine forest and grass land meets the eye, and through
a chain of rocky hills formed of the most fantastic
masses and boulders of granite of every shape the
road leads on to Usekhé.

A species of hyrax or rock-coney abounds in the
crevices and holes of these rocks.

These boulders remind one of logans, churches,
and the Druidic monuments of Stonehenge and
elsewhere, but their enormous size precludes the
possibility of their having been erected by human
hands.

A narrow strip of jungle divides Usekhé from
Khoko.   This district, though inhabited by Wagogo, may be considered, as indeed might Usekhé,
as belonging to a geographical division separate
from that containing the Marenga Mkali and
Eastern Ugogo, which ends at Kanyenyé.   Khoko
is a fertile undulating plain, with many trees
and a few of those boulders which form such a
conspicuous feature in Usekhé.

Khoko is also remarkable for a species of sycamore or fig closely allied to the banyan-tree which grows to an enormous size, spreading out its branches over a large area. Three of these trees near the village of the chief sheltered the camping-ground, and under one side of a single tree our caravan of over three hundred found ample room and shade.

When Burton went from Khoko to the next sultanat of Mdaburu there was a long tract of jungle to be passed. This has now nearly disappeared and the ground has almost entirely been brought under cultivation.

Mdaburu is another large fertile district extending as far as the eye can reach, with a large population owning great herds of cattle, and is drained by the Mdaburu nullah—a line of creeks and pools where plenty of good water is to be found even in the driest seasons, becoming in the rains an impetuous stream running to the Ruaha, which was here within fifty miles of our route.

The soil of the vale of Mdaburu is a rich red loam, and the people are able to cultivate sweet potatoes and various pulses in addition to the matama which formed the main crop of their eastern relatives.

Between Mdaburu and Unyanyembé lies a tract of country which is known as the Mgunda Mkali or "Fiery Field," and in former days was considered one of the worst · pieces of travelling between Unyanyembé and the coast. It was once nearly an unbroken mass of forests with few watering-places, and nowhere could provisions be procured. But now all is changed; and although there are still many long and weary marches to be endured and caravans constantly suffer from scarcity of water, much of the forest has been cleared by the Wakimbu, a branch of the Wanyamwési driven from their former homes by war.

At many of the settlements they have formed provisions can now be obtained, and waterholes have been dug and natural watering-places discovered, so that the dreaded Mgunda·Mkali of yore, where every caravan expected to leave the bodies of a considerable percentage of its numbers, is now faced without fear and traversed without much difficulty.

The country immediately after leaving Mdaburu is broken and hilly, the granite showing in sheets and patches on the hillsides. After three marches the Mabunguru nullah is crossed, very similar in its character to the Mdaburu, the easternmost affluent of the Ruaha passed on the road to Unyanyembé.

After the Mabunguru the country rises considerably, and soon the highest levels before reaching Unyanyembé are attained. Many pools, mostly dried up, lay on this small portion of the route and several small watercourses; but the direction they took was so tortuous that it was

impossible to trace whether they belonged to the
area of drainage supplying the Nile, the Tanganyika, or the Ruaha.

Where the land is cultivated around settlements,
as at Jiwé la Singa, it everywhere presents a scene
of wondrous fertility, and the whole of this level
might hereafter be made a wheat-producing
country.

From Jiwé la Singa onwards the drainage decidedly belonged to the Nile area.

Just beyond that settlement is a small range of
rocky hills, where the road leads over an *aréte*
about fifty yards in length, which blocks the
pass between two of the hills. Few villages are to
be seen in the country beyond, which is mostly
covered with jungle. Water is scarce, though no
doubt it lay in the hollows of the granite rock
which in places showed out in great sheets, and
probably is to be found everywhere within thirty
feet of the surface.

The most cultivated portion of this district is
near the village of the chief of Urguru, four long
marches from Unyanyembé, and there, for the first
time since leaving the coast mountains, rice cultivation was seen in the damp hollows. The country
between Urguru and Unyanyembé is tolerably level
and almost entirely jungle. At Marwa, half-way
on the road, numerous boulders and granite hills
stand out from the plain, and many fan-palms
grow near them.

At the outskirts of Unyanyembé is a small dry watercourse, an affluent of the Tura nullah, which in the rainy season spreads out a short way to the N.N.W. into a lagoon or swamp called the Nya Kuv, which drains ultimately into the Victoria Nyanza. This is according to Arab information, and I think worthy of credence.

It may be worth remarking the presence of the root *Nya*, in Nyanza, Nya-ssa, Ma-nya-ra and Nya Kuv. In Kisuahili, Ku-nya means "to rain," and, the "Ku" being only the prefix of the infinitive mood, Nya is the enclitic form of the verb.

This "dry stream" is the boundary of Unyanyembé proper, which is mostly cleared of jungle and has long been pre-eminent for the large number of its population and the extent of their husbandry.

Indeed, the name Unyanyembé points to the extensive cultivation. *U*, country; *nya*, a form of the preposition *ya*, signifying "of," the *n* being introduced for the sake of euphony, and *yembé*, hoes: the whole meaning "country of the hoes," or "cultivated country."

This country is dotted with innumerable villages surrounded by impenetrable hedges of the milk-bush. The juice of this plant is so acrid that if a small portion gets into the eye it gives almost intolerable anguish and frequently causes blindness. Wheat, onions, and different sorts of herbs and vegetables, as well as fruit-trees imported

from the coast, are cultivated by the Arabs round
their settlement.

The southern part of Unyanyembé is intersected
with numerous small rocky hills; but to the north
it is more level, running into the plains of the
Masai in one direction, and to those bordering the
mid-course of the Malagarazi on the other.

Large herds of cattle are possessed both by Arabs
and natives, but their numbers have of late years
been much diminished by constant petty wars.

South-west of Unyanyembé the rocky hills
cease, and the broad alluvial plain is partly
occupied by jungle and partly by the plantations
of the people of Ugunda. Ugunda also means a
cultivated country, *Mgunda* being synonymous
with the Kisuahili *Shamba*, meaning a farm or
plantation, and *Ugunda* a country of farms.

The drainage here is very partial, large tracts
being in the rainy season only fit for growing rice.
The main drain of the country is the Walé nullah,
which afterwards joins the Southern Ngombé and
forms part of the system of the Malagarazi.

Beyond the furthest settlements of the Wagunda
lies a broad plain, bounded on the west by the
Southern Ngombé. This plain is swampy in places,
and it is well wooded in many parts, but there is
little or no tangled undergrowth. Open and park-
like stretches form the feeding-grounds of innumerable herds of game, amongst others the
rhinoceros, lion, and buffalo.

The Southern Ngombé in the dry season and
at the commencement of the rains consists of long
reaches of open water separated from each other
by sand-bars—what our Australian brothers would
call creeks—but which unite towards the end of
the rainy season and form a noble stream flowing
to the Malagarazi, and often spreading three and
four miles over the adjacent country.

Ugara, lying beyond Southern Ngombé, is a flat
plain covered with forest and jungle, except in
places where the natives have made a clearance and
formed a settlement.

From the summit of some small hills an unbroken
horizon of tree-tops was seen in every direction
save N.N.W., where two or three small conical hills
appeared.

To the westward the country becomes more
undulating; a series of hills of wave-like form
rising gradually on their eastern sides, and on the
west falling precipitously to the level of the plain,
whence many streams flowed towards the Malagarazi.

The Kawendi mountains, on the west of Ugara,
rise sometimes to the height of 7,000 feet above the
sea-level, and are principally of granite formation;
but patches of sandstone and a sort of immature
clay-slate are also seen. The cliff-like sides and
jutting promontories of this range suggest the idea
of its having once been an archipelago.

The first part of Uvinza is very similar to Ka-

wendi until the plain of the Malagarazi is reached
at Ugaga.   The river then works along the northern
face of the mountains of Kawendi.   This plain is
intersected by the valleys of the Luviji, Rusugi,
and other affluents of the Malagarazi, the waters of
which, curious to relate, are perfectly fresh though
the soil is in many places impregnated with salt.

Drawing nearer to the Tanganyika the country
becomes more broken and hilly, forming a link
between the mountains of Ujiji and Urundi and
those of Kawendi.

In a jungle in Ukaranga—"the country of
ground-nuts"—I picked up some nutmegs, well
flavoured and of good size, and various kinds of
indiarubber plants abounded.

CHAPTER XVI

THE LAKE-SYSTEM OF CENTRAL AFRICA.—A FLAW IN SOME ANCIENT UP-
HEAVAL. — CORRECT POSITION OF THE TANGANYIKA. — KAWÉLÉ. — RAS
KUNGWÉ.—KABOGO ISLAND.—RUGUVU.—COAL.—RAPID ENCROACHMENT OF
THE LAKE UPON ITS SHORES.—FORMATION OF CLIFFS.—REMAINS OF AN
INLAND SEA.—MAKAKOMO ISLANDS.—GRADUAL DISAPPEARANCE.—CONSTANT
ADDITIONS FROM MAINLAND.—RAS MUSUNGI.—LOOSE MASSES OF GRANITE.—
WEATHER-WORN CLIFFS.— FANTASTIC FORMS.— NUMEROUS LANDSLIPS.—
BLACK BEACHES.— THE WEST OF TANGANYIKA.— A NEW GEOGRAPHICAL
REGION.—THE RUGUMBA.—BLACK SPECULUM ORE.—THE KILIMACHIO HILLS.
—AFFLUENTS OF THE LUALABA.—UNDERGROUND DWELLINGS.—THE LUALABA
AND KONGO.—CHANGES IN RIVER CHANNELS.—BEE CULTURE.—A BARREN
WASTE.—A FERTILE FLAT.

THE existence of a wonderful lake-system in
Central Africa, of which Tanganyika forms
part, seems to have been known to the ancients,
and if not actually ascertained was at all events
conjectured by the earlier European explorers in
Africa. Latterly this lake-system has been re-
placed in the ideas of geographers by expanses of
desert.

The suppositions of the first Portuguese travellers
and missionaries are wonderfully near the truth,
and maps of Africa of two hundred years ago gave
a far more accurate idea of the interior of the
continent than those of this century, before the
eyes of the world were opened by the discussion

of old travels, the theories of Mr. Cooley and the
discoveries of Burton and Livingstone. .

The Tanganyika, Nyassa, and Albert Nyanza in
my opinion—though of course this is only advanced
as a theory—are in the line of a great flaw in some
ancient upheaval.

Until I found the variation on Tanganyika to
be 17° westerly, that lake was laid down on the
maps as running due north and south. And I
believe that when variation is allowed for, Lake
Nyassa will also be found to have a similar
inclination to the meridian, both being parallel
to the lines of upheaval of the mountains of the
coast range and of Madagascar.

The Albert is parallel to the curve the coast
mountains take to the eastward of north in running
out to form the high land extending up to Cape
Guardafui, and of which Socotra Abd-al-Kuri and
the neighbouring islets and rocks are the outlying
fragments.

These three lakes therefore seem to lie in an in-
terrupted fissure on the outside of one in a series
of concentric upheavals.

In support of my belief that Lake Nyassa lies at
an angle to the meridian ,like the Tanganyika, I
am inclined to refer the reader to Mr. Cooley's
"Geography of the Nyassa," a paper in which,
notwithstanding the disadvantages of having to
work with defective and in many cases erroneous
data, the scientific writer made an immense

advance towards breaking through the darkness which for so long had shrouded the interior of Africa.

Lake Victoria Nyanza owes its existence to some other cause, whilst of the many lakes to the westward of this line, some are apparently formed by rivers dammed back by ranges of hills at the edges of tablelands, whilst others are simply lacustrine expansions of varying size of the rivers themselves.

The name of Tanganyika means "the mixing-place," being derived from *Ku-tanganya*—in some dialects *Changanya*—"to mix or shuffle."

The fact that I found no less than ninety-six rivers besides torrents and springs flowing into the portion of the lake which I surveyed proves this name to be well deserved.

Behind Kawélé towered lofty hills which could be seen long after the low land on which the town was built had disappeared below the horizon.

Proceeding southwards from Kawélé, the shore of the lake at first consisted of dwarf cliffs of red sandstone broken by landslips and fringed at their base by "matélé," or cane-grass, whilst behind were wooded hills rising higher and higher as they receded from the lake.

A level marshy plain extends at the mouth of the Ruché, whence the coast rises gradually until it culminates in the double promontory of Kabogo. This section is broken into deep inlets and bays by the mouths of the Malagarazi and other rivers;

the Malagarazi running into the lake by the side
of a long red quoin which can be seen from Ujiji.
The cape at Kabogo is not very striking, but it is
well known as the point of departure of canoes
bound to the islands of Kisenga on the west.

South of Ras Kabogo the lake forms a deep bay
into which many streams flow. The shores are low
and marshy, though a short way back from the
coast large mountains rise abruptly, and it was from
one of these, Mount Massowah, that Livingstone
and Stanley took their last look of the lake.

The southern limit of this bay is defined by Ras
Kungwé, formed by a groyne of the mountains of
Tongwé. The first steps are seen rising almost
precipitously out of the lake as soon as the cape is
rounded, and down their faces rushing torrents are
here and there visible through the tangled verdure
which clothes the cliffs.

Grand masses of mountains rise behind, but
being hidden by those near the coast are only
visible from the western side of the lake, whence
they present a magnificent *coup-d'œil*.

The mountains continue to overhang the lake for
some way to the south, then receding from the
shore allow secondary lines of smaller grassy and
wooded hills to rise between them and it.

At Ras Kiséra Miaga the main ridge seems to
turn back to the eastward, and after a time to meet
another range which again overhangs the lake from
the mouth of the Ruguvu to Ras Makanyazi.

In the angle between these two ranges lies a low
country with small rounded hills where many fan-
palms and timber-trees flourish.   Off this land
lies the large, level, and fertile island of Kabogo.
It is separated from the main by a channel in places
nearly a mile wide, but narrows at both ends, where
there are sand-bars.

The hills overhanging the lake beyond the Ruguvu often take the form of cliffs, and on the face
of one of these I saw a patch of what I believed
to be coal lying in a great synclinal curve of other
strata.   The lake was so rough when we passed
that it was impossible to land to get a specimen;
but a piece of coal from Itawa was given me,
and is probably of the same sort.   It is a light
bright splintery coal, very slightly bituminous.

The other strata showing close to the coal,
which was lying on granite, were limestone
and red sandstone, marble and slaty rocks, some
patches of soft-looking grey chalk, and a reddish
soil like that of the Wealden area with lumps
of stone looking like Kentish rag.

All the faces of the cliffs were so much torn and
seamed by torrents and rains that it is almost
impossible, from merely a passing glance, to give a
reliable description.

Just beyond Ras Makanyazi a sharp line seemed
to divide the granite overlaid with sandstone from
limestone cliffs, and shortly afterwards the cliffs
came to an end and the mountains trended back

a long way from the coast, the intervening country
being formed of low and rounded hills and level
plains.

The lake here is rapidly encroaching on the shores,
and the contour is constantly changing. Near the
mouth of the Musamwira, the drain of the Likwa
lagoon, where large villages stood a year or two
ago, sand-banks only are now seen and these are
hourly decreasing in size.

After passing the Musamwira the hills again
approached the lake, but I observed a few inlets
which might be utilised as boat harbours. At Ras
Kamatété the hills run back again something in the
same manner as near the island of Kabogo, forming
a deep bay with low-lying level land around it.
The southern horn of this bay is Ras Mpimbwé, a
promontory consisting of enormous blocks of granite
piled on each other in the wildest confusion.

The land is composed of a light red sandstone,
though it is hardly stone at all, with large masses
of granite and harder sandstone embedded ; the
water washes away the soft sandstone and leaves the
harder rocks either in piles or half-sunken reefs.

I believe that exactly the same process is going
on here which in earlier ages formed the hills and
mountains we came across between Liowa's and
Ugogo, the rocky hills of Unyanyembé, and
deposited the rocks in Ugogo about Usekhé and
elsewhere. The whole country was apparently
at one time an enormous lake with a soft sand-

stone bottom overlying granite; and as it con-
tracted, either through a general elevation of the
bottom or from some other cause, the surf on the
shores cut away the sandstone and left the harder
rocks standing out in their present forms.　Of this
sea, most probably a fresh-water one, Tanganyika,
the Nyanzas, and the Livingstone Lakes are probably the remains.

It may have been salt—witness salt soil of
Uvinza and Ugogo—and freshened by the continued rainfall of thousands of years.　The
country, except for a gradual elevation of the
whole mass, was most probably left unvisited by
any great geological convulsion after the days
when subterranean fires formed the granite which
constitutes the great mass of the whole.

The hills now again overhang the lake, and
navigation is rendered dangerous by the number of
sunken pinnacle and other rocks, some being only a
foot or two below the surface of the water.

The Makakomo islands which were next passed
had, according to the guides, once been part of the
mainland—some within their own remembrance—
and the outer island, which a few years back was
populated and fertile, is now a mere barren heap
of rocks half-submerged by the waters of the lake,
proving that the wasting action is rapidly progressing.

A short way beyond the Makakomo islands some
remarkable masses of granite were seen, two in

particular towering up above the rest to a height
of seventy or eighty feet like a pair of giant
brothers.   Wooded hills now again formed the
boundaries of the Tanganyika, but every here and
there landslips exposed the stony nature of their
formation.   The line of hills continued for some
time nearly parallel to the shore.

At Ras Masungi, near the island of Polungo, the
hills consist of loose masses of granite, looking as if
they would slide down into the lake beneath at the
slightest jar of an earthquake; indeed they appeared
so insecure that it seemed scarcely safe to camp
at their base.   Soon afterwards white limestone
cliffs rising up like columns and pillars were seen
from the lake.

At Ras Yamini the cliffs were very high and
composed of innumerable thin strata of a red stone
about the thickness of a Roman brick.   These cliffs
were worn and broken by the action of weather and
waves into fantastic forms bearing much resemblance
to ruins of castles and fortresses, arches being
honeycombed in their bases, and turret-like projections standing out in advance of the main portion.
In some places two or three of the small strata
projected slightly beyond the rest, forming a sort
of band or string course, which added greatly to
the resemblance of masonry.

The southern end of the lake had now been
nearly reached.   It lies niched into the edge of a
tableland which overhangs it some four or five

hundred feet. These cliffs are some of the grandest in the world.

The lake is still extending its sway in this direction as well as on the eastern shore, as testified by the numerous landslips which form picturesque groynes to the upright cliffs. Several grand waterfalls pour down the face of these cliffs, the streams which supply them running tranquilly on the tableland till they take the sudden plunge which precipitates them into the lake.

Westward of the lake this tableland runs into a fine range of mountains, and another range running up northwards from them forms the western boundary of the trough in which the Tanganyika lies.

This range of mountains continues without any great change right up to Ras Mulango—the southern of that name—where they turn off to the westward and most probably join the range damming back the waters of Moero.

Thence northward, to the southern end of the mountains of Ugoma, also called Ras Mulango, all the country is low, consisting principally of small flat-topped hills of soft sandstone of a dark red colour covered with grass and trees. In one or two places the beaches were perfectly black, but as the surf was much too heavy for me to attempt to land I could not ascertain the cause.

Mulango or M'lango signifies a door, and it is worthy of remark that the two Ras Mulango are situated at the northern and southern extremities

of the low-lying land which here makes a break in
the continuous fringe of mountains surrounding the
lake, the two capes standing as it were at the doorway or opening through which the Lukuga flows.

Northward of Kasengé the mountains of Ugoma
rise abruptly from the lake to a height of two or
three thousand feet.

To the west of Tanganyika a new geographical,
ethnological, zoological, entomological, and botanical
region is entered. Close to the lake the road leads
over the southern spurs of the Ugoma, the habitat
of the Mvuli, a tree very valuable to the natives, as
the large "dug-out" canoes which they use in
navigating the Tanganyika are made of the trunk.

The Rugumba flows into the lake just to the
west of the south extremity of the Ugoma mountains,
through the northern edge of the flat plain near the
entrance into the Lukuga; whilst the Rubumba,
which takes its rise close to the source of the
Rugumba, is found at a very short distance from
the lake, flowing away from it. The country is
hilly with occasional plains until Ubûdjwa is passed,
when it becomes mountainous in character.

Uhiya and Uvinza, the two next countries, are a
series of ridges running in different directions from
the Bambarré mountains, which are the most
important range in this part of Africa. Beyond
them is another lesser ridge divided from them
by a well-watered and fertile plain, and beyond
this the country is practically level, with the

exception of a few rocky hills, till the Lualaba is reached.

The mountains and hills are as usual composed of granite, gneiss and quartz, with here and there a few patches of porphyry.

The lower levels consist of strata of sand and water-worn pebbles, and present the appearance of having been once the bottom of some great sea. These beds of sand and pebbles vary much in thickness and extent.

Between the Bambarré mountains and the Tanganyika a red hæmatite ore is worked, but not in very large quantities.

After the mountains are passed the soil on the surface in the plains is a rich red sandy loam, but in some of the watercourses a dark grey shaly sandstone. Round Manyara and its neighbouring villages this red soil is wanting; but whole hills are composed of a black speculum ore. The iron obtained from it being of excellent quality accounts in great measure for the goodness of the smith's work.

The country near the Lualaba is again composed of sand and water-worn pebbles; but the river is clearly working down the dip of the strata, for the country on the left bank stretches back for miles and rises very gradually, whilst the right side is in many places bordered by cliffs. On the face of these cliffs are often to be seen numerous small strata of shaly sandstone, and in some places there are curious round marks exactly like those caused by a round-shot striking brickwork too solid for it to breach.

Beyond the Lualaba, and all along near the Lomâmi, the country is generally level, with deep gulches grooved out by the innumerable streams, the sides showing more water-worn pebbles, sand, and a light yellow sandstone resting on the granite.

The Kilimachio hills are the commencement of a system of rocky hills composed of granite, gneiss, and a peculiar sort of vesicular rock with occasional small pieces of granite embedded in it, which had the appearance of being the granite really melted and not simply metamorphosed by heat. It did not look like lava or slag, though no doubt somewhat of their nature.

These hills are the western extremity of the "Mountains of Rua," which Livingstone mentions as damming in the northern part of Lake Moero, and are also the same range that turn back from Lake Tanganyika, at Ras Mulango, to the south of the Lukuga.

It will be well here to trace the affluents of the Lualaba. The one that extends furthest west, and which, except for rapids, might be navigable to within one hundred and fifty miles of the Nyassa, is the Chambèzi, the principal feeder of Lake Bangweolo. From this lake it issues as the Luapula, and, flowing past the town of Ma Kazembé, is the chief supply of Lake Moero. From Moero it bursts

through the Mountains of Rua and is then known
by the natives as the Luvwa, though the Arabs
call it Lualaba, and Dr. Livingstone adopted that
name from them. Between the Lakes Moero and
Lanji it joins with the Lualaba proper, which is
the central and lowest line of drainage.

The Lualaba rises near the salt marshes of
Kwijila, and, flowing through Lake Lohemba, makes
a considerable drop before entering Lake Kassali or
Kikonja. Into Lake Kassali also flows the Lufira,
beneath which river are the underground dwellings
at Mkanna and Mkwamba.

According to the accounts I received, these caves
pass right underneath the bed of the river and are
high and lofty. There are several openings on
both sides of the river, and stories are told of
strangers who had come to attack these Troglodytes
being hotly engaged at one entrance and then
suddenly finding themselves attacked in rear by a
party which had sallied out from another. The inside of these dwellings is described as being of great
beauty with columns and arches of white stone.

The people here are greatly afflicted with goître,
and strangers residing amongst them are said to
feel symptoms of that disease after drinking the
water for a few days. This no doubt points ot
the existence of a limestone formation.

Other affluents of the Lualaba are the Luama
and Lomámi—both navigable streams—and the
Lowa, described as coming from the north, and it

is said to be as large as the Lualaba some distance to the west of Nyangwé. The Uellé of Dr.
Schweinfurth may be an affluent, or perhaps the
head-waters of this great stream, which must
receive the drainage of a very large portion of the
continent.

The Lualaba if it be the Kongo, of which I
think there can be no doubt, must also receive
the drainage of all the country north of the
Zambési basin, until that of the Kwanza is reached.

The volume of the Kongo was roughly estimated
by Tuckey at two millions of cubic feet per second,
and even if this estimate be too large there can be
no doubt that the mighty river, over a thousand
feet deep at its mouth, must receive the drainage of
an enormous area.

The Kongo also rises very slightly when compared with other tropical rivers, and its rising takes
place twice a year. This may be accounted for by
the fact that its basin extends on both sides of the
equator, and that therefore some of its affluents are
in flood when others are low.

Beyond the ranges of Kilimachio and Nyoka
are broad and well-watered plains extending to
Kilemba, east of which is a shallow basin about
five or six miles across, where the soil is salt and
there are some salt springs. Several of these
basins were said to be near, but this was the only
one visited.

From Kilemba to Lunga Mândi's the country

consisted of wooded hills, flat-topped tablelands
of sand and broad marshes bordering the streams.

The channel of the river is continually changing,
and in a year or two no trace remains of its former
course. This is owing to the growth of the semi-
aquatic vegetation, which quickly chokes up every
space where the water does not flow rapidly; and
this accounts for the fact that towards the end of
the dry season the actual channel is much smaller
than in the rains.

If these swamps prove to be the modern representatives of the old coal measures, we should find
ferns, papyrus—especially its roots—trees, some
fallen on their sides and half-rotten, others still
standing, and stumps and grasses amongst the vegetable fossils; whilst those of the animal kingdom
should include skeletons of mud fish and frogs, and
also of an occasional crocodile, buffalo, or hippopo-
tamus. Small thin sheets of sand might perhaps in-
dicate where the different channels had once been.

The country in Ussambi consisted mostly of flat-
topped sandstone hills. Strata of red and yellow
sandstone alternated, and between them and the
granite were usually masses of water-worn pebbles.

Ulûnda is a thickly wooded country with gentle
undulations and occasional savannahs or meadows
watered by numberless streams, most of them
running northwards to the Kongo.

At its western side broad plains stretch right
across Lovalé. They are light and sandy in the

dry season, with belts of trees along the different watercourses intersecting them, but during the rains become quagmires and morasses. The watershed between the Zambési and Kongo basins lies along the centre of these plains—which in the annual rainy season are waist-deep in water—and the two basins then actually join.

West of Lovalé is the country of Kibokwé, where the rise out of the central depression becomes very marked and the country is nearly all covered with forests.

Bee culture is here the chief occupation of the natives. The large trees are utilised to support their beehives, the produce of which forms a considerable and profitable item of barter. They exchange the wax for all the foreign trade goods they require, and from the honey make a sort of mead which is strong and by no means unpalatable.

The people work iron tastefully and well. They obtain the ore from nodules found in the beds of the streams.

The basins of the Kongo and Zambési terminate in the western portion of Kibokwé, where that of the Kwanza commences. The country of Bihé is entered after the Kwanza is crossed, the eastern portion being formed of wooded hills of red sandstone with many running brooks and rills, whilst in the western part are wide prairies and bare downs with a few patches of wood.

A peculiar feature is the number of streams

which flow underground for a portion of their
course; the most remarkable instance of this being
the "Burst of the Kutato," the boundary between
Bihé and Bailunda.

The eastern portion of Bailunda is moderately
level, with rocky hills, on the summits of which
are situated the villages of the chiefs; but as the
western portion is reached the country breaks into
mountains of every shape and form, amongst which
are needles and cones of granite. In, the foreground the hills are of red sandstone crowned with
groves of magnificent trees festooned with jasmine
and other sweet-scented creepers.

At the western side of Bailunda the caravan
reached the culminating point of the section across
the continent.

A mountainous and rocky tract lies between
this and the West Coast. In some of the passes
the solid granite hills are cupola and dome shaped,
like the Puy-de-Dôme in Auvergne. But even
amongst this mass of rocky sterile mountains lie
fertile valleys where the people cultivate large
quantities of corn, which they carry down to the
coast to exchange for aguardienté and cloth.

After passing Kisanji, forty miles from the sea,
no more human habitations are seen till Katombéla
is reached. Nearly thirty miles of this part of the
road is through one continuous pass of bare granite
rocks with only the occasional shelter of a baobab-
tree or a giant euphorbia.

To this pass succeeds a barren waste of sand
nd gravel, separated from the sea by limestone
ills fringed by a low flat strip of land on the
eaward side; and here the towns of Katombéla
nd Benguella are situated. This strip only needs
rrigation to make it yield all tropical productions,
nd, as water is obtained everywhere close to the
urface, large and productive gardens are easily
ultivated.

CHAPTER XVII.

AFRICA'S FUTURE.—SLAVES AND OTHER ARTICLES OF COMMERCE.—TRADE
ROUTES.—EXPORT OF INDIARUBBER INCREASING.—INTERNAL SLAVE-TRADE.
— IVORY SUPPLY. — PRODUCTS. — SUGAR-CANES. — COTTON. — OIL-PALM. —
COFFEE. — TOBACCO. — SESAMUM. — CASTOR-OIL. — THE MPAFU-TREE. —
NUTMEGS.— PEPPER.— TIMBER.— RICE.— WHEAT.—KAFFIR CORN.— INDIAN
CORN.— INDIARUBBER.— COPAL. — HEMP. — IVORY. — HIDES. — BEESWAX.—
IRON.—COAL.—COPPER.— GOLD.— SILVER.— CINNABAR.— MISSION WORK.—
COMMERCIAL ENTERPRISE. — ESTABLISHMENT OF DEPÔTS. — SCHEME FOR
ADVANCING INTO THE INTERIOR.—LIGHT RAILWAYS.—STEAMERS ON RIVERS.
—PROBABLE RESULTS.—SHALL SLAVERY CONTINUE?—HOW TO STAMP IT OUT
AND MAKE AFRICA FREE.

IT now only remains to discuss the present state
of trade and communication in Africa, and the
future of this vast continent. To speak of the
regions of the Sahara, the Cape, the Niger basin
and Somáli land is of course out of my province.

I only desire to show the present condition of
the large and fertile country I have traversed, the
different routes by which it may be approached,
and in what manner they may be utilised; and,
above all, how the utilisation of these routes may
best serve to develop the vast latent resources of
the country, and remove that blot on the boasted
civilisation of the nineteenth century, "the cursed
slave-trade."

Slaves, ivory, beeswax, and indiarubber are now

the only articles exported from either coast, with the exception of a small and local trade from the eastern littoral in gum-copal and grain.

Of these, ivory and slaves occupy such a prominent position that it would be hardly worth while to mention the others were it not that the existing trade in them proves that commerce in other articles besides slaves and ivory may be made profitable.

The trade routes at present are—Firstly, from the East Coast ports by land; which is in the hands of the subjects of the Sultan of Zanzibar from Brava to Cape Delgado, and in those of Portugal from that point to Delagoa Bay.

Secondly, the Nile route, on which the advance of traders has been accompanied by so much aggression and cruelty that, in the words of Colonel Gordon, "it is impossible for an explorer to push his way except by force, as the natives are suspicious of the intentions of all strangers." Indeed, Mr. Lucas, after a considerable expenditure of time and money, has been obliged reluctantly to yield and abandon all idea of proceeding to Nyangwé from the Nile basin.

Thirdly, the routes from the West Coast; of which those only at present used by Europeans or their agents are viâ Bihé and Kasanji. But here the Kongo would seem to offer a highway to the remotest parts of the continent.

Lastly, a route from Natal through the

Transvaal by the Drakensberg to the tropical highlands, which has the advantage of possessing a terminus in British territory and of avoiding the unhealthy coast districts; two facts which point to it as likely to prove hereafter one of the great highways into the interior.

The export of indiarubber to the value of £40,000 from the Zanzibar·ports, and the stoppage of the export of slaves from the East Coast—in which we have been so loyally aided by the Sultan —are circumstances the significance of which it is impossible to overrate, showing that a brighter future is already dawning upon Africa. The fact that a new article of export has thus been profitably worked at a time when the depression of trade at Zanzibar is very great—owing to the suppresion of the traffic in slaves—proves incontestably that a portion of the capital hitherto employed in that detestable traffic has been diverted into a more legitimate channel.

The whole trade of tropical Africa is at present dependent on human beings as beasts of burden, and valuable labour which might be profitably employed in cultivating the ground or collecting products for exportation is thus lost.

Besides this, in the countries where ivory is cheapest and most plentiful none of the inhabitants willingly engage themselves as carriers, and traders are obliged to buy slaves to enable them to transport their ivory to a profitable market.

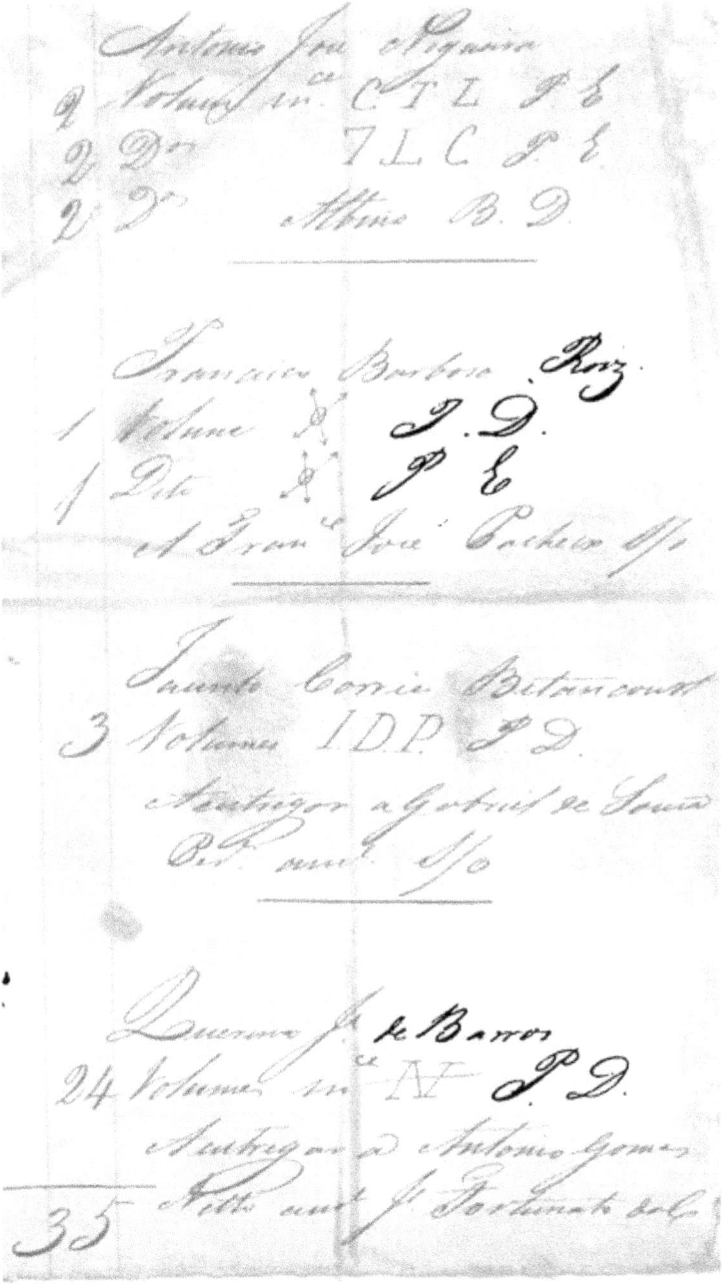

Antonio Joze Siqueira

4 Volumes in^{ce} C T L ♂ ♀

2 D^o 7 L C ♂ ♀

2 D^o Albino B. 2

Francisco Barbose Roiz

1 Volume ⚹ J. 2.

1 Dito ⚹ ♂ ♀

á Fran^{co} Joze Pacheco S/o

Jacinto Correa Bitancourt

3 Volumes I.D.P. ♂ 2

Entregar a Gabriel de Souza

Por conta S/o

Querino J^h de Barros

24 Volumes in^{ce} A^b ♂ 2

Entregar a Antonio Gomes

35 Netto and J^o Fortunato do C^o

PART OF A BILL OF LADING FOR SLAVES FROM LOANDA.

When the export slave-trade was flourishing, the carriers who brought the ivory to the coast were sold and added to the gain of the trader. And it is to be feared, now that there is no market for these people, that they will be even more recklessly expended than hitherto by the lower classes of East Coast traders.

Many of the larger merchants are wise enough to see that slave-carriage is the most precarious and costly of all means of transport, and they would be glad to avail themselves of any other method that might be introduced.

On the lines occupied by the Portuguese, especially that from Bihé to Urua and Katanga, there is a vast amount of internal slave-trade; but the greater portion of those captured—for they are nearly all obtained by rapine and violence—are not taken to the coast, but to Kaffir countries where they are exchanged for ivory. I should not be at all surprised to hear that much of "the labour" taken to the diamond fields by the Kaffirs is obtained from this source.

The traders are not a whit behind their fore-fathers—who invoiced their slaves as bales of goods, and had a hundred baptized in a batch by the Bishop of Loanda, by aspersion, in ·order to save a small export duty—in their bad treatment of slaves, or their recklessness as to the means by which they are obtained.

The internal trade is principally carried on by

slaves of merchants residing at the coast, and—as
is always the case with those equally low in the
scale of civilisation—they are the most cruel op-
pressors of all who fall into their clutches.

Ivory is not likely to last for ever (or for long)
as the main export from Africa; indeed the ruth-
less manner in which the elephants are destroyed
and harassed has already begun to show its
effects. In places where elephants were by no
means uncommon a few years ago, their wanton
destruction has had its natural effect and they are
now rarely encountered.

Having this probable extinction of the ivory
trade in view, and allowing, as all sensible people
must, that legitimate commerce is the proper way
to open up and civilise a country, we must see
what other lucrative sources of trade may hereafter replace that in ivory.   .

Fortunately we have not far to go; for the vegetable and mineral products of this marvellous land
are equal in variety, value, and quantity to those
of the most favoured portions of the globe. And if
the inhabitants can be employed in their exploita-
tion, vast fortunes will reward those who may be
the pioneers of commerce; but the first step necessary towards this is the establishment of proper
means of communication.

Africa for some time to come will lack a
sufficiency of labour to carry on the necessary
mining and agricultural. operations, and to supply

men for making roads. But this will prove by no means an unmixed evil, for when the chiefs find it more profitable to employ their subjects in their own country than to sell them as slaves they will lose the most powerful incentive towards complying with the demands of the slave-dealer.

An enumeration of some of the products which may form valuable articles of trade, and the localities in which they are found, will assist in giving an idea of the great wealth of the country.

The vegetable products are—

Sugar-canes.—Which flourish wherever there is sufficient moisture.

Cotton.—Cultivated almost everywhere, and grows wild in Ufipa and some other countries.

Oil-palm.—Flourishes in marvellous profusion to a height of two thousand six hundred feet above the sea, all along the broad valley of the Lualaba, and in some places to a height of three thousand feet. This palm also grows on the island of Pemba and might doubtless be cultivated with advantage on the East Coast.

Coffee.—Grows wild in Karagwé and to the west of Nyangwé. The berry of Karagwé coffee is said to be small; but that of the plant near Nyangwé is as large as the Mocha bean, which it greatly resembles in appearance.

Tobacco.—Is grown almost throughout the continent, and in some places is of very excellent quality. Ujiji excels in this respect; the leaf being smooth and silky, like that of the best Cuban plants.

Sesamum.—Flourishes on the East Coast, near Zanzibar, from which place large quantities are exported to France, "the finest olive oil" being made from it at Marseilles. It also grows in Unyamwési, near the Tanganyika, and in Urua, and its cultivation might be indefinitely extended.

The Castor-oil plant.—Two varieties are met with everywhere, sometimes cultivated and sometimes growing wild.

The Mpafu.—A large and handsome timber-tree, with a fruit something like an olive from which a sweet-scented oil is extracted, and under the bark an aromatic gum is found; is common from the western side of the Tanganyika to the commencement of Lovalé.

Nutmegs.—Were found close to the eastern shore of Tanganyika, near the town of Russûna, and at Munza. The fruit was very strong and pungent.

Pepper.—The common black pepper was common at Nyangwé. Chilies, large and small, are found everywhere; and in Manyuéma and Urua there grows a pepper so excessively hot that Arabs who would eat bird's-eye chilies by handfuls were unable to touch it. It is a small, round, red fruit about the size of a marble.

Timber-trees.—There are trees available for every purpose—some hard and others soft—and sufficiently numerous to supply all the wants of the country and no doubt to form profitable articles of export.

Rice.—Is profitably cultivated by the Arabs wherever they have settled, and in Urua is said to yield a hundredfold. In Ufipa it grows wild.

Wheat.—Abundant crops of wheat are raised by the Arabs at Unyanyembé and Ujiji, and they were trying, apparently with success, to introduce it at Nyangwé. On the high lands round Unyanyembé and in those of Bihé and Bailunda it might undoubtedly be made profitable.

Holcus sorghum.—Better known as Matama or Kaffir corn; is grown throughout the country, both in dry and wet situations. In the latter it is not planted till the end of the rainy season, but in both its yield is enormous.

Indian corn.—Is grown everywhere, and where there is a long rainy season three crops are often produced by the same patch of ground in eight months. Each crop yields from a hundred and fifty to two hundredfold.

Indiarubber.—Vines, trees, or small shrubs producing this valuable article of commerce are to be met with nearly everywhere.

Copal.—May be considered as a vegetable, though now a semi-fossil. It is principally obtained near the Lufiji river, though some is found near Mbuamaji, Laadani, and other places. The tree still grows near the coast, and in the very centre

of the continent is again met with, and Arabs have
assured me that they have found the semi-fossil
gum when digging pits.

Hemp.—A very long stapled hemp is found on
the island of Ubwari, in the Tanganyika, and the
fibrous barks of many trees are made into such
excellent cordage that the place of hemps is quite
supplied by them.

The animal products are—

Ivory, of elephants and hippopotami, their
hides, and those of other wild animals.

Hides of cattle might also be obtained in great
quantities from the countries of the Masai, the
Gallas, the Wasukuma, the Wagogo, Waganda,
Wahumba, and others.

Beeswax forms an important article of export
from Kibokwé and Lovalé ; and as bees are common throughout Africa and in many places are
hived in order to obtain the honey easily, a very
large trade might soon be established in wax,
which at present is often thrown away as useless.

Amongst minerals—

Iron takes the first place. It is worked in
the north-west portion of Unyanyembé, whence
it is carried in all directions. Hoes made there
are even exported to the coast by down caravans. Hæmatite ore is common all. about the
country of Unyamwési, and is found in Ubûdjwa
and Uhiya, as also at and about Munza in Urua.
In Manyuéma there is a beautiful black specu-

lum ore in great quantities, and the iron produced from it is much valued. Dr. Livingstone
also discovered much iron to the westward of Lake
Nyassa. In Kibokwé nodules of ore are dredged
up from the streams.

Coal has been for some time known on the
Zambési and I heard of it near Munza, in Itawa,
from which place I obtained a specimen, and I
believe that I saw it on Lake Tanganyika.

Copper is found in large quantities at Katanga
and for a considerable distance to the westward.

Gold is also found at Katanga, and when I was
with Haméd ibn Haméd he showed me a calabash,
holding about a quart, full of nuggets varying in
size from the top of my little finger to a swan-shot.
I asked whence they came and he said that some
of his slaves at Katanga found them while clearing out a waterhole, and brought them to him
thinking that they might do for shot. He said he
had not looked for more, as he did not know such
little bits were of any use.

The natives, too, know of the gold, but it is so
soft they do not value it, preferring "the red
copper to the white."

I heard when at Benguella that gold had been
found in copper brought from Katanga, and that a
company was buying all the Katanga copper it
could obtain in order to extract the gold.

Silver.—From a man in Urua I bought a silver
bracelet produced in or near this district.

Cinnabar is found in large quantities in Urua, near the capital of Kasongo.

Salt, which forms an important article in internal trade, is produced in Ugogo, Uvinza, Urua, near Nyangwé, and in Ussambi, near Kanyoka.

Enough has been said to prove the existence of incalculable wealth in tropical Africa.

Already the rind of the continent has been pierced, and the Scotch missionaries on Lake Nyassa have demonstrated the feasibility of transporting a steamer past rapids, and have established a settlement on the shores of that lake. Mr. Cotterill is now engaged in tentative trade in the same direction, and I have no doubt that his efforts will be crowned with success. Bullocks have been driven from the coast to Mpwapwa by Mr. Price, of the London Missionary Society, and the Church and University Missions are pushing their way forward.

Missionary efforts, however, will not avail to stop the slave-trade and open the country to civilisation unless supplemented by commerce. Commercial enterprise and missionary effort, instead of acting in opposition as is too often the case, should do their best to assist each other. Wherever commerce finds its way, there missionaries will follow; and wherever missionaries prove that white men can live and travel, there trade is certain to be established.

The philanthropic efforts of his Majesty the

King of the Belgians, if they meet with the support they deserve, although not either of a missionary or commercial character, must also materially
assist in opening up the country.

The establishment of depôts or stations on a
trunk route across the continent, where the tired
and weary explorer may find a resting-place and
fresh stores and men to carry on his task, cannot
fail to do much towards systematising the work of
discovery, instead of leaving every man to hunt for
his own needle in his own bundle of hay.

The establishment of these stations would neces-
sitate the maintenance of regular means of communication between them, and therefore each new
explorer would be able to travel direct to the one
which is to serve as the base of his operations,
without wasting time, money, and energy in
getting into a new country. These stations might
either be commanded by Europeans, or by men of
character amongst the Arab merchants, who might
be thoroughly relied on to do their duty in an upright and honourable manner.

By commencing from both coasts, a chain of
stations some two hundred miles apart, might be
established in a comparatively short space of time;
but money is needed.

There are many men well fitted to take charge
of these expeditions whose means do not allow
them to travel on their own account, but who
would volunteer in hundreds if they could see their

way to aiding in the work without endangering
their scanty fortunes.

The promoters of the Nyassa mission are already
talking of establishing stations between the coast,
the north end of Nyassa and the south of Tanganyika, and then by placing steamers on that lake
to draw a cordon between the East Coast and the
countries from which the greater portion of the
slaves are derived. This is a practical and feasible
plan, but whether it would not be a line of action
that comes more under the scope of Government in
suppressing the slave-trade is a question that may
well be asked.

I would recommend the acquirement of a port
—Mombasah for instance—from the Sultan of
Zanzibar, by treaty or purchase, and thence to
run a light line of railway to the Tanganyika, *viâ*
Unyanyembé, with branches to the Victoria Nyanza,
and to the southward through Ugogo. Such a line
may be constructed for about £1,000 a mile.

I allude here to the " Pioneer " form of railway,
which seems to be best adapted to a new country.

Such a railway advancing into the country would
at once begin to make a return, for the present
ivory trade to Zanzibar should be sufficient to pay
working expenses and leave a margin for profit,
without making any allowance for the increased
trade. Numbers of Indian merchants at Zanzibar
would at once push into the interior if they could
do so without physical exertion.

On the Zambési, Kongo, and Kwanza there should at once be placed steamers of light draught, good speed, and capable of being taken to pieces and transported past rapids that might be encountered. A steamer should be stationed on each section of a river, depôts should be formed at the rapids for provisions and merchandise, and the goods should be carried past them by men stationed there for the purpose, or by bullock-carts, or small lines of tramways.

The affluents of the Kongo would enable our traders and missionaries to penetrate into the greater portion of the at present unknown regions of Africa.

The Kongo, at its mouth, is not under the dominion of any European power, and the principal merchants there are the Dutch. They would be delighted to see the trade of the interior in the hands of Europeans instead of being dependent on the caprice of some of the most depraved of the West Coast tribes, who, ever since the Kongo has been discovered, have been engaged—in company with Europeans even more vile than they—in slave-trade and piracy.

A hundred and ten miles from the coast are the Yellala rapids—*Yellala* really means "rapids"— the furthest point hitherto reached by any European since the unfortunate expedition of Captain Tuckey, R.N., in 1816.

A portage of by no means a difficult character,

and past which a tramway might be constructed, would conduct an expedition to the upper waters of the river described by the gallant Tuckey "as a noble placid stream from three to four miles in width."

We may well ask ourselves why we allow such a noble highway into regions of untold richness to lie neglected and useless. Why are not steamers flying the British colours carrying the overglut of our manufactured goods to the naked African, and receiving from him in exchange those choicest gifts of nature by which he is surrounded, and of the value of which he is at present ignorant?

The Portuguese hold the keys of the land route from Loanda and Benguella and keep out foreign capital and enterprise, and are morally accomplices of slave-traders and kidnappers. If they threw open their ports, and encouraged the employment of capital and the advent of energetic men of business, their provinces of Angola and Mozambique might rival the richest and most prosperous of the dependencies of the British crown. But a blind system of protection, carried on by underpaid officials, stifles trade and renders these places hot-beds of corruption.

Many of the Portuguese are aware of this and lament it, but say they are powerless. The Marquis Sa de Bandeira—now, alas! dead—was, and M. le Vicomte Duprat is, wiser than the majority of their countrymen. If their suggestions

and advice, and that of men like Admiral Andradé,
lately Governor-General of Angola, were followed,
we might soon see a vast stride made towards the
civilisation of Africa.

A charter has lately been granted by the Portuguese Government to a company to place steamers
on the Zambési, and if the project is carried out
vigorously some results may soon be heard of from
that quarter.

Many people may say that the rights of native
chiefs to govern their countries must not be inter-
fered with.   I doubt whether there is a country in
Central Africa where the people would not soon
welcome and rally round a settled form of government.   The rule of the chiefs over their subjects
is capricious and barbarous, and death or mutilation is ordered and carried out at the nod of a
drunken despot.

The negroes always seem prone to collect round
any place where they may be comparatively safe
from the constant raids of their enemies, and thus
the settlements of both East and West Coast traders
frequently become *nuclei* of considerable native
populations.   These people, throwing off the yoke
of their own rulers, soon fall under the sway of the
strangers, and in any scheme for forming stations
in Central Africa—be they for missionary, scientific,
or trading purposes—the fact that those in charge
would soon have to exercise magisterial powers
must not be lost sight of.

If the great river-systems of the Kongo and
Zambési are to be utilised for commercial purposes,
they ought either to be under the control of a great
company like the H.E.I.C., able to appoint civil
and military servants ; or consular officers should be
appointed for each district as it is opened up, to
ensure both the native and the new comer having
fair play.

By a glance at the map the extraordinary rami-
fications of the twin systems of the Kongo and
Zambési will be seen, and it is plain that the
distance which the products of the interior would
have to be carried before being placed on ship-
board would be materially lessened if the rivers had
flotillas on them, instead of having to provide transport over the three or four thousand miles of the
Nile valley.

The advance of trade and civilisation into the
interior from the southward may be left to take
care of itself. Every year the ivory traders push
further north, and now they meet the Portuguese
from Bihé in the country of Jenjé, and we shall not
have to wait long ere the fertile and healthy lands
round the Zambési are colonised by the Anglo-
Saxon race.

The question now before the civilised world
is, whether the slave-trade in Africa, which
causes, at the lowest estimate, an annual loss of
over half a million lives, is to be permitted to
continue ?

Every one worthy of the name of a man will say, No!

Let us then hope that England, which has hitherto occupied the proud position of being foremost amongst the friends of the unfortunate slave, may still hold that place.

Let those who seek to employ money, now lying idle, join together to open the trade of Africa.

Let those interested in scientific research come forward and support the King of the Belgians in his noble scheme for united and systematic exploration.

Let those who desire to stamp out the traffic in slaves put their shoulders to the wheel in earnest, and by their voice, money, and energy aid those to whom the task may be entrusted.

Let those interested in missionary efforts aid to their utmost those who are labouring in Africa, and send them worthy assistants, prepared to devote their lives to the task.

It is not by talking and writing that Africa is to be regenerated, but by action. Let each one who thinks he can lend a helping hand do so. All cannot travel, or become missionaries or traders; but they can give their cordial assistance to those whose duty leads them to the as yet untrodden places of the world.

But I would impress upon all who approach this question the necessity for not being too sanguine. Many a name must be added to the roll of those

who have fallen in the cause of Africa, much
patient and enduring labour must be gone through
without flinching or repining, before we see Africa
truly free and happy.

I firmly believe that opening up proper lines of
communication will do much to check the cursed
traffic in human flesh, and that the extension of
legitimate commerce will ultimately put an end to
it altogether.

But I am by no means so certain of the rapid
extinction of slavery as a domestic institution.
The custom is so deeply engrained in the mind of
the African that I fear we must be content simply
to commence the task, leaving its completion to
our descendants.

And with regard to education and civilisation,
we must be satisfied to work gradually, and not
attempt to force our European customs and manners
upon a people who are at present unfitted for
them. Our own civilisation, it must be remembered, is the growth of many centuries, and to
expect that of Africa to become equal to it in a
decade or two is an absurdity. The forcing system,
so often essayed with so-called savages, merely puts
on a veneer of spurious civilisation; in the majority
of cases the subject having, in addition to the vices
of his native state, acquired those belonging to the
lowest dregs of civilisation.

Let us therefore work soberly and steadily, never
being driven back or disheartened by any apparent

failure or rebuff; but, should such be met with, search for the remedy, and then press on all the more eagerly. And so in time, with God's blessing on the work, Africa may be free and happy.

COLOUR PARTY.

APPENDIX I.

ENUMERATION OF PLANTS COLLECTED IN THE REGION ABOUT LAKE TANGANYIKA.

Drawn up by D. Oliver, F.R.S., F.L.S., Keeper of the Herbarium, Royal Gardens, Kew.

[The following notes comprise an enumeration of the species contained in a small parcel of plants received at Kew in February, 1875, and which had been collected by me in the southern basin of Lake Tanganyika. The flora of the region round the lake may be taken as belonging to the basin of the Kongo. The enumeration has been drawn up by Professor Oliver; the descriptions of new species are by him and by Messrs. Baker and Spencer Moore, assistants in the Herbarium.]

The new species described below are marked *.

Clematis Kirkii, Oliv.
Cleome hirta, Oliv.
Courbonia decumbens, Brongn.
Abutilon? sp.
Hibiscus cannabinus, L.
Gossypium barbadense, L.
Dombeya spectabilis, Boj. (M. T. M. in Flora Trop. Afr. p. 227).
Waltheria americana, L.
Triumfetta semitriloba, L., or *T. rhomboidea*, Jacq.
Ochna macrocalyx, Oliv.
Vitis, sp. nov.?
V. serpens, Hochst., var.??
Polycarpæa corymbosa, Lam.
Crotalaria laburnifolia, L.
Pueraria?
Indigofera (§ *Trichopodæ*) *cuneata*, J. G. B.*

I. (§ *Dissitifloræ*) *dissitiflora*, J. G. B.*
I. hirsuta, L.
I.: an *I. torulosa*, J. G. B.?
I. (§ *Tinctoriæ*) *Cameroni*, J. G. B.*
Phaseolus, sp.
Erythrina tomentosa, R. Br.
Eriosema rhynchosivides, J. G. B.*
Dolichos? sp.
Cassia, sp.
Cæsalpineacea. Allied to the "*Kobbo*" of Dr. Schweinfurth, referred by him to *Humboldtia.*
Dichrostachys nutans, Benth.
Rhus insignis, Del., var.? Leafy specimen only.
Kalanchoe platysepala? Welw.

Jussiæa villosa ? var.

Cephalandra ? sp.

Vernonia obconica, Oliv. & Hiern, ined.

V. pauciflora ? Less.

Conyza ægyptiaca, Ait.

Sphæranthus. Perhaps a new species allied to *S. peduncularis.*

Gutenbergia polycephala, Oliv. and Hiern.*

Leptactinia heinsioides, Hiern, sp. nov. ined.

Oldenlandia. Near *O. parviflora* ?

Kraussia congesta, Oliv.*

Jasminum auriculatum, var. β. *zanzibarense* ? (*I. tettense*, Kl.)

Strychnos ? sp. Leafy specimen only (perhaps the same from Batoka country, Dr. Kirk).

Strychnos ? sp. Leafy aculeate specimen.

Asclepiadaceæ (*Raphionacme* ?)

Convolvulus (*Breweria malvacea* ? Kl).

Ipomæa. Allied to *I. simplex* and allies.

Convolvulus ? sp.

Trichodesma zeylanicum, R. Br.

Heliophytum indicum, D. C.

Leonotis nepetæfolia, R. Br.

Ocymum canum, Sims., var. ?

Ocymum near *O. obovatum*, E. Mey.

Ocymum, sp. ?

Sesamum. Not in a state to describe, with very narrow leaves.

Sesamum. Perhaps the same species. Similar to a specimen collected by Dr. Kirk in S.E. Africa, but not in fruit.

Striga elegans, Benth. ?

Rhamphicarpa tubulosa, Benth.

Rhamphicarpa. Perhaps *R. tubulosa*, with oblique rostrate included capsule.

Rhamphicarpa Cameroniana, Oliv.*

Rhamphicarpa ? Too imperfect for description.

Cycnium adonense ? E. Mey.

Thunbergia near *T. oblongifolia*, Oliv.

Nelsonia tomentosa, Willd.

Barleria limnogeton, Spencer Moore.*

Hypoëstes, sp. Insufficient for description.

Lantana ? sp.

Lantana near *L. salviæfolia.*

Vitex ? Leaves simple. Not in state to describe.

Vitex. Leaves 3-foliolate; leaflets oblanceolate, obtuse, or broadly pointed, entire, glabrescent, more or less tomentose toward the base of the midrib beneath. Not in flower.

Cyclonema spinescens, Oliv.*

Plumbago zeylanica, L.

P. amplexicaulis, Oliv.*

Arthrosolen glaucescens, Oliv.*

Amarantaceæ, dub. Perhaps *Achyranthes.* Too decayed to describe.

Euphorbiaceæ an *Phyllanthus* ? sp. Not in flower.

Acalypha, sp. ?

Habenaria ? ?

Lissochilus, sp.

Walleria Mackenzii, Kirk.

Gloriosa virescens, Lindl. The typical plant, and also a form with very broad subopposite leaves.

Asparagus racemosus, Willd.

A. asiaticus, L.

A. Pauli-Gulielmi, Solms.

Anthericum Cameroni, J. G. B.*

Chlorophytum macrophyllum, A. Rich.

Cienkowskia ? sp.

Hæmanthus, sp.

Gladiolus near *G. natalensis* ?

Aneilema longifolia, Hook.

Commelyna, two species.

Nerine, sp.

Fuirena pubescens, Kunth.
Cyperus rotundus, L.
C. coloratus, V.
Setaria glauca, Beauv.
Tricholæna rosea, Nees.

Stipa, sp.
Eragrostis poæoides, Beauv.
E. Chapelieri, Nees.
Eragrostis, sp.
Hymenophyllum polyanthos, Sw.

INDIGOFERA CUNEATA, *Baker*. Suffruticosa, ramulis gracillimis dense pubescentibus, foliis perparvis subsessilibus simplicibus vel ternato-digitatis, foliolis minutis obovato-cuneatis crassis pilosis complicatis, floribus solitariis raro geminis, pedunculis gracillimis folio multo longioribus, calyce minuto dense setoso dentibus linearibus, petalis minutis rubellis, legumine cylindrico glabrescente atro-brunneo, seminibus pluribus.

Belongs to the section Trichopodæ, and closely resembles *I. trichopoda* in the flowers and their arrangement, but differs entirely in the leaves.

Stems very slender, suffruticose, terete, copiously branched, with ascending branchlets densely clothed with fine, variously directed, white, pellucid hairs as long as, or longer than, their diameter. Stipules minute, setaceous. Leaves very minute, nearly sessile, simple and trifoliolate intermixed; leaflets obovate, cuneate in the lower half, usually not more than a line long, complicate, digitate, subacute, clothed with hairs similar to those of the branches, but shorter. Flowers copious, solitary or rarely geminate on a thread-like, nearly naked, ascending peduncle 3–4 lines long. Calyx ½ line deep, densely firmly pilose; teeth deep, linear. Corolla reddish, three times as long as the calyx, externally pilose. Staminal sheath ½ inch long. Pod cylindrical, sessile, ½–⅔ inch long, at first obscurely hispid, finally glabrescent, dark brown, straight, many-seeded, not at all torulose.

I. DISSITIFLORA, *Baker*. Suffruticosa, ramulis gracillimis teretibus obscure pilosis, stipulis setaceis, foliis petiolatis pinnatis, foliolis 1–4-jugis lineari-subulatis oppositis pallide viridibus setis paucis adpressis, racemis laxe 3–5-floris pedunculatis, calyce minuto dense griseo-hispido dentibus lanceolatis, petalis parvis purpureis, ovario cylindrico multiovulato.

Belongs to section *Dissitifloræ*, next *I. pentaphylla*, Linn., which it closely resembles in the flowers, but differs entirely in its leaflets and shrubby habit.

Stem erect, suffruticose, with copious, very slender erecto-patent branches clothed only with a few scattered, adpressed, bristly hairs. Stipules minute, setaceous, persistent. Leaves of main stem an inch long, distinctly stalked, with 3–4 distant pairs of opposite, linear-subulate leaflets, which are ¼ inch long, grey-green, pointed, narrowed at the base, rather thick in texture, clothed only with a few obscure adpressed hairs like those of the branches. Leaves of branches often with only 3–5 leaflets. Racemes about as long as the leaves, laxly 3–5-flowered, distinctly stalked. Bracts minute, subulate. Pedicels nearly or quite as long as the calyx. Calyx ½ a line deep, densely bristly; teeth lanceolate, as long as the broadly funnel-shaped tube. Corolla purplish, three times as long as the calyx, shortly bristly. Ovary cylindrical, multiovulate. Ripe pod not seen.

I. CAMERONI, *Baker*. Fruticosa, ramulis gracillimis teretibus obscure pilosis, stipulis minutis setaceis, foliis pinnatis breviter petiolatis foliolis 2–3-jugis oblongis subcoriaceis utrinque tenuiter pilosis, racemis densis brevibus conicis sessilibus folio brevioribus, calyce, minuto oblique campanulato argenteo-sericeo dentibus deltoideis, petalis angustis elongatis extus brunneo-sericeis, ovario cylindrico multiovulato.

Belongs to section *Tinctoriæ*, next *I. torulosa*, Baker, from which it differs by its pilose leaves and branchlets, argenteous calyx, &c.

Habit quite shrubby. Branches slender, terete, thinly clothed with minute, adpressed, white hairs. Stipules and stipellæ setaceous. Leaves short-stalked, 1½–2 inches long; leaflets 2–3-jugate, oblong, subcoriaceous, mucronate, ¼–¾ inch long, rounded at the base to a short petiolule; side ones opposite; both surfaces, especially the lower, clothed with short minute white hairs. Flowers in dense racemes, an inch long, which are sessile in the axils of the leaves. Bracts lanceolate-navicular, minute, argenteous, caducous. Pedicels very short. Calyx obliquely campanulate, scarcely ½ a line deep, densely argenteo-sericeous; teeth deltoid. Corolla ¼ inch long, densely brown-silky. Ovary cylindrical, multiovulate. Ripe pod not seen.

ERIOSEMA RHYNCHOSIOIDES, *Baker*. Volubilis, dense griseo-pubescens, stipulis parvis lanceolatis persistentibus, foliis longe petiolatis ternato-pinnatifidis subcoriaceis conspicue venulosis, foliolo terminali oblongo distincte petiolulato obtuso minute mucronato, floribus 4–8 in racemum capitatum densum longe pedunculatum dispositis, pedicellis brevissimis, calyce campanulato dentibus magnis lanceolatis, petalis purpureis extus pilosis, legumine oblongo applanato piloso inter semina haud constricto.

Of the Tropical African species this will have to be placed next *E. parviflorum*, E. Meyer; but it is very different in leaf and calyx, and has entirely the general habit of a *Rhynchosia*—so much so that it would be inevitably referred to that genus if the seeds were not examined.

A voluble herb, with long internodes. Branches densely clothed with short, rather spreading, grey hairs. Stipules small, lanceolate, persistent. Petioles ¾–1 inch long, spreading, densely pilose. Leaflets 3 subcoriaceous, oblong, 1–2 inches long, both sides thinly pilose, the lower with its veins and veinlets raised; the point bluntish, with a minute mucro, the end one largest, distinctly stalked, the side ones shorter and rather oblique. Flowers 4–8, crowded at the top of an axillary peduncle which much exceeds the leaf. Pedicels very short. Calyx 2 lines deep, densely clothed with short, spreading, grey hairs, the lanceolate teeth much exceeding the tube. Corolla twice as long as the calyx, much recurved, densely silky on the outside. Pod oblong, flat, $\frac{1}{2}$ inch long, $\frac{1}{4}$ inch broad, densely pilose, two-seeded, abruptly rounded at the base, not constricted between the seeds. Flattened funiculus attached obliquely to the extremity of the hilum.

GUTENBERGIA POLYCEPHALA, *Oliv. et Hiern, Fl. Trop. Afr.* iii. ined. Herba plus minus incano-tomentella; ramis teretibus striatis; foliis superioribus sessilibus lanceolatis v. ovato-lanceolatis acutiusculis basi obtusis cordatisve amplexicaulibus integris v. subintegris, supra glabratis v. scabriusculis, subtus albido-tomentosis; capitulis parvis numerosis in paniculas cymosas dispositis, squamis involucralibus pauciseriatis, exterioribus lineari-lanceolatis, interioribus 8–12 sub-æqualibus ovali-oblongis 3-nerviis, achænio obovoideo 10–12-costato glabro v. parce breviter pilosulo.

We have the same from Kilwa (Dr. Kirk).

KRAUSSIA CONGESTA, *Oliv.*, sp. nov. Glabra, foliis ellipticis tenuiter coriaceis breviter obtuse acuminatis basi in petiolum brevissimum angustatis, floribus in cymis brevibus paucifloris axillaribus sessilibus v. subsessilibus congestis, pedicellis bracteolatis brevissimis sub-nullisve, calycis lobis rotundatis tubo obovoideo æquilongis, corollæ lobis tubo æquilongis fauce hirsuta, antheris apice appendicula gracili terminatis, stylo bifido glabro, ovulis in loculis paucis (circ. 4).

Folia 3–3$\frac{1}{2}$ poll. longa.

RHAMPHICARPA ·CAMERONIANA, *Oliv.*, sp. nov. Herba verisimiliter 1–2-pedalis, caule ramoso tetragono 4-sulcato parce pilosulo v. glabrato, foliis sessilibus v. subsessilibus lineari-lanceolatis linearibusve basin versus sæpe utrinque grosse 1–2-dentatis v. pinnatifido-dentatis, floribus racemosis breviter pedicellatis, pedicello calyce brevioribus, calyce tubuloso-campanulato 10-costato, lobis lanceolatis acutis tubo subæquilongis, corollæ hypocrateriformis tubo ($\frac{3}{4}$–1 poll. longo) gracili limbo amplo (1$\frac{1}{4}$ poll. lato) paulo longiore, labio superiore breviter et obtuse 2-lobato, labio inferiore profunde 3-fido lobis subæqualibus late obovato-rotundatis, filamentis apice piloso-barbatis, capsula calycem paulo superante subtruncata v. obcordata vix aut leviter obliqua, valvis coriaceis retusis.·

Remarkable in the retuse fruit, which is neither beaked (except the persisting style-base) nor distinctly oblique.

BARLERIA LIMNOGETON, *Spencer Moore*, sp. nov. Caule subtereti, leviter tomentoso; foliis petiolatis, oblanceolatis, acutis, integris, primo tomentosis demum supra pubescentibus; floribus spicatis spicis terminalibus; bracteis strobilaceis, inermibus, late ovatis, obtusis, sericeo-tomentosis; bracteolis linearibus, acutis; calycis laciniis exterioribus late lanceolatis, interioribus subulatis; corolla hypocraterimorpha, glabra, tubo quam calyx duplo longiore, segmentis limbi patentis obovatis; staminibus fertilibus 2 exsertis, sterilibus 3; capsula ignota.

Caulis erectus. Folia matura 3–3½ unc. longa; petiolus ½ unc. longus. Bracteæ ½ unc. longæ, nervosæ. Calycis laciniæ pubescentes, exteriores ½ unc., interiores ¼ unc. longa. Corolla 1 unc. longa. Ovarium compressum, villosum; stylus crassus, glabrescens.

A very distinct species of the genus, with the habit of a *Crossandra*. Indications in some of the leaf-axils would lead to the presumption that the inflorescence may be axillary as well as terminal.

CYCLONEMA SPINESCENS, *Oliv.*, sp. nov. Piloso-pubescens, ramulis teretibus interdum spinis rectis recurvisve supraaxillaribus oppositis folio brevioribus armatis, foliis late ellipticis rotundatisve obtusis v. mucronatis brevissime petiolatis v. subsessilibus, utrinque piloso-pubescentibus, pedunculis 1-floris axillaribus patentibus folio æquilongis v. eod. longioribus supra medium 2-bracteatis, bracteis auguste linearibus, calycis villosi tubo campanulato, limbo 5-lobo, lobis ovato-lanceolatis acutis, corollæ tubo cylindrico calycem superante, limbo 5-partito lobis obovatis integris apice obtuse rotundatis v. late acutatis venuloso-reticulatis, staminibus longe exsertis glabris, ovario glabro.

Folia ⅔–1¼ poll. longa. Bracteæ 3–4 lin. longæ. Flores 1–1¼ poll. diam.

PLUMBAGO AMPLEXICAULIS, *Oliv.*, sp. nov. Ramis glabratis v. puberulis, in sicco longitudinaliter sulcatis, foliis obovato-ellipticis late acutatis integris v. undulatis glabris reticulatis subtus nervo medio venisque secundariis prominulis, lamina in petiolum late alatum continua basi conspicue rotundato-auriculata, auriculis amplexicaulibus, floribus cærulois spicatis, spicis paniculatis glandulosis, bracteis ovatis breviter apiculatis, calyce anguste tubuloso costato puberulo parce glanduloso, corollæ hypocrateriformis tubo gracili poll. longo, limbi lobis obovatis obtusis nervo medio gracillimo excurrente mucronatis, antheris exsertis.

Folia 2–5 poll. longa, 1½–3 poll. lata. Calyx ⅓–½ poll. longus.

ARTHROSOLEN GLAUCESCENS, *Oliv.*, sp. nov. Glabra, glaucescens, ramulis foliiferis (circ. ½-pedalibus) teretibus lævibus, foliis alternis adscendentibus linearibus planis utrinque leviter angustatis acutiusculis, floribus tetrameris capitatis, capitulis solitariis terminalibus multifloris, foliis involucralibus ovatis acuminatis glabris floribus brevioribus, receptaculo dense hirsuto-piloso, floribus puberulis, tubo perianthii gracili, lobis limbi patentibus ovato-lanceolatis acutis, antheris subsessilibus lineari-oblongis lanceolatisve plus minus apiculatis, squamulis hypogynis nullis.

Folia ⅝–¾ poll. longa, 1–1½ lin. lata. Perianthium tubo ½ poll. longo.

ANTHERICUM (DILANTHES) CAMERONI, *Baker*. Caule pedali, foliis
caulinis 4 anguste linearibus duris glabris persistentibus, racemo
simplici laxifloro rachi insigniter flexuosa, bracteis parvis deltoideis,
floribus semper geminis, pedicellis brevibus prope basin articulatis,
perianthii segmentis lanceolatis dorso nervis 5 laxis purpureis vittatis
margine angusto albido, staminibus perianthio vix brevioribus,
antheris magnis papillosis, ovulis in loculo pluribus crebris.

This comes nearest the common Cape *Anthericum triflorum*, Ait.,
wrongly placed by Kunth in *Chlorophytum ;* but it may easily be known
from that and all other species by the nervation of the perianth-segments.

Root not seen. Stem a foot high, with 3-4 leaves, which vary in length
from 6 to 15 inches, narrow, linear, firm, persistent, acuminate, 3-4
lines broad, quite glabrous, with a thickened keel, and about 20
close distinct ribs on each side of it, the uppermost one rising from
half-way up the stem, and reaching as high as the top of the raceme.
Raceme simple, half a foot long, with a slender very flexuose rachis.
Bracts minute, deltoid. Flowers laxly placed, all up to the tip in
pairs. Pedicels unequal, ascending or spreading, 1-3 lines long,
articulated just above the base, and the flowers easily falling away by
this articulation. Perianth ¾ inch long; segments lanceolate, 1½-2
lines broad at the middle, rather reflexed when fully expanded, with
five distinct purple ribs in the centre, leaving only a narrow white
border on each side. Stamens nearly as long as the perianth ; anther
linear, papillose, as long as the rather flattened filament. Ovary
minute, oblong, with a large number of horizontal ovules in each cell.
Style ½ inch long, filiform, declinate.

APPENDIX II.

KIRUA VOCABULARY.

THE system of spelling native names and words has been adopted from Bishop Steere's "Handbook of Kisuahili." The accent is almost without exception on the penultimate syllable. Vowels are broad, and the letter "G" always hard. The verbs marked with an asterisk are not in the infinitive.

1	Kamo.
2	Tuwili.
3	Tusatu.
4	Tana.
5	Tutano.
6	Tusamba.
7	Tusambalawili.
8	Mwanda.
9	Kitema.
10	Di Kumi or Kikwi.
11	Di Kumi na Kamo.
12	Di Kumi na Tuwili.
20	Vikwi viwili.
30	Vikwi visatu.
100	Katwa.
200	Tutwa tuwili.

I	Amiwa.
Thou	Avè.
He	Ayè.
We	Atwè.
You	Awè.
They	Acha.
Mine or our	Mina.
Thine or your	Avè.

His, hers, its, or theirs	Ayè.
These	Longangengè.
Who	Naimboka.
Bad (thing)	Chi-vipi.
Good (thing)	Chi-ampi.
Full	Ki-sanku.
Much	Chi-kwavo.
Perhaps	Sika kasangava.
Close to	Pèpi-pèpi.
Not yet	Kulingivili.
After	Chansuma.
Above	Kulo.
Under	Anshi.
Again	Wu-bia.
Now	Wino-wino.
Before	Likomeso.
Across	Kavukita.
God	Vidie.
Father	Tata.
Mother	Lolo.
Brother	Tula
Sister	Kaka.
Child	Mwana.
Son	Mwana malumè.
Daughter	Mwana m'kazi.
Youth	Kalukèkè (young person).

Person	Mukalumbè.	Blood	Mashi.
Man	Mukalumbè malumè.	Skin of a man	Kova-kova.
		Skin of a beast	Kiséva.
Woman	Mukalumbè m'kazi.	Sun	Minyia.
All men	Angola kwambu.	Moon	Kwési.
European	Msungu.	Star	Kanyenya.
Europeans	Wasungu.	Day	Mfuko.
Friend	Mlunda.	Night	Cholwa.
A great person, high in rank	Mukalenjè.	To-day	Lélo.
		To-morrow	Usikwa.
		Yesterday	Kesha.
Master	Mfumwami.	Cold	Masika.
Guide	Kina meshinda.	Wind	Luvula.
Slave	Mahika.	Clouds	Malè.
Fool	Kinèma-nèma.	Heat	Changa.
He has no wits	Kadi manango.	Fire	Miriro.
		Hunger	Njali.
A carpenter (a man that adzes)	Msonga.	Thirst	Nafwa kiluka.
		Food	Wulio or Viliwa.
An iron-worker	Mvisendi.	Water	Méma.
		Rain	Mvula.
Wizard	Mganga.	Fear	Ulimoyo.
Witch	Mfwishi.	Anger	Bomana.
Idol	Kavita.	War	Luana.
Ghost	Kilui.	Sweat	Changa.
Soul	Miliwa.	Dirt	Visha.
Body	Vili vili.	Strong	Mumi.
Heart	Mula.	Long	Mulampi.
Leg	Mienga.	Short	Mwipi.
Foot	Uswaya.	Large	Mkata.
Arm	Kuwoko.	Small	Kishéshè.
Fingers	Minwè.	Slim	Mshu.
Finger-nail	Mala.	Heavy	Chaléma.
Head	Kutwè.	Light	Chaperlu.
Mouth	Makanu.	Good	Viyampi.
Tongue	Lulimi.	Bad	Chawola.
Teeth	Néno.	Old	Mununu.
Nose	Miona.	Slowly	Vishi-vi-hi.
Eyes	Masa.	Quickly	Bukiti-bukiti.
Eyebrow	Mazigi.	Raw	Muvichi.
Eyelash	Kofio.	Cooked	Kukenda.
Ears	Matwi.	Bare	Vitupu.
Hair	Mwènè.	Bitter	Kisuku.
Beard	Mwèvu.	Half	Kipongo.
Stomach	Mumunda.	Sick	Uvéla.
Breasts	Mavélè.	Black	Afita.
Bone	Chikupa.	White	Sitoka.
Flesh	Mwita.	Red	Ushila.

Other	Wangi.	Oil	Mâni.
Ants	Menyo *and* Mpazi.	Oil-palm	Ngazi.
„ (white)	M'swa.	Pepper	Lungito.
Antelope	Kashia.	Pumpkins	Mâni.
„ (small sort)	Kabruka.	Rice	Mwêlè a mpunga.
Ape	Buya.	Semsem	Ulongo.
Bees	Nyuki.	Sugar-cane	Miongè.
Bird	Ngoöni.	Tobacco	Fanga.
Buffalo	Mboö.	(Pipe	Mtonga.)
Cat (jungle)	Paka.	Yam	Kulungu.
Crocodile	Nandu.		
Dog	Mbwa.		
Duck	Kisulolo.	Fever	Pachési.
Eggs	Mayi.	Hole	M'kina.
Elephant	Holo.	Salt	Mwèpu.
Fish	Mwita wa luwi.	Thing	Kintu.
Fly	Lanji.	The game of Bao	Kisolo.
Fowl	Zolo.		
Frog	Nyunda.	The seeds they play it with	Masoko.
Goat	Mbuzi.		
Guinea-fowl	Kanga.	Country	Nshi.
Hippopotamus	Chobu.	Earth	Vilowa.
Hornets	Matembo.	Sand	Vilowa a vitanda.
Hyæna	Kumungu.	Mud	Vilowa a mèsa.
Leopard	Nge.	Stone	I. Uivè.
Lion	Tambu.	Hill	M'kuna.
Lizard	Sambatu.	River	Luwi.
Monkey	Kima.	Opposite bank	Ushiga.
Ox	Ngombè.	Pond	Liziwa.
Pig (jungle)	Nguruwè.	Road	Mishinda.
„ (tame)	„ . a mbuzi.	Tree	Chiti.
Rat	Mkoswè.	Fork of tree	Kihanda.
Scorpion	Kaminiò.	Bough	Mikamba.
Sheep	Mkoko.	Bush	Tusondè.
Snake	Nyoko.	Thorn	Miba.
Bananas	Makondè.	House	Mzuo.
Bamboo	Sununo.	Roof	Mukalo.
Beans	Kundè.	Wall	Bilu.
„ (small red)	Atandawala.	Chair	Kipôna.
Castor-oil	Mono.	Bedstead	Mtangi.
Flour	Ukula.	A wooden head-rest	Msama.
Flower	Kulongo.		
Fruit	Kuha.	Spoon to scoop up	Lutuwa.
Ground-nuts	Nyumu.		
(Voiandzeia	Konkota.)	To stir with	Mpanzi.
Indiarubber	Kudimbo.	Farm	Kurimi.
Indian corn	Mavèlè a wahemba.	Boma	Kihango.
Matama	Mavèlè a lua.	Load	Misélo.

Earthen pot	Kisuku.
Bowl	Luvu.
Basket	Kisaku.
Gourd	Mungu.
Mat	Chata.
Cloth	Mbwisha.
„ (grass)	Kissandi.
Cowries	Mbéla.
Beads	Malungo.
Bag	Mkolo.
Box	Kipówa.
Net	Wanda.
String	Sondè.
Firewood	M'kuni.
Coals	Makaa.
Medicine	Wanga.
Honey	Bukè.
Gunpowder	Bwanda.
Cartridge	Vissongho.
Bow	Uta.
Bowstring	Kiremba.
Arrow	Mikétu.
Quiver	Chibungo.
Spear	Mkovè.
Club	Kavombogoni.
Shield	Ngao.
Sword	Lupete luwando.
Knife	Lupétè.
Axe	Kasolo.
Adze	Chongo.
Hoe	Lukaso.
Iron	Kilonda.
Copper	Mwambo.
Canoe	Watu.
Paddle	Kwuho.
To be able	Ku misashani.
„ ache	„ fimpa.
„ alter	„ shintani.
„ amuse	„ shikuta kipona.
Annoy	Ulilukampo.*
Answer	Wavinga.*
To arrive	Ku fika.
Assemble	Mulwi.*
To bake	Ku shia.
„ bathe	„ vamèmu.
„ bear fruit	„ vutala.
„ beat	„ kupila.
„ beg	„ lomba.

Behave	Ndi kuva.*
To believe	Ku mambo.
(To say it is well.	Meiyampi.)
To bend	Ku téma.
„ bite	„ musumè meno.
*„ blaze	„ wanka.
„ bleed	„ tamba.
„ boil	„ vila.
„ break	„ kata.
„ build	„ waka.
„ burst	„ wala jika.
„ buy	„ ota.
Call	Mwitè (call him).*
To carry	Ku éla.
„ chew	„ aukao.
Clean	Kiampi.*
To clothe	Ku vala.
„ come	„ henga.
„ cook	„ ipika.
„ cross	„ chalakata.
„ cry	„ malilo.
„ cut	„ tèla.
Delay	Kafia.*
To die	Ku taha.
„ dig	„ kola.
Draw water	Kusoka.
To drink	Ku toma.
„ eat	„ shia.
„ enter	„ twéla.
„ excel	„ pita.
„ fall	„ fiona
„ fasten	„ téi.
„ fatten	„ nuni.
„ fear	„ china.
„ feed	„ awana.
„ fight	„ pulwa.
„ „	„ luana.
Fill	Chintè.*
Fly	Chatambaka.*
Forget	Nailuwa.*
To follow	Ku mlonda.
„ get	„ sambuuganyo.
„ give	„ mavire.
„ go	„ onda.
„ heal	„ watuba.
„ hear	„ omvana.
„ hoe	„ ndima.
„ kill	„ taha.

To know	Ku wonwa.	To be sick	Ku véla.
„ „	„ juka.	„ sing	„ vemba.
„ laugh	„ séka.	„ sit	„ shikuta.
„ leave	„ vika.	„ shave	„ tenda.
„ lie	„ uwerla.	„ show	„ lambóla.
„ like	„ awacho.	„ shut (the door)	„ shita (kuchiwèlo).
„ love	„ zîmina.	„ sleep	„ lala.
Make	Kanguvilè. *	„ smear over	„ isinga.
„	Kivéla kové.*	„ smell	„ muku.
Measure	Wiku viku *	„ smoke (tobacco)	„ toma (fanga).
To meet	Ku sambaganyu.	„ spoil	„ chavola.
„ order	„ wambana.	„ suck	„ fwama.
„ open	„ shita lamo.	Swim	Kóya.*
„ pay	„ futa. *	Take	Kamutvalitè.*
„ pick up	„ wóya.	To take away	Ku fundula.
„ plaster a house	„ bua.	„ tell	„ sapwila.
„ play	„ wakuiya.	„ throw	„ sumbu.
„ pull	„ koka.	„ thunder	„ ngulu.
„ put	„ vika.	„ wait	„ nga.
„ put down	„ tula.	„ wake	„ taluka.
„ run	„ enda uviro.	„ want	„ wakacho.
„ run away	„ wanyoma.	„ walk	„ kananga.
„ say	„ nèna.	„ wash	„ kenda.
„ see	„ tala.	Work	Weïla mingéla.*
„ sew	„ fuma.		

I will beat you	Nsaka niku kupilè.
When a sultan dies what do the Warua do?	Lufa a Mlohhè tulonga na mini la lèlo Warua ?
Give me water to drink	Navila méma nitomè.
He is very drunk	Wakolwebo katoma vibi.
Is there a big dance to-day ?	Wazia an-ngoma ikata lèlo ?
No, yesterday	Vituu kesha.
Where do you get iron ?	Waboya hi kilonda ?
Does Kasongo pay tribute to Muta Yanfo ?	Kasongo ulambulakwé Mwata Yanfo ?
No, he does not	Vituu, kalumbuluho.
Kasongo is afraid of Daiyi a Kèjèra	Kasongo aliuo moyo na Daiyi a Kèjèra.
How many children has Kasongo ?	Kasongo wana wangavo a watula ?
Kasongo goes to war to steal food and people's children : he has nothing	Mlohhè renda kuli luana wakeva udio ni wana waneni : kali luhéto.
Where has Kasongo gone ?	Kasongo (Mlohhè) aendi hi ?
Kasongo has been cutting off ears and noses to-day	Ya lèlo Mlohhè wuchiwa matwi na mulu.
Do the Warua eat men ?	Waluu nawo walia wantu ?
No, they don't	Vituu, viso.

Who make the knives of tho Warua?	Walongo lupéto Warua?
People near Munza work iron	Wantu walipépi a Munza wafula kilonda.
Where do they get copper?	Wawè ahi mwambo?
Do they make knives of stones?	Walongo lupétè uivè?
No	Vituu.
Warua pray to God, and He gives them what they want	Walua sakakèsè Vidie, angavilè chonsuka.
Have the Warua any songs?	Waluu nè nimbo?
Can you get a man to tell me one?	Wasamba kania muntu unéna mkwao?
Have the Warua any tales?	Walua né vishima?
I want to hear both songs and tales	Nsaka kunyukisba 'wami wawili mimbo na vishima.
Warua shave their heads	Walua watenda mévu.
Women tattoo their bellies	Wakazi wataa añ tappo chali.
When the Warua want fire, what do they do?	Walua wusoka mililo walangukka?
They rub sticks	Mufio wavié mililo.
Is that a heavy load?	Kisaka chaléma.
No, it is a light one	Vituu, chapèrla.
What have you in it?	Mulichika ukisaka?
Sugar-canes and bananas	Miongè na makondè.
Put your load down	Sela kisaka chovè.
Carry the box	Usélè kitundu.
Catch hold of the rope	Tambula mionzi.
The cloth is spoilt	Mbwisha yavola.
The axe cuts	Kasolo kawiti.
Give me your bow and arrows	Gawilè uta na mikétu yovè.
The bowstring is broken	Kilemba wachivika.
What have you to sell?	Wasela ka a kuota?
What do you want?	Usakaka?
Tell a man to bring some grass cloth	Sowili muntu a kalétè kissandi.
Where do they get the stuff to make grass cloth black?	Kiaviloha ya afiti ha vissandi ushiti kwéhi?
I want some fat goats	Nsaka mbuzi munumè.
Bring goats and six fowls	Letè mbuzi na wazolo tusambi.
He has some beans	Muntu waïanè kundè.
Give my slave an earthen pot	Gavilè mabika mwavilé a kisuku.
Bring me some ivory (a tusk) and I will give you some knives	Letélè lino, nikwavilè lupèto.
Go and cut some firewood and I will give you salt	Enda katiavé kuni na mkwavilè mwépu.
Have you any potatoes to sell?	Dinè wambala sakatè notè?
I want eggs and bananas	Nsaka mayi a zolo na makondè.
There are none	Hatupu.
Sell me the skin	Niotà kiséva.
He does not want to sell it, he will give it you	Kiswe kuota, usaka kungavila.
I will drink palm wine	Nitoma malovu.
He shot two guinea-fowl	Nataba wakanga tuwili.

Let the sheep go .... Mkutuhila mkoko.
They eat frogs .... Walia vyula.
The pot is full .... Kisuku chayala.
The water has flies in it .... Méma mabi.
He is eating .... Ulia.
Monkeys eat fruit................. Mpuyè walè matungulo.
Birds drink water................. Ngoöni utoma méma.
Bamboos grow near water .... Sunumu ili papa na méma.
Ask if pigs (tame) are good.......... 'Nge wakwata nguruwè a mbuzi.
The cat stole a fowl .... Paka wawata zolo.
Rats (large jungle rats) are very large. Sonzi a kuno vukata.
Rats eat ivory .... Wampuku walia méno.
The meat stinks.................... Mivita lina vinio. ▪
What is the name of that animal ? ..Mwita la lisua mwitaka ?
He has told people to kill a goat ..... Wanèna wantu wakatabè mbuzi.
Pound this corn.................... Utwè matava.
Make a fire....................... Wanza mililo.
Go and draw water .... Wendè katéka méma.
Does he drink pombé ?............. Walintoma malwa ?
He does not, but he smokes bhang ..Kashwè malwa, liloma liamba.
How many fowls have you there?....Zolo wanga wo waïa navo ?
Does the water boil ? .... Méma avila.
I am very hungry, I want to eat .... Nafanzala, usaka kulia.
Give me food .... Ngavilè wulio.
Is this a river, or what ?............ Keki luwi ikika ?
He has bidden .... Wafia.
He is clever .... Kalima langa.
He is a bad man .... Tambula mionzi.
Do all the people carry shields, or { Wanzololo wangerla ngao
  only the chiefs ? .... { Mlobhè ?
All the chiefs carry them .... Wanzerla Mlobhè wonzolo.
He knows the road .... Wayuka ushinda.
The caravan has crossed the river ....Wulwondo wawukakala luwi.
How many days till he comes back ?..Mafuku wanga wahingili ?
What is he doing ? .... Wakalangaka ?
Will you show the road ?............ Unombolè mishinda?
Follow this road .... Enda diè la mishinda.
Take him to the river .... Mutwatè ku luwi.
Tell me what your name is.......... Lisè yovè lisina wiani.
I have come from Kiremba .... Narya wa Kiremba.
Have you seen my men ?............ Uwaono watu wami ?
I have not seen them, that man { Vitupu chamwénévo, wamkona
  yonder has .... { ava.
Tell my men to go back ....Tunénè tu hingi wakwétu.
I want a boat and guide .... Nisaka watu na kilima nashinda.
Where are the paddles ? .... Wavilè masuki ?
Go quickly and tell him I am waiting..Enda ukatè ukumkugila kogo.
Are you ready ?.................... Uliwa kiti ?
Let us be going.................... Twendè wosololo.

English	Translation
That man is telling a lie	Muntu awa anénà ovéla.
Some one has stolen a gun	Muntu waiva utawa mputa.
It is very hot	Awalénè ulovu.
The sun has come out	Mwina amkata.
There are many clouds above	Makumbi avangevila kélu.
The rain is very heavy now	Mvula unoko ulovu.
Is to-day's camp far or close to reach?	Makumbi a lélo kuteka palumbi a pépi?
Where do you come from to-day?	Wataluka hüya lélo?
Where are you going?	Windapi shangali?
Have you any news?	Tala ipo?
He killed his brother	Wataha tula yani (tula, big brother—mkasandi, small brother).
He has lost his axe	Kasola kasimina.
He laughed, he cried	Useha, ulila.
He dreams bad dreams	Nalota nvibi.
Is that a magician or a witch?	U kilè mganga é mfwishi?
What will that idol do?	Kishi kilongoka?
Antelopes' horns are a great medicine	Kisengo tambuluku wanza mkatampè.
He is a poor man	Mulanda.
He has no wealth	Kalilo pato.
He is a good man (he speaks well)	Ayo muntu miyampi.
He has bad anger	Uli nésungu ibi.
He beat his people, and they all ran away	Wakupila wantu wanti, wanyuèma wanololo.
The men only make war	Wantu waluu luana.
The women do all the work	Wanawakaza wusaka mingilo wosolola.
Truly she has no children	Uinè vinè uli wanawo a watula.
She is pregnant	Uinè limi.
To-day I have seen a woman who has borne eight children	Lélo tuamono malwa mnakazi avutula wana mwanda.
They love their children	Usaka wana wandi.
Little children are mischievous	Waléwakaiya numo wana wachè.
That man is dead	M'ntu wafu.
Where do you bury people?	Kwzika m'ntu kwéhi?
He has killed an elephant	Wataha holo.
A crocodile has caught a man	Nandu kikwata m'ntu.
Shut the door	Shita kutiwélo.
Go and bathe	Enda koyè méma.
This is dirty	Ulina uko.
Make it clean	Katokè si viyampi.
Wait a bit	Kungila kashi.
Don't be in a hurry	Likà kulonga ukili.
Don't make a noise	Kisotunwa.
Go away	Talaka nano.
He is here	Ulipano.
He is not here	Patspungè.
He is yonder	Akwanaku kutupwiyè.

He is not yonder	Uliakwa kulampò.
This is a tall tree	Munti mulampi.
That is a big house	Mzuo kata.
How are you?	U lina mini?
I am not well, sickness has seized me much	Hili viyampi, luva luanka ména.
I am quite well	Pikomo.
He is blind	Fofa.
He has lost an eye	Kisongo.
He is deaf	Mbulu.
He is thin	Wanyanyè.
He is getting fat	Mwita mununé.
He has long hair	Visuki mulampi.
To chip the teeth	Kuku la néno.
That is a short man	Muntu mwéka mwipi.
He is a strong and brave man	Mwiyampi kayukila uzenzanyi.
He is a bad man	Awè mubi.
He is a thief	Ngivi.
He threw a stone	Waela uiwè.
The stone hit me	Wantabè uiwè.
He rejoiced much	Washalmi or Shelengami.
I cut my finger	Makéka chàla chàmi.
Dig a big hole	Kola kina mkata.
Let go	Ulékè.
Build a house quickly	Wakanzu nozuo ukiti.
A very large dog	Mbwa ukata katà.
A lion is fierce	Tambu mukali.
The leopard has torn the goat	Ngè wakwatà mbuzi.
Dogs like men	Mbwa uli viyampi wantu.
The goat has borne two kids	Mbuzi yavutula wana tuwili.
Good-bye	Enda ku lala.

NAMES AND TITLES OF KASONGO.

Mkonzo	Means	fleet of foot.
Kirenga	,,	killer of men.
Kowimbi	,,	,, ,,
Moena Tanda	,,	king of all countries—of the whole world.
Mwéné Munza	,,	chief over all other men.
Vidiè	,,	God—he claims divine power.

Kungwe Banza is the name of the great devil of the Warua, and is applied to Kasongo, as he is supposed to be descended from or related to him.

Mlua, or Mrua, means that he is the great Mrua.

Mlunda means that he is the great Mlunda; it also means friend.

A man or woman uses as a second name the name of his or her mother. For instance, Kasongo is called Kasongo Kalombo, Kalombo being his mother's name.

Mwéné and Mona are titles.

KIRUA NAMES.

There is no distinction between male and female names.

Bambarré.	Kassali.	Lukunga.	Nabanda.
Bula.	Katwamba.	Lunga Mândi.	Nandu.
Buya.	Kendélé.	Lupandu.	Ngàwa.
Chala.	Kifwamba.	Luwangwè.	Ngöi.
Chikara.	Kikonja.	Luwendi.	Ngöi Mani.
Choöni.	Kilo.	Luwéti.	Nionè Ooté.
Daiyi.	Kimè Kinda.	Malalé.	Numbi.
Darambo.	Kingo.	Malova.	Poiyo.
Darla.	Kirua.	Mamjania.	Pomwimba.
Deri.	Kirumba.	Manana.	Pupundu Lan-
Fuma Juorla.	Kirunga Sungu.	Masengo.	gu.
Fuma Mwana.	Kisiko.	M'kunjila.	Sambi.
Fumé a Kenna.	Kitambara.	Mombèla.	Sanga Tambi.
Fumo.	Koga.	Mona Kaiyi.	Senga.
Irunga.	Kokolo.	Mona Kasanga.	Senga Wana.
Kadièra.	Koma Swinzi.	Mpanga.	Shèkè Shèkè.
Kaiyumba.	Komwimba.	Mshina.	Sungu.
Kajiri.	Kongwa.	Mtombo.	Tambwi.
Kalala.	Kopa Kopa.	Mtuwaji.	Tooté.
Kalalína.	Kowemba wem-	Musena.	Twitè.
Kali èlè.	ba.	Mwambaiyi.	Ukwa Kanuno.
Kalu Kulako.	Kulu.	Mwèhu.	Wana Mpunga.
Kalulu.	Kusèka.	Mwènè Kasovo.	Wana Ngao.
Kamwania.	Kwâdi.	Mwenzi.	Wapana Visiwè.
Karenga.	Luchilu.	Mwèpa.	Wondo.
Kasongo.	Lukonja.	Mza Kulla.	

INDEX.

A.

Abdallah ibn Habib, i. 309.
Abdallah ibn Nassib, i. 154, 196.
Abdul Kader, i. 124.
Abdûllah Dina, i. 12, 14, 95.
Acacias, i. 52, 77, 85, 90, 99; ii. 287.
Accident, an, i. 321.
Aden, arrival at, i. 17.
Africa, formation of continent of, ii. 281.
Akalunga, i. 291.
Alexanderson, Captain Carl, ii. 275.
Alowy ibn Zain el Aidûs, letter of recommendation from, i. 7.
Alvez, José Antonio (Kendélé), ii. 57, 86, 117, 121, 135, 198; his settlement, ii. 201.
Ambriz, ii. 276.
American, an, ii. 269.
Ammunition, i. 320.
Andradé, Admiral, Governor-General of Angola, ii. 273.
Ants, a delicacy, ii. 29; hills, ii. 127.
Antelopes, i. 54, 90, 132, 135, 139, 140, 142, 199, 202, 213; ii. 150.
Apple, custard, ii. 287.
Arabs, extortions of, i. 9; defeat of an Arab expedition, i. 93; caravan, i. 132; kindness of, i. 163; slaves of, i. 212; old camp, i. 299; kirangosi, i. 349; settlement, i. 373.
Arms, carried by expedition, i. 72; by elephant-hunter, i. 82; native, at Mpwapwa, i. 88; Wadirigo, i. 88; Wagogo, i. 96; Wahumba, i. 121; at Hisinéné, i. 192; Wagara, i. 210; at Mikisungi, i. 279; Watuta, i. 285; Warua, i. 325; Wabiya, i. 348; Manyuéma, i. 353; Lovalé, ii. 165.
Arrows, poisoned, i. 82; ii. 9.
Askari, i. 20, 179, 208, 255.

B.

Asmani, Bilâl Wadí, i. 170, 182, 195, 199; ii. 13.
Asparagus, i. 13.
Atlantic, first sight of the, ii. 259.
Attacks, i. 145; ii. 34, 40.
Auction, an, i. 163.

Badger, Dr., i. 7.
Bagamoyo, arrival at, i. 11; fire, i. 19; return to, i. 25.
Bailunda, country of, ii. 224, 318.
Baker, letter from Sir Samuel, i. 153.
Balomba, R., ii. 251.
Balooches, i. 151.
Bamharré (Kasongo's father), chief wife of, ii. 66.
Bambarré Mountains, i. 351.
Bamboo, i. 53, 236; ii. 152, 286.
Bananas, i. 245, 350.
Band, Kusongo's, ii. 93.
Bangwè, I. of, i. 248.
Banyan-tree, i. 201.
Baobab-trees, i. 49, 84; ii. 257.
Bark, boxes, i. 191; cloth, i. 192; sack, i. 198.
Basins, river, ii. 282.
Bastian, José Perez, ii. 132, 165.
Beans, i. 57, 224.
Bed-places, i. 191.
Bees, i. 213; ii. 152, 317.
Belgians, the King of the, ii. 331.
Belmont, settlement of Silva Porto, ii. 221.
Benguella, arrival at, ii. 267; the town of, ii. 269; leave, ii. 272.
Betsy, the, i. 248, 315.
Bihé, country of, ii. 196, 318.
Bilâl, i. 298, 308; ii. 62.
Bombay, i. 9, 20, 35, 102, 108, 155, 170, 196, 224, 236, 300, 309, 311; ii. 13, 62, 114, 268.

Books, box of, left at Ujiji by Dr. Livingstone, i. 168, 242.
Bowls, wooden, i. 329.
Bradshaw, Captain, R. N., ii. 279.
Bread-fruit trees, i. 13.
Bridges, natural, i. 222; a suspension. i. 365; fishing-weir, ii. 14, 34, 134; over the rivers Kukéwi and Kuléli, ii. 240.
Brother-making, i. 332, 369.
Buffaloes, i. 61, 132, 142, 202, 214, 220, 235, 327; ii. 222, 287.
Burghash, Syud, i. 150.
Burials, i. 120; ii. 110.
Burton, Captain, i. 108, 122, 149, 201; ii. 290.
Butterflies, i. 130.

C.

Cairo, i. 6.
Calasso, Dr., ii. 267.
Cameron, the Frances, ii. 275.
Camping, i, 38.
Camp at Rehenneko, i. 67; remains of Arab, i. 299.
Cannibals, i. 349, 357.
Canoes, at Malagarazi, i. 230; hiring at Ujiji, i. 246, 314; at R. Lulwu, i. 362; near Nyangwé, i. 376; at Nyangwé, ii. 6; on Lake Mohrya, ii. 65; at R. Kwanza, ii. 197.
Caravan, an Arab, i. 47, 51, 132; a Wanyamwési, i. 81; at Pakhúndi, i. 338; from Bihé, ii. 182; from West Coast, ii. 248, 251.
Carpentry, good, ii. 30.
Carving, i. 348.
Cassava, i. 41, 43, 323; ii. 241.
Castor-oil, ii. 285, 326.
Caterpillars, a delicacy, ii. 237.
Cattle, i. 94, 133; ii. 167, 184, 199.
Cauchoix, M., his great kindness, ii. 263, 267; news of his death, ii. 264.
Caves, i. 216.
Cemetery, a, ii. 211.
Chakuola, Ras and R., i. 273.
Chankoji, R., ii. 77.
Charlie, French, i. 23.
Chase, a, i. 214.
Chief, a young, i. 225; of Ujiji, i. 244; of Msknkira, i. 276.
Chikumbi, ii. 184.
Children, mode of carrying, i. 89.
Christmas, a miserable, i. 188; another, ii. 92.
Chuma, i. 166.
Chunyo, i. 89.

Cinnabar, ii. 48, 330.
Claims, extortionate, i. 225.
Cloth, bark, i. 192: cotton, i. 276.
Clubs, village, i. 181.
Coal, i. 266, 329.
Coffee, ii. 325.
Coimbra, Lourenço da Souza (Kwarumba), ii. 95, 179.
Coneys at Usekhé, i. 117.
Congo, s.s., ii. 278.
Convolvuli, i. 50.
Copal, ii. 15, 287, 327.
Copper, i. 134, 319; ii. 149, 329.
Corn i. 57, 324; grinding, i. 193, 344; ii. 235, 327.
Corn, Indian, i. 44, 53; ii. 241, 285.
Corn, Kaffir or Matama, i. 53, 193, 285, 327.
Cotton, i. 278; ii. 325.
Cows in Lovalé, ii. 167.
Crane, a, i. 204.
Crew, hiring a, i. 249.
Crocodiles, in R. Kingani, i. 34; in the South Ngombé, i. 202; in Lake Tanganyika, i. 252; in R. Luguvu, i. 265; in R. Lualaba, i. 375.
Crystalline pebbles, i. 49.
Cucumbers, i. 150, 245.
Cultivation, i. 133, 297; instruments of, i. 325.
Currency, at Kawélé, i. 246; on Kongo, i. 310; at Nyangwé, ii. 3.
Customs, curious, i. 79, 95, 101, 120, 190, 333.
Cygnet, H.M.S., ii. 273.

D.

Daisy, yellow, i. 50.
Daiyi, ii. 79, 84.
Dance, native, i. 190, 258, 263, 353; ii. 91.
Daphne, H.M.S., i. 22, 30.
Darters, on Lake Tanganyika, i, 238.
Date, wild, ii. 288.
Dawson, Lieut. L. S., expedition of, i. 2.
Depredations, by Wadirigo, i. 83.
Deserts, ii. 282.
Desertions, i. 35, 47, 75, 95, 122, 135, 138, 152, 163, 172, 177, 179, 200, 315; ii. 13, 27, 108.
Destruction and desolation, i. 209.
Devils, sham, in Kibokwé, ii. 188.
Dillon, Mr. W. E., i. 5, 33, 35, 39, 43, 58, 63, 66, 152; letter from, i. 157; 160, 169, 171; his death, i. 174.
Dilolo, legend of Lake, ii. 171.

Dinah, my goat, i. 211, 350; ii. 39; Fort, ii. 44.
Disturbance, a, i. 128, 366.
Divers and darters, i. 238.
Donkeys, buying, i. 11; harness, i. 69; death of a, i. 85, 138; Muscat, i. 185; birth of a, i. 234, 309.
Dress, at Kawélé, i. 243; of Watuta, i. 285; of Warua, i. 325; at Ubûdjwa, i. 336; of Wahiya, i. 344; in Manyuéma, i. 353, 372; in Ulûnda, ii. 157; in Lovalé, ii. 165; in Kisanji, ii. 257.
Drum, wooden, i. 329.
Ducks, i. 377.
Duthumi, or Kungwa, Hills, i. 53; ii. 286.
Dwarfs, i. 357.
Dwellings, underground, ii. 89, 314.

E.

Earthquake, an, i. 362.
Ebony, i. 53.
Eclipse of the sun, i. 282; ii. 192.
Eggs, i. 57, 197.
Eland, i. 214; ii. 154.
Elephants, near the Makata, i. 61; hunter, i. 82; a herd, i. 136; tracks of, i. 114, 235, 290, 322; ii. 124, 154.
England, a work for, i. 209.
Expedition, personnel of, i. 170.

F.

Fauna, the, of Africa, ii. 288.
Ferry at R. Malagarazi, i. 225, 229; at R. Lulwu, i. 362.
Festival, Arab, i. 20.
Festivities, i. 130, 134; ii. 229.
Fetish, i. 101; man, i. 230, 304, 330, 336; ii. 67, 117, 159, 164, 168, 211, 218.
Fever, i. 32, 42, 152, 157, 249, 252, 322; ii. 14, 78.
Fire, at Bagamoyo, i. 19; at Kawélé, i. 312; of grass, i. 364; at Totéla, ii. 113; of country, ii. 134; of neighbouring camp, ii. 139.
Fireplaces, i. 191.
Fish, dried, i. 326, 361; in market at Nyangwé, ii. 5; in Lovalé, ii. 169.
Flogging, a, i. 241.
Forest, a, i. 351.
Fort Dinah, ii. 44.
Fortune-telling, ii. 219.
Foundries, iron, i. 338, 340, 371.

Fowl, Guinea, near Lake Ugombo, i. 82; near Simbo, i. 142; in Ulûnda, ii. 155.
Fowl, jungle, i. 142.
Fowl, water, on Lake Ugombo, i. 82.
Fowls, ii. 286.
Fracas, a, i. 26; ii. 15.
French beans, ii. 13.
Frere, Sir Bartle, mission of, i. 6; comes to Bagamoyo, i. 32.
Frogs, i. 267.
Frost, ii. 161.
Fumé a Kenna, ii. 60, 115.
Fundalanga, ii. 152.

G.

Gags, for slaves, i. 341.
Game, mode of preserving, i. 192.
Garrison of Benguella, ii. 270.
Gateways, i. 141, 201.
Gazelles, i. 184, 188.
Geography, physical, ii. 285.
Germain, Père, i. 32.
Ghee, i. 89.
Giraffes, i. 61, 142, 199; ii. 287.
Gnu, or mimbu, i. 139.
Goats, i. 41, 355; ii. 286.
Goître, ii. 315.
Gold, ii. 329.
Gonçalves, Senhor, ii. 204; settlement of, ii. 212.
Gorillas (Soko), i. 296.
Gourds, i. 191.
Granaries, i. 191, 199, 292, 346, 363; ii. 198.
Grandy, Lieutenant, i. 6.
Granite, i. 52, 84; rocks at Usekhé, i. 114; at Pururu, i. 130; near R. Ruguvu, on Lake Tanganyika, i. 296; near the West Coast, ii. 254, 294.
Grant, Col., i. 149.
Grapes, wild, i. 299.
Grass, tall, i. 340.
Graves, of chiefs, i. 49; of slaves, ii. 256.
Grinding corn, i. 193, 344; ii. 235.
Guava, ii. 205, 287.
Gulls, on Lake Tanganyika, i. 238.
Gum-copal, ii. 15, 287, 327.

H.

Habed ibn Salim, alias Tanganyika, i. 378.
Haméd ibn Haméd (Tipo-tipo), ii. 11, 20.

Hamees, i. 170.
Hamees ibn Salim, i. 51, 58.
Hanyoka, ii. 48.
Harmonium (?), Pakwanywa's, i. 333.
Hassan ibn Gharib, i. 310.
Hawks, fish, on Lake Tanganyika, i. 252.
Head-dress, of Wagogo, i. 96; of Wanyamwési, i. 194; of Wagaga, i. 227; of Wajiji, i. 244; at Kitata, i. 275; at Mikisungi, i. 279; of Watuta, i. 286; of Waguhha, i. 303; of Warua, i. 325; ii. 48, 73; of Mrs. Pakwanywa, i. 335; of Wahiya, i. 343; in Manyuéma, i. 363, 373; in Lovalé, ii. 165, 176; in Kirfoandi, ii. 193; at Kapéka, ii. 199.
Heat, great, i. 330, 340; ii. 142.
Hemp, i. 245; ii. 328.
Henn, Lieut., i. 3.
Herons, at R. Kwanza, ii. 196.
Hides, ii. 328.
Hippopotami, in R. Kingani, i. 34; in Lake Ugombo, i. 82; in the South Ngombé, i. 202; in Lake Tanganyika, i. 252; in R. Luguvu, i. 265; in R. Lulwu, i. 363; in R. Lualaba, i. 375.
Hisinéné, i. 184.
Home, letters from, i. 308; ii. 272; safe, ii. 280.
Honey, i. 57, 101, 266.
Honey-birds, i. 54.
Hopkins, Consul, ii. 272.
Horner, Père, i. 12, 22.
Hospitality, Arab, i. 149.
Houses, thatched, at Khoko, i. 119; to be built for Kasongo, ii. 105.
Humbi, Hill of, ii. 241.
Huts, tembé, i. 87.
Huts, at Pururu, i. 129; at Jiwé la Singa, i. 133; at Hisinéné, i. 191; at Pakwanywa's, i. 332; in Uhiya, i. 345; near Nyangwé, i. 375; at Kituma, ii. 30; in Ulúnda, ii. 159; in Lovalé, ii. 162; near R. Kwanza, ii. 198.
Hyænas, near Lake Ugombo, i. 83; at Kanyenyé, i. 113.

I.

Ice, ii. 161
Idols, i. 304, 330, 347; ii. 71.
Iki, L. (or L. Lincoln), ii. 12.
Illusion, an optical, i. 270.
Incident, an amusing, ii. 273.
Incivility, i. 343.

Indiarubber, vines, i. 329; ii. 288; export of, ii. 322.
Inspection, a minute, i. 226.
Iron, i. 245, 338, 340, 371; ii. 165, 181, 317, 328.
Islands, floating, i. 222, 256, 272; ii. 79, 84.
Issa, i. 35, 101, 128, 156, 170
Itaga, i. 231.
Itambara, i. 223.
Itumvi, i. 173.
Ituru, i. 145.
Ivory, i. 124, 245, 374; trade in, ii. 321, 328.

J.

Jacko, i. 170, 229.[1]
Jasmin, i. 185, 198, 217; death of, i. 219.
Jemadar Issa, i. 12, 13, 15, 27.
Jemadar Sabr, i. 15, 18, 28.
Jenjé (country of the Kaffirs), ii. 174.
Jiwé la Singa, i. 133; ii. 297.
João, ii. 174.
João, Baptista Ferreira, settlement of, ii. 216.
Jumah Merikani, i. 299; ii. 51, 54, 86, 107, 129.
Jumah Wadi Nassib, i. 315; ii. 40, 88, 113, 179.

K.

Kabba Rega, i. 154.
Kabongé, islands of, i. 315.
Kabogo, I. of, i. 216.
Kabogo, Ras, i. 253.
Kabongo, i. 252.
Kaça, R., i. 323.
Kadetamaré, i. 78.
Kafundango, ii. 162.
Kagnombé, town of, ii. 206; chief of, ii. 209.
Kamasanga, i. 272.
Kambala, village of, ii. 231.
Kambemba, Ras, i. 271.
Kamwassa, i. 368.
Kamwawi, ii. 37.
Kanyenyé, i. 104, 107; ii. 204.
Kanyumba, ii. 190.
Kaoli, i. 17.
Kapéka, ii. 198.
Karungu, i. 366.
Karyan Gwina, i. 262.
Kasékerah, i. 177.
Kasongé, i. 308.
Kasongo, ii. 20.

Kasongo, chief of Urua, ii. 69, 86;
  his return, ii. 92.
Kassabé, R., ii. 161.
Kassali, L., or Kikonja, ii. 26, 67, 78.
Kasuwa, i. 47.
Katamba, R., i. 338.
Katanki, Ras, i. 272.
Kutendé, ii. 169.
Katimba, Ras, i. 260..
Katombéla, ii. 262.
Katupi, i. 296.
Kawala, ii. 143.
Kawélé, arrival at, i. 237; house at, i.
  240; return to, i. 308; fire at, i. 312;
  second start from, i. 315.
Kawendi Mountains, ii. 300.
Kebwé, Ras, i. 253.
Kendélé. (See Alvez.)
Khedive, letter of recommendation
  from the, i. 6.
Kboko, i. 118; ii. 294.
Kibaiyéli, ii. 74.
Kibokwé, ii. 186, 317.
Kifuma, ii. 30.
Kigambwé Hills, i. 56.
Kigandah, i. 179.
Kihondo Hills, i. 58.
Kikoka, i. 32, 35.
Kikonja, ii. 83.
Kilemba, ii. 64, 65, 316.
Kilimachio Hills, ii. 313.
Kilolo, I. of, i. 260.
Kiluilui, R., ii. 123.
Kilwala Hills, ii. 51.
Kimbandi, ii. 190.
Kingani, R., i. 32, 34.
Kingfishers, i. 252.
Kinsembo, ii. 276.
Kinyari, i. 258.
Kipireh, i. 136.
Kirangosi, or guides, i. 349; ii. 26, 33.
Kirk, Dr., i. 24, 30.
Kiroka, i. 55.
Kirua, collecting a vocabulary of, ii.
  110.
Kirumbu, i. 276.
Kisanji, country of, ii. 257, 319.
Ki Sura Sura, i. 137.
Kisémo, i. 49.
Kisenga, ii. 160.
Kisima, ii. 78.
Kisimbika, i. 364.
Kisokweh, i. 89.
Kitata, i. 275.
Kivira, I. of, i. 308, 315.
Kokéma, R., ii. 200.
Kolomamba, i. 348.
Kolqualls, i. 84.

Kombéhina, i. 66.
Kombo, i. 171.
Kongasa, i. 53.
Kongo, chief of Bailunda, ii. 231.
Kongo, R., i. 310; ii. 315.
Konongo, i. 175.
Kowamba, L., ii. 67.
Kowédi, ii. 78, 85.
Kowenga, I. of, i. 273.
Kukéwi, R, ii. 239.
Kungwa Hills, i. 53; ii. 286.
Kungwé, Ras, i. 254.
Kutato, the burst of the R., ii. 224.
Kwakasongo, i. 373.
Kwanfrora Kasén, i. 324.
Kwanza, R., W. 191, 196.
Kwarumba, chief in Urua, ii. 37.
Kwarumba (Coimbra), ii 95.
Kwaséré, i. 339.
Kwatosi, i 206.
Kwihuruh ("village of a chief"), i. 180,
  197.
Kwikuruh, i. 147.
Kwinbata ("chief's residence"), in
  Urua, ii. 80.

L.

Lake dwellings, ii. 64.
"Lake Regions of Central Africa," ii.
  290.
Lake-system of Africa, ii. 302.
Lanji, streams flowing to Lake, i. 351.
Lecture, a, i. 217, 348.
Lee, Mr. F., R.A., ii. 277.
Lemons, sweet, ii. 287.
Lemur, a, i. 135.
Leo, i. 73, 136, 200, 210; death of, i.
  234.
Leopard, a, i. 78.
Lepidosiren, a, i. 270.
Leprosy, ii. 90.
Letters from home, i. 308; ii. 272.
Levée, a, ii. 102.
Lilies, i. 43, 50, 128, 133, 203, 262.
Lilwa, R., ii. 10.
Limes, i. 163; ii. 287.
Lindi, R., ii. 10.
Lindo (bark boxes), i. 191.
Lincoln, Lake (or Iki), ii. 12.
Lions, i. 44; ii. 87.
Liowa, chief of Western Ugara, i. 208,
  211.
Livingstone, Dr., news of, i. 111;
  death of, 166; arrival of body, i.
  167; particulars of death, i. 168;
  manner of transporting body, i. 181
  his papers at Kawélé, i. 240, 311,

355; at Nyangwé, ii. 2; in Lovalé, ii. 170.
Livingstone, Oswell, i. 3.
Livingstone Search Expedition, first one, i. 2; second one, i. 5.
Loanda, arrival at San Paul de, ii. 272.
Locusts, ii. 243.
Lomâmi, R., ii. 11.
Longevity, instances of, i. 108, 109.
Lovalé, ii. 161, 317.
Lovoi, R., ii. 78, 138.
Lovuma, R., i. 299.
Lowa, R. (or Uellé ?), ii. 10.
Lualaba, R., i. 305; first sight of, i. 374; at Nyangwé, ii. 8; country near, ii. 312; affluents of, ii. 314.
Luama, R., ii. 152.
Lubiranzi, R., ii. 152.
Luhji, R., i. 122.
Lufunga, R., i. 260.
Lugerengeri, R., i. 49; crossing it, i. 51.
Lugowa, i. 232.
Lugumba, R., i. 321.
Lugungwa, R., i. 327.
Luguvu, R., i. 265, 290.
Lukazi, R., ii. 34.
Lukoji, R., ii. 159.
Lukuga, R., i. 302, 305.
Lulindi, R., i. 365.
Lulu, Ras, ii. 10.
Lulumbijé, R., i. 347.
Lulumbiji, R., i. 305.
Lulwu, R., i. 362.
Lumeji, R., ii. 176, 184.
Lunga Mândi, ii. 127, 129, 316.
Lungi, ii. 225.
Lungu, i. 282.
Lupanda, ii. 145.
Luuluga, R., i. 258.
Luvijo, R., ii. 48.
Luwaziwa, R., i. 294.
Luwembi, R., ii. 12.
Luwika, R., i. 344.
Luxuries, ii. 202.

M.

Mabruki, i. 170; ii. 13.
Mabunguru Nullah, the, i. 131; ii. 296.
Machachézi, i. 253, 308.
Madété, village of, i. 82.
Magic, i. 116.
Magomba, grandson of, i. 104; great age of, i. 108; great grandson of, i. 111.

Majuto, ii. 243; death and burial, ii. 244.
Makakomo, islands of, i. 273.
Mukanyazi, R., i. 266.
Makata Swamp, i. 48, 61; crossing it, i. 63.
Makukiza, i. 275.
Makurungwe, Ras, i. 273.
Malagarazi, R., i. 224, 230.
Mangos, i. 17; ii. 287.
Manioc, i. 17; ii. 285.
Mûn Komo, i. 216.
Manoel, ii. 201.
Manyara, i. 371.
Manyuéma, country of, i. 352.
Mapalatta, i. 100, 183.
March, a desperate, ii. 247.
Marenga Mkali, the, i. 86, 90.
Marimba, a musical instrument, i. 357.
Market, at Kawélé, i. 244; at Nyangwé, ii. 3.
Markham, kind help of Mr. C., i. 5.
Marrows, vegetable, i. 57.
Marwa, i. 143.
Massanga, i. 272.
Massi Kambi, i. 269.
Masungwé, R., i. 235.
Matama, or Kaffir corn, i. 78, 85, 94, 224, 323; ii. 145, 293, 327.
Matomondo, i. 84.
Mata Yafa (chief in Lovalé), ii. 178.
Mata Yafa (Muato Yanvo, chief in Ulûnda), ii. 58, 148.
Mbumi, i. 79.
Mdaburu, i. 121; ii. 295.
"Medium," a, ii. 66.
Meginna, ii. 8.
Mékéto, i. 322.
Mello, Lieutenant, ii. 273.
Melons, water, i. 91.
Men, breakdown of my, ii. 241; relief sent to, ii. 266; arrival at Benguella, ii. 268; sent to Zanzibar, ii. 277.
Merikani, Jumah, i. 299; ii. 51, 54, 86, 107, 129.
Methusaleh, a veritable, i. 108.
Mfomdo Point, i. 251.
Mfuv, the, ii. 287.
Mganga, or medicine man, ii. 81, 118.
Mgunda Mkali, or Fiery Field, i. 125, 127; ii. 295.
Mhongo, i. 45, 49, 94, 100, 110, 118, 125, 205, 216, 224.
Michikichi, or palm-oil tree, i. 285.
Miguu Mifupi, i. 118.
Milk-bush, the, i. 145.
Mimba, or gnu, i. 139.
Minstrels, Negro, i. 250.

Mirambo, i. 77, 124, 139, 150, 195, 227.
Miriro, chief of Akalunga, i. 292.
Mission, French, at Bagamoyo, i. 13; Scotch, on Lake Nyassa, ii. 330.
Mkombenga, i. 65.
Mkwembwé, i. 171.
M'Nchkulla, ii. 47.
Moéné Bugga and Gobé, i. 356.
Moéné Kula, ii. 158.
Moffat, Robert, i. 33, 43, 71.
Mohalé, R., and village, i. 56.
Mohammed ibn Gharib, i. 309.
Mohammed ibn Salim, i. 240, 309.
Mohammed Malim, i. 170, 188, 196, 315.
Mohrya, L., ii. 26, 62.
Mona Kasanga, ii. 26, 36, 49.
Mona Lamba, ii. 185.
Mona Pého, ii. 186.
Monkeys, i. 140, 253, 280.
Mpafu-tree, the, i. 326, 326 ; ii. 15, 113, 326.
Mpanga Sanga, i. 101.
Mpara Gwina, i. 277.
Mparamusi-tree, the, i. 77 ; ii. 288.
Mpeta, i. 230.
Mpimbwe, Ras, i. 270.
Mpwapwa, i. 83, 85.
Mrima Ngombé, chief of Ugunda, i. 180, 195.
Mshiri, chief of Katanga, ii. 140.
Msou, ii. 139.
Msuwah, i. 44.
Mtamba, R , i. 213.
Mtésa, King, i. 153.
Mtonga, i. 46.
Muinyi Bokhara, i. 356.
Muinyi Dugumbi, ii. 2.
Muinyi Hassani, i. 367, 374.
Muinyi Useghara, i. 78.
Mukondokwa, R., i. 76, 82.
Mulattoes, ii. 249.
Mulongo, Ras, i. 308.
Munza, ii. 61.
Murphy, Lieutenant C., i. 8, 23, 32, 70, 152, 158, 168, 172, 178, 181, 198.
Musamwira, R., i. 268.
Music, i. 333, 356 ; ii. 93.
Mutilation, of women, i. 294 ; of men, ii. 98.
Mutiny, a, 156.
Mutwalé ("chief"), i. 224.
Mvumi, i, 94.
Mwêbu, ii. 77.
Mwéré Torrent, i. 57.
Myambarau, the, ii. 287.

N.

Nassiba, the ibn, i. 154, 167, 172.
Needlework, ii. 91.
New, Mr., death of, i. 3.
Ngombé Nullah, the South, i. 202.
Niamtaga, i. 236.
Nile, R., impossibility of identity with Lualabu, ii. 10.
Njivi Marsh, ii. 125.
Nullah, the, Mabunguru, i. 131.
Nuts, ground-, i. 324 ; ii. 285.
Nutmegs, in Uvinza, i. 236 ; at Rusûna's, ii. 15, 326.
Nyangwé, arrival at, i. 378; ii. 1 ; departure from, ii. 13.
Nyanza, Lakes Albert and Victoria, ii. 303.
Nyassa, L., ii. 303.

O.

Oak, African, ii. 15.
Oil, palm, i. 245 ; ii. 4.
Omens, i. 150.
Ophthalmia, i. 159, 162, 171.
Oranges, i. 17, 214 ; ii. 287.
Ornaments, at Rehenneko, i. 66 ; Mpwapwa, i. 88 ; Wagogo, i. 95, 141 ; Wanyamwési, i. 194; Wagara, i. 210 ; Wagaga, i. 227 ; at Kawélé, i. 243 ; Karyan Gwina, i. 264 ; Mikisungi, i. 279 ; Watuta, i. 285; Akalunga, i. 335 ; Waguhha, i. 304 ; Warua, i. 325 ; ii. 48; Mrs. Pakwanywa's, i. 325 ; Wabûdjwa, i. 366 ; Wavinza, i. 348; in Manyuéma, i. 335.
Outlet of Lake Tanganyika, i. 301.

P.

Pagazi, difficulty of procuring, i. 10, 25 ; death of a, i. 85; duties of, i. 107, 152, 177 ; an accident to a, i. 321 ; breakdown of the, ii. 241 ; death and burial of a, ii. 244.
Painting, oil, i. 332 ; face, ii. 48.
Pakhûndi, i. 337.
Pakwanywa, i. 327, 331 ; Mrs., i. 334.
Palaver, a, i. 369.
Palms, fan-, i. 62, 65, 262 ; -oil tree, i. 285 ; date-, i. 306 ; oil, i. 350 ; ii. 29, 138, 325 ; cocoa-, ii. 287.
Palmyras, i. 135.
Panic, a, i. 215, 220, 272.
Papaw, the, ii. 287.
Parks, public, i. 342.
Partridges, i. 142.

Payment, curious mode of, i. 246.
Pechel, Dr. Loesche, ii. 278.
Pembereh. great age of, i. 109.
Pepper, ii. 326.
Pickle, the, i. 248, 298, 315.
Pig, wild, i. 54.
Pigeon-shooting, i. 117, 359.
Point, highest reached, ii. 248.
Poisoned arrows, i. 62.
Polunga, I., i. 280.
Pombé, i. 130, 183, 190, 197, 245, 276; ii. 198.
Pombeiros, the, ii. 157.
Ponda, i. 262.
Poporla, chief of Kawala, ii. 143.
Porridge, i. 192.
Portuguese, the, i. 292; ii. 51, 56.
Pottery, i. 191, 245, 289; ii. 4.
Potatoes, sweet, i. 44, 53, 85, 191, 224, 245, 324.
Prerogative, a chief's, i. 358.
Primulas, i. 50.
Public-houses in Unyamwési, i. 181.
Pumpkins, i. 44, 57, 191; ii. 293.
Pururu, i. 128.

Q.

Quail, i. 202.
Quartz, i. 49, 52, 84; ii. 286.

R.

Rain, in Ugogo, i. 94; in Ugara, i. 208, 212; in Uvinza, i. 220, 235; on Tanganyika, i. 300; in Bibé, ii. 221; at Humbi, ii. 242.
Raphia, the, ii. 288.
Reception, a warm, ii. 202.
Rehenneko, arrival at, i. 66; stay at, i. 69; start from, i. 75.
Relief sent to men, ii. 266.
Rhinoceros, skull, i. 132; a white, i. 202, 214.
Rice, i. 53, 188; ii. 286, 327.
Rohombo, i. 349.
Rosako, village of, i. 38.
Rosan, i. 24.
Roses in Bihé, ii. 214.
Routes, trade, ii. 321.
Roubu, R., ii. 14.
Rusha, R., i. 122.
Ruanda, i. 317.
Rubumba, i. 327.
Ruga-Ruga, i. 143, 145, 182.
Ruguvu, R., 235.
Rusugi, R., i. 234.
Ruseűna, ii. 12, 16.

S.

Sack, manufacture of a, i. 198.
Said ibn Salim al Lamki, i. 124, 147, 172, 182, 196.
Sail-making, i. 147.
Sale, a, i. 313.
Salt, i. 105, 134, 232, 245; ii. 4. 52, 330.
Salutations, i. 226, 342.
Samaritan, a good, ii. 263.
Sambo, i. 112, 170, 197, 231, 254; ii. 181.
Sandstone, i. 49.
Sankorra, L., ii. 12.
Scene, a lovely, i. 280.
Scheme, for exploration, i. 4; for commerce stations, ii. 331.
Scurvy, attacked by, ii. 260, 267.
Secretary-birds, i. 202.
Sem-sem, ii. 285.
Seruia, Mr., ii. 262.
Sesamum, ii. 326.
Sha Kélembé, ii. 175.
Shamba Gonèra, i. 26.
Shaykh ibn Nassib, i. 154.
Sheep, i. 355; ii. 286.
Showman, a, i. 350.
Signals, i. 194.
Silva Porto, settlement of, 220.
Silver, ii. 329.
Simbawéni, i. 56.
Simbo in Useghara, i. 58.
Simbo in Urguru, i. 142.
Sindy, R., i. 221, 222.
Sirius, H.M.S., ii. 277.
Skeletons of slaves, ii. 256.
Slaves, i. 164; of Arabs, i. 212, 373; ii. 27; of Portuguese, ii. 106; of Coimbra, ii. 136; of Alvez, ii. 147; escape of a gang, ii. 163; of Silva Porto, ii. 191; export of, ii. 246.
Slave-trade, the, i. 209, 246, 255, 257, 277, 324, 341; ii. 4, 141, 168, 217, 256, 321.
Small-pox in Kanyenyé, i. 106.
Smithies, i. 372; ii. 189.
Snakes, i. 135, 189; ii. 146; the supper of a, ii. 192; a trader in, ii. 269, 289.
Snipe, i. 188.
Snuff, liquid, i. 233.
Soap, ii. 24.
Soko (gorillas), i. 296.
Soorghi, i. 17.
Sona Bazh, ii. 161.
Speke, Captain, i. 149.
Spiders, i. 298; ii. 289.
Spinning, cotton, i. 278.

Spiteful, H.M.S., ii. 274.
Springs, hot, i. 302, 337.
Stanley, Mr., news of success of his first expedition brought to Bagamoyo, i. 2 ; second expedition, i. 4.
Stores, i. 23, 163, 320.
Storms, i. 259.
Story, an improbable, i. 115; a curious, i. 204.
Strike, a, i. 68.
"Suahili Tales," i. 312.
Sughr-cane, i. 245 ; ii. 286, 325.
Superstitions, i. 144, 189, 253, 272, 302 ; ii. 83, 118, 188, 192.
Surgery, ii. 24.
Suspension bridge, a, i. 365.
Susi, i. 166.
Sycamores, i. 119, 262.
Syde ibn Habib, i. 246.
Syde ibn Omar, i. 80.
Syde Mezrui, i. 250, 310, 332 ; ii. 2.
Syud Burghash, i. 150.

T.

Taborah, i. 162.
Taka, chief of Eastern Ugara, i. 185, 205.
Tales, Suahili, i. 312 ; strange, ii. 87.
Tamarinds, i. 163 ; ii. 287.
Tanganyika, first sight of Lake, i. 237 ; start for circuit of, i. 250; enlargement of, i. 268; how fed, i. 295; leaving, i. 317 ; last sight of, i. 322 ; ii. 302.
Tanganyika, *alias* Habed ibn Salim, i. 378; ii. 2.
Tarya Topan, i. 23.
Tattooing, i. 193, 227, 336, 343.
Teak, ii. 15, 288.
Teal, bird like, near Mvumi, i. 98.
Teeth, chipping, i. 193, 286, 343.
Temba Lui ("Devil's Finger"), ii. 236.
Tembé huts first met with, i. 87.
Temé, i. 176.
Terekesa, a, i. 83.
Terraces, i. 297.
Téwéré, i. 205.
Thieving, i. 236, 241, 282, 298, 365 ; ii. 32.
Thrashing, a, ii. 34.
Thunderstorm, a, ii. 77.
Timber-trees, ii. 326.
Tingi-tingi, i. 285 ; ii. 84.
Tipo-tipo (Haméd ibn Haméd), ii. 11, 20.
Tobacco, i. 224, 245, 258 ; ii. 86, 205, 293, 325.

Tomatoes, i. 245.
Totéla, ii. 106.
Traders, at Kawélé, i. 242 ; at Karungu, i. 367 ; on Lake Sankorra, ii. 25 ; a Portuguese, ii. 228.
Trade, slave-, i. 209, 246, 255, 257, 277, 324, 341 ; ii. 41, 141, 168, 217, 256 ; various articles of, 321.
Traps, for game, i. 136 ; for fish, i. 269 ; 302 ; ii. 160.
Trees, giant, i. 351.
Tribal marks, i. 193, 286.
Turk, a, i. 177.

U.

Ubûdjwa, i. 327 ; ii. 311.
Uellé, R. (or Lowa ?), ii. 10.
Ufipa, i. 281.
Ugaga, i. 225.
Ugali, or porridge, i. 192.
Ugara, i. 185, 205 ; ii. 300.
Ugarowwa R. (same as Kongo and Lualaba), i. 310 ; ii. 10.
Ugogo, i. 91 ; ii. 292.
Ugoma, Mountains of, i. 307 ; ii. 310.
Ugombo, R. and L., i. 82.
Uguhha, i. 317.
Ugunda, i. 179, 200 ; ii. 299.
Uhha, i. 225.
Uhiya, i. 343 ; ii. 312.
Ujiji, i. 237 ; return to, i. 308 ; second start from, i. 315.
Ukaranga, i. 236 ; ii. 301.
Ulegga, ii. 9.
Ulûnda, ii. 152, 317.
Ulungu, i. 281.
Umbrella, an, i. 207 ; gay, ii. 248.
Underground dwellings, ii. 89, 314 ; streams, ii. 318.
Unyanyembé, Arab governor of, i. 124, 147, 172, 182, 196.
Unyanyembé, arrival at, i. 145 ; departure from, i. 171 ; ii. 298.
Urguru, i. 140 ; ii. 297.
Urua, ii. 68.
Useghara, Muinyi, i. 78 ; ii. 285, 289.
Usekhé, i. 114 ; ii. 294.
Ussambi, ii. 133, 316.
Utendé, i. 207.
Uvinza, East, i. 217, 224 ; ii. 300.
Uvinza, West, i. 347 ; ii. 312.

V.

Village, of Msuwah, i. 45 ; stockaded, i. 145 ; ii. 139, 159 ; Kasékerah, i. 178 ; in Ugunda, i. 201 ; Téwéré, i.

206; Mán Komo, i. 216; destroyed by Miramibo, i. 228; deserted, i. 234, 340, 345; ii. 15; Kinyari, i. 258; Karyan Gwina, i. 263; in Munyuéma, i. 352; burning, i. 368; Russúna's, ii. 19; in Urua, ii. 36; Mussumba, ii. 60; in Lovalé, ii. 167; in Bihé, ii. 205.

Visits, a round of, i. 149; a state, ii. 21, 57, 60, 170, 207, 233.

Visitors, i. 69, 100, 123, 225, 255.

W.

Wadirigo, predatory tribe, i. 83, 88.
Wagenya, i. 375.
Wagogo, i. 92.
Waguhha, i. 245, 303.
Wahumba, i. 120.
Wainwright, letter from Jacob, i. 165.
Wakimbu, i. 127.
Wamerima, i. 9, 36, 119, 164.
Wanyamwési caravan, i. 81, 88.
Warori, i. 164.
Warua, i. 323.
Warundi, i. 245.

Wasuahili, i. 9, 164.
Water, lack of, i. 83, 127; contrivance for carrying, i. 87; green, ii. 48.
Watersheds, i. 133; ii. 283.
Watosi, i. 195.
Watuta, i. 285.
Wedding, a, ii. 76.
"Westward Ho!" i. 171.
Wheat, i. 150; ii. 327.
Whindé, i. 44.
Wine, palm, i. 245.
Women, mutilation of, i. 294; fisher-, i. 362.

Y.

Yacooti, ii. 229, 237.
Yamini, Ras, i. 283.
Yams, i. 16, 245.
Yellala Cataracts, i. 310; ii. 333.

Z.

Zambési, R., ii. 161.
Zanzibar, arrival at, i. 8; leave, i. 11.
Zebra, i. 90, 139, 188; ii. 161, 288.
Ziwa, or pond, i. 98, 104, 145; ii. 293.

THE END.

PRINTED BY VIRTUE AND CO., LIMITED, CITY ROAD, LONDON.